"It is often said that an outsider sees [...]
Neil Humphreys' witty, insightful, wa[...]
Singapore (warts and all) proves that p[...] over again."
Shamini Flint, author, *Inspector Singh Investigates* mystery series

"Neil Humphreys sheds a good humoured and tolerant light on Singaporeans. After a sojourn Down Under he is back in town, revealing his fondness for all our foibles—vomit, *kaka*, casinos and more! Give him honorary citizenship!"
Lim Kay Tong, actor, *Growing Up, Mee Pok Man, Perth, The Photograph, The Pupil*

"Singapore is lucky to have Neil Humphreys—an *ang moh* visiting places we have never been to, recounting histories we are unaware of and, most importantly, showing us how to laugh, love and forgive all the imperfections of this little island we call home."
Chew Gek Khim, executive chairman, The Straits Trading Co. Ltd.

"Whenever Singaporeans gripe about 'foreign talent' crowding our shores, they always give Neil Humphreys an exemption, and with good reason. Not afraid to be critical, but also clearly affectionate about the people of our crazy little republic, Neil's work is always astute and filled with generous humour. Not say I say what, but Singapore can't be all bad if we managed to lure someone as talented as he is back."
Colin Goh, writer/director, *Talking Cock the Movie, Singapore Dreaming*

"Neil Humphreys is a believer—he believes that the human spirit will prevail to make things better all around. So he writes his stories with humour, an eye for detail and, most importantly, an empathy for the downtrodden. I'm glad that he has always

reserved a special place in his heart for migrant workers—
'maids', construction workers, undocumented workers. In his
own unique way, he has given a nudge or two, jabbed us once
in a while in the ribs, asking us to see how migrant workers
are human beings with similar aspirations, quirky habits, fears,
as many of us. Singapore has become richer with Humphreys'
observations and commentaries."

Braema Mathi, former NMP, founder-president of
Transient Workers Count Too and President of MARUAH,
a human rights NGO

"We should do a Neil Humphreys Musical. It would be
completely Singaporean, in Singlish, absolutely irreverent but
at the heart of it, true. With so many 'Notes' already written,
all we need to do is to put them together and we've got a hit
musical on our hands. Double confirm!"

Hossan Leong, actor, *The Singapore Boy*

"Neil Humphreys has that rare gift of telling non-Singaporeans
what they would never in a million years otherwise know about
our glorious Island, and telling Singaporeans about what we
think we already know about ourselves, and making us go, "****
... I never thought about it that way!" Reading his book once
made me laugh so hard I squirted *kopi* out of my nostrils onto
my Bermudas. And now he returns to find that our island has
got its sexy back. Warning: This book is a High Squirt Zone
and can be hazardous to your shorts."

Adrian Pang, actor, *Forever Fever, Spy Game, The Pupil*

"A more local kind of *ang moh*
You'd be severely pressed to find
A jaundiced view, nay, honest
His musings come to mind

The chap is tall as gangly
For useful observations found
The bits they say are dangly
Five feet off the ground

We've claimed for our own, Neil Humphreys
In truth forsooth, God knows
Long stick his nose in our business
And his business long stick in our nose."
Will Xavier, veteran broadcaster

"I read what he wrote. I read what was written about him.
Then I met him. He was all of what I thought he would be.
And more. The *Ang Moh* who lived in Toa Payoh. The *Ang Moh*
who wrote local stories. Of course the stories are coloured. With
a different sensibility. But at long last we have reached a point
where we have a foreign local writer, if there is ever such a thing.
As a filmmaker, I am looking forward to working with Neil.
Someone with a perspective from within and without. Someone
who may just connect this red dot with the world. In local and
international colours."
Daniel Yun, film producer, *I Not Stupid,
The Eye, 881, Painted Skin*

"Singapore is almost impossible to understand adequately if you use outsider measures to gauge it. Though British humour columnist Neil Humphreys is anything but a native, he writes so knowingly—and so well—that if Singapore's Ministry of Culture had any sense of humour at all, it would hire him as a consultant to lighten the place up some more. But the Ministry doesn't. Fortunately Humphreys does—in warmly agreeably huge doses."

Tom Plate, university professor, author of *Conversations with Lee Kuan Yew: Citizen Singapore—How to Build a Nation*

"Whatever you may think about the man, Neil Humphreys is never ever boring. The hours will melt away when you have got a book of his in your hands. And his latest effort, *Return to a Sexy Island*, is no exception. Told in his inimitably humorous, wickedly irreverent style, *Sexy Island* is one side of Singapore that many of us have suspected was always there but thank God for Neil, the man has the rare ability to put such indelicate thoughts into words. Lesser mortals would have been hounded into bankruptcy for daring to say what he has. And *Sexy Island* says it all. Reading his latest, sexy masterpiece, he talks about ladies of the night cavorting in Goodwood Park Hotel (fancy that) and the most impressive phallic symbol at the waterfront—gave me a tingly feeing (quite a rare experience these days for a man in his twilight years). I especially liked that part when Neil went skinny dipping in MacRitchie Reservoir ... No, I won't go on. That would be spoiling your fun."

Clement Mesenas, *Pinoy Star* editor, author of *The Last Great Strike—The untold story of the Straits Times shutdown of 1971*

"Most part Brit, generous portions of Singaporean and an all round hoot of an author, Neil is nothing less than a national treasure."
Hamish Brown, veteran broadcaster

"You think you got balls? This *ang moh* writer got bigger balls."
Royston Tan, writer/director of *Sons, Hock Hiap Leong, 48 on AIDS, Mother, 15: The Movie, 4:30, 881, 12 Lotus*

" 'Irreverent' is probably the word most commonly used to describe our author and his work(s). But it is not the only one. A random review might reveal a few we all recognise: provocative, controversial, cheeky, naughty, outrageous. Some may go further and include blasphemous, saucy, profane, impertinent."
Kirpal Singh, author of short stories and poems

"The rock star of authors in Singapore. His never-run-of-the-mill quips on this little red dot will either make you boil or chuckle like a little boy on nitrous oxide. A rebel with a cause you may call him, he explores and documents facets of the Lion City that you may find taboo or plainly refuse to acknowledge. Despise or embrace his coherent perspective, I am one of the lucky ones to have found a friend in this "Red Haired" man. Or, more accurately, he should be referred to as 'Sir' Neil Humphreys."
Taufik Batisah, singer, songwriter, producer

Return to a Sexy Island

NEIL HUMPHREYS

Marshall Cavendish
Editions

© 2012 Marshall Cavendish International (Asia) Private Limited
Reprinted 2012

Cover image and design by Bernard Go Kwang Meng

The publisher would like to thank Marina Bay Sands for their assistance
and use of the Sands SkyPark.

Published by Marshall Cavendish Editions
An imprint of Marshall Cavendish International
1 New Industrial Road, Singapore 536196

Other Marshall Cavendish Offices
Marshall Cavendish Corporation. 99 White Plains Road, Tarrytown NY 10591-9001, USA
• Marshall Cavendish International (Thailand) Co Ltd. 253 Asoke, 12th Flr, Sukhumvit 21
Road, Klongtoey Nua, Wattana, Bangkok 10110, Thailand • Marshall Cavendish (Malaysia)
Sdn Bhd, Times Subang, Lot 46, Subang Hi-Tech Industrial Park, Batu Tiga, 40000 Shah
Alam, Selangor Darul Ehsan, Malaysia

Marshall Cavendish is a trademark of Times Publishing Limited

National Library Board, Singapore Cataloguing-in-Publication Data
Humphreys, Neil.
Return to a sexy island / Neil Humphreys. – Singapore : Marshall Cavendish Editions, 2012.
p. cm.
Other title: Notes from a new Singapore
ISBN : 978-981-4382-67-0

1. Singapore – Anecdotes. 2. Singapore – Humor. I. Title. II. Title: Notes from a new
Singapore

DS609
959.57 — dc23   OCN793373104

Printed in Singapore by Chung Printing Pte Ltd

Acknowledgements

Uncle Leslie and Chris have been asking for a new island book ever since I hit the final full stop in the last one. When I finally returned to Singapore, they called the following morning to check if the new island book was ready. I appreciate their support and hope I can switch my phone back on now.

Stephanie, Mei Lin and the MCIA team soon whipped me into shape. Bernard made sense of my journey with a damn fine map and took the terrifically sexy cover shot of new Singapore. (All at Marina Bay Sands were good sports to finally let me get my feet wet.) As for the peerless Katharine, well, she remains an editor beyond compare. We started our island journey more than 10 years ago and she still scares the crap out of me.

Honourable handshakes must also go to Ben Slater for supporting my search for Saint Jack and Singapore's Otterman, N. Sivasothi, for answering my daft questions about wildlife, mangroves, escaped fugitives and haunted houses.

As always, I must thank my wonderful wife for tolerating my lost days in the jungle and my daughter for occasionally playing Dora to my Diego. I now look forward to her notes on Singapore.

Neil's Return to Singapore Tour

MALAYSIA

Johor Bahru

Chek Jawa

PULAU UBIN

Singapore FreePort

Tampines Mountain Biking Trail

Bedok Reservoir

NEWater

Coney Island

Treelodge @Punggol

Yishun

Bishan Park

Aljunied

Singapore Flyer (end of tour)

Marina Bay Sands (start of tour)

Marina Barrage

Toa Payoh Town Park

Woodlands

D'Kranji Farm Resort

Bukit Brown Cemetery

Jacob Ballas Children's Garden

Dempsey Hill

Pinnacle @Duxton

Tanjong Pagar Railway Station

Jewel Box

Universal Studios

Bukit Timah Railway Station

Rochester Park

Labrador Park

Railway Corridor

Fusionopolis

Jurong Lake

Tuas

Prologue

MY next-door neighbour was going to hit me. He was actually going to punch me in the face. This wasn't the Australian Dream, not a sober Australian dream anyway. Owning your own home—now that's the Aussie dream and I'd already done that. I had bought into the whole suburban ideal, complete with lawnmower, cream-coloured picket fence, leaf-blowing machine, the lot. My garage was filled with household items that had once been obscure but were now apparently essential: weed killer, lawn fertiliser, *L*-shaped lawn-edge cutting thingies, tins of paint and even secateurs. I didn't even know what secateurs were but I still knew that I had to have them. I still don't know how to spell the damn things (I had to spellcheck these ones). Once I was bending over the driveway trimming my beloved, hand-reared indigenous plants when the neighbour said, "That's a nice pair of secateurs you've got there." I thought I had a hole in my shorts. In truth, I often did have a hole in my shorts but that only added to my newfound Australian masculinity. Weekends were spent oiling decks, painting window frames, assembling bookcases, landscaping gardens and adjusting garage roller doors (usually by smacking them with a hammer and shouting, "Open, you little bastards."). I even had my own paint-spattered, oil-stained work shirt. I really was living the Australian Dream.

Singapore, my former home, my spiritual home, had never seemed further away.

My next-door neighbour took a step towards me and raised a malevolent fist. The Aussie dream was assuming nightmarish proportions. When my wife and I scratched the travel itch again back in September 2006 and left Singapore for Australia, we hadn't anticipated a close encounter with the next-door neighbour's clenched mitt. Being wide-eyed nature lovers, we had hoped for the odd date with a dopey, but adorable, echidna, the occasional sighting of a sleeping koala and a lolloping Eastern grey kangaroo bounding home across the paddocks in its daily race to beat the sunset. We had wanted to follow in the footsteps of the irreverent Steve Irwin and explore Australia's sizeable backyard.

Steve Irwin was killed by a stingray before we'd even had a chance to unpack our suitcases. Perhaps that was an ominous sign. It certainly was for Steve Irwin.

Using the hand that wasn't balled into a fist, my next-door neighbour pointed at the water tanks along the side of my house. It made him look like an unhinged air traffic controller.

"I'll tell you what my problem is," he bellowed, after I'd asked gently what his problem was. "It's them fucking water tanks."

Ah, the water tanks. They were my financial contribution to tackling climate change, Australia's crippling drought and the global decline of the world's most precious resource. I fancied myself as the Public Utilities Board (PUB) of the Aussie suburbs. If I couldn't acquire water from Malaysia or, in my case, the neighbouring suburb (I had tried but all that bucket-carrying at 4 a.m. was getting suspicious), I decided I would trap and harvest the rainwater in my gutters like a conscientious global citizen and filter it through to the toilets and washing machine. In Singapore,

I would have been applauded for demonstrating such initiative, even rewarded for fulfilling my civic duties (and possibly fined for installing two 2500-litre water tanks in the common corridor). In Australian suburbia, I was being castigated because the cream-coloured tanks blocked the view of ... the cream-coloured bricks of my house. People get publicly flogged for less in the suburbs.

"You didn't ask for my permission," the rocking, fist-waving, pointing neighbour cried, making a fine stab at replacing Andy Serkis, should the actor ever grow tired of the ape-acting, motion capture game.

"Your permission for what?" I enquired. "The tanks are on my property. They block no views. They are up against my brick wall, which is the same colour, cover no windows and are tucked beneath the gutter."

"They're a bloody eyesore. You should've asked for permission."

My next-door neighbour took another step towards me, his bluster swiftly giving way to outright belligerence. Now I'm not a fighting man by any means. The last time I had a fight was with Matthew Vickers back in Secondary 2. Vickers had cut the queue so I unleashed a sneaky knee to his ribs before he landed a sly blow to my eye. I then proceeded to pummel him with a series of punches that elicited a number of giggles from the gaggle of onlookers. I was well on top when Mr White, an English teacher who, despite the cool name, looked nothing like Harvey Keitel and had a ginger moustache, hauled us off to the principal's office, where I promptly shit myself. The fact that I remember this petty punch-up so proudly indicates how woefully inadequate I am in such circumstances. But I was still twice the size and half the age of my next-door neighbour. He was certainly brave. Nevertheless, his vacant, absent stare indicated that the point of no return had long since passed. Violence was the only conceivable option now.

This wasn't supposed to have happened. I loved Australia. I still love Australia with its dramatic landscapes, its endearing but exasperating weather patterns, its admirable sense of "fair go" for all, its quaint obsession with domestic football codes that are irrelevant beyond most state borders (let alone national ones) and the country's ability to produce the stupidest animals. (Kangaroos will wait patiently in a paddock for that solitary car to approach at 100 km/h and only then will they decide to cross the road, staring wide-eyed at the speeding vehicle as if to say, "Shit. Where did you come from?" I rest my case.)

Australia had been a prosperous place for my family for more than five years, in every sense. Our beautiful daughter was born Down Under and one of her first words was "echidna", swiftly followed by "Your dad's a Pommy bastard." (It is a state and federal law in Australia that the adjectival "Pommy" must always be affixed by "bastard". Traditionally, "Pommy" was usually followed by "poofter" but we now live in enlightened times.) We bought our first home in Australia, made many dear friends there and I somehow found the time to write three books that didn't have "island" in the title.

But something wasn't quite right. After five years, the travel itch needed scratching again. But it was more than that. I was starting to sound like That Really Annoying Expat. You know the one. He drones on endlessly about how wonderful the mother country is without ever actually returning there, rather like the Irish expats in New York or Indian expats living anywhere but in India. It's all superior culture this and superior cuisine that while overlooking the more obvious negatives such as the flailing economy in Ireland and the horrendous poverty in India.

I had become That Really Annoying Expat. But instead of championing the wonders of my hometown of Dagenham in East London (which is rather difficult to do when teenage residents are caught on camera mugging injured Malaysian students during a looting spree), I would tediously begin every sentence with "This would never happen in Singapore ..." or "In Singapore, you'd never see such municipal inefficiency ..." or "In Singapore, the prospect of running out of water would not be allowed ..." or "In Singapore, the airlines are more cost-effective. Tiger Airways is going to take down Jetstar."

You see. I wasn't always right.

But the sentiment was proving to be stubbornly consistent. The Little Red Dot rants were not anti-Australian or anti-British, just pro-Singaporean, pro-efficiency, pro-progress, pro-just-getting-the-bloody-job-done. Distance was making the heart grow if not fonder, then certainly more appreciative. I had swapped one country with no natural resources for one with natural resources in comparative abundance and before you could say, "Let's just dig it all up and sell it to China", I found myself saying things like "Singapore went from third world to first world in a single generation, yet I can't post a letter here after 5 p.m. ... Singapore has no natural resources and yet Australia is sending delegations there to learn how to manage its water supply ... Singapore is selling knowledge to the world, Australia is selling brown coal. Which one will last longer?"

I sounded like a recorded People's Action Party (PAP) rally stuck on repeat mode.

Of course, this was my fault. The old travel curse had struck again. Should you live in a country in need of a sudden injection of luck and prosperity, just insist I never stay there. When I left England in 1996, the country was tumbling towards the abyss of post-Thatcher monochrome mediocrity. Six months later, New Labour rode the brash technicolour wave of national euphoria for the next few years while I swiftly took care of Singapore and the Asian Currency Crisis. In 2006, I departed for Geelong, Victoria, and thereby gave my consent for Singapore to transform into the Monaco of Southeast Asia. Hotels, casinos, museums, conference and heritage centres, nature trails, theatres, Grands prix, giant flyers, eco-tourism and *ah longs*, or loan sharks, all flourished in my absence. After a mere five years, Singapore had become sexy. Who would have thought it? With my usual impeccable timing, I had swapped a sexy island for a pair of suburban secateurs.

Like a jilted lover jealously watching from afar as a former girlfriend goes through a lusty makeover, I read all the *Time* and *Newsweek* articles about shiny, sparkly, shimmery Singapore wooing visitors and winning over sceptical locals (some of them anyway, we'll get to Aljunied later) while I went about my business of cutting the lawn and contemplating slicing through the electrical cord just to bring a bit of spark to suburban life. After a particularly stimulating Saturday morning applying weed killer to the cracks in the driveway, sentimentality got the better of me. I took out my old map of Singapore, the one that had accompanied me around the island for my valedictory tour back in 2006. On the map, Sentosa still boasted tourism delights such as Fantasy Island and the Asian Village (before nitpickers write in, the map was bought earlier than 2006). Marina Bay had nothing to offer except Clifford Pier and the old Change Alley. Curious, I compared my tattered, former travel companion with the latest efforts from Google's cartographers. The changes were breathtaking, even as tiny symbols on a laptop screen. I was examining two different maps—two different islands—less than a decade apart.

In Australia, it is possible to pinpoint the location of a single tree after 30 years. I kid you not. *Mad Max*, the cult classic of Australian cinema, was filmed in Geelong in 1979 and to mark its 30th anniversary, an exhibition was staged with mini-tours arranged to revisit filming locations. Biker gangs came from all over the world and I remember an excited Japanese gang member, decked out in black leathers, tapping me on the shoulder as we gazed at an empty paddock before exclaiming, "The tree ... same tree ... There, the tree ... Mel Gibson ... He stand in front of tree ... Same tree ... never change ... same tree." I agreed with him, largely because I was alone and I wasn't sure how far his homage to post-apocalyptic, psychopathic mass-murdering bikers went. The man had flown from Japan to look at a tree, for heaven's sake. I checked the DVD later and the Japanese Easy Rider was right. In Australia, it is possible to locate a solitary tree in an unchanged environment after 30 years. In Singapore, a futuristic metropolis topped with a swimming pool in the clouds can mushroom around Marina Bay in less than five.

Singapore was offering me the unique opportunity to tour a country for the second time in five years and not visit the same place twice—unless it had been transformed in the interim. Would such a tour even be possible in any other country? It was an intriguing premise. And then there was also a chance for our daughter to learn conversational Mandarin. And Singapore has *pasar malams*, or night markets, region-free DVD players and cheap *hor fun*. The pull factors were too many to mention. I just needed a final push.

My next-door neighbour continued to dribble on about the trivial tanks, gesticulating aggressively and prodding me in the shoulder to emphasise a point (usually something about a camouflaging screen for water tanks being more important in the suburbs than life itself). To my credit, I had a sudden lucid moment of clarity. I heard a voice laughing. It was my voice. My subconscious had assumed control, mocking the insanity of the situation and forcing me to take stock. I was not going to get into a street fight with a neighbour over a pair of water tanks. I was not.

"I'm an intelligent man," I muttered and walked away. I think I was going for profundity, a kind of "less is more" philosophy, and for a few precious seconds I lived up to the billing. The worldly, much-travelled author was leaving the trivial little man to poison the air with his colourless invective. The trouble is the much-travelled author occasionally gets overruled by the kid from Dagenham who is less verbose, but more pertinent.

"Oi, moron," I heard myself shout as I marched back to the ranting one.

I had somehow convinced myself that retreating to my suburban kingdom was not a dignified, noble act, but one of cowardice. Surprisingly, the neighbour did not take kindly to being called a moron. He hurried across his garden, narrowly avoiding his manicured rose bushes of course, and held his paw up to my jaw.

"Don't you call me that," he screamed. "I'll smash your fucking face in. I'll smash your fucking face in. I'll smash your fucking face in."

I wasn't sure if he was repeating himself for dramatic effect or he really did intend to smash my face in three times, but it was at that moment—that exact moment—that I knew it was time to return to Singapore.

One

THE woman beside me was talking to herself. It was barely audible at first, but then she got louder and I peered up from my notepad. In my experience, I believe it's not the people who have a little natter with themselves in public places that one should be wary of, it's the people who suddenly increase the volume. They're the ones whose shoulder you generally peek over to see if anyone is standing behind them holding a syringe. Personally, I enjoy a disarming chat with myself. It affords me the opportunity to pass the time and arrange my diary for the week. But I never start talking loudly. That has mothers shielding their children.

I did that scratching-my-right-shoulder-with-my-chin thing to sneak a peek. The young businesswoman was muttering a few words aloud as we trundled along Nicoll Highway on the top deck of the No. 14. She needed to adjust the volume slightly but there was no cause for alarm. When I was a kid growing up in Dagenham, everyone engaged in healthy discourses with themselves on buses between generous swigs of cider.

I found myself seated beside The Woman Who Talked Too Loudly because I had decided to begin the tour of new Singapore where my previous valedictory jaunt around old Singapore had almost ended: at Marina Bay. The former gateway to the country—and the very spot where dear old Stamford Raffles popped by in the first place—now linked a nation's history with its prosperous future and, quite literally, marked Singapore's spot at the centre of Asia's blitzkrieg march through the 21st century. Marina Bay brought rubber, tin and coffee merchants into Singapore's waterways two hundred years ago. Now it's bringing bankers, Formula 1 drivers and gamblers.

Besides, it was a humid, headache-inducing hazy day and I was desperate for a bit of backstroke in the world's sexiest swimming pool. But I had to find it first.

Now, Marina Bay Sands, with its three hotel towers symbolising three decks of cards, can be seen from East Coast Park. On a sunny day, or when Indonesian farmers are not playing Guy Fawkes, the resort can be spied from the neighbouring island of Batam. The gambling resort boasts Singapore's largest hotel, one of the biggest conference centres in Asia, an art science museum, more celebrity chefs than an IKEA bookshelf and, some 57 storeys in the air, a canoe-shaped viewing platform from which you expect Boba Fett to fall off and tumble into the sarlacc pit. From travel magazine readers sitting on Singapore Airlines flights to leathery-faced fishermen lazily casting off from the jetty at East Coast Park, Marina Bay Sands is inescapable. And yet, do you think I could find the bloody thing from Suntec City?

In my new shiny street directory—I never leave home to write a book without one—Suntec City and the Sands are linked by both Bayfront Avenue, a road that did not exist five years ago (just extraordinary), and The Helix, a pedestrian bridge (ditto). But I failed to track down either as I continued to stagger around the monstrously long levels and soporific shopping stretches that fill the lost world of Suntec City. It is only a matter of time before anthropologists discover a forgotten tribe of people beside the Suntec City fountain whose descendents only popped into Carrefour for some cheap croissants.

I wandered aimlessly into a Suntec City public toilet, more for the change of scenery than anything else, and sat down to re-examine the directory. The chap in the cubicle beside me was talking animatedly on the phone in Mandarin. He was also straining. Did the guy think I couldn't hear him? More pertinently, did he not consider the possibility that the listener might discern the straining down the line? This neither happened during my five years in Australia nor growing up in the UK. Yet in Singapore, I'm no stranger to overhearing another man's toilet talk. For a society preoccupied with saving face, some Singaporeans are not shy when it comes to conducting a business meeting while having a crap.

Motivated to push on immediately, I powered on through the underpass of Esplanade MRT Station and was thoroughly entertained by an absorbing temporary visual arts exhibition. A puppet and video installation had been hung along the otherwise pristine walls of the underpass (roll your eyes all you want but I grew up with urine-stained walls in London underpasses, some of it was my own, so I'll take pristine over piss every time). The exhibition depicted Singapore's aunties and uncles going about their daily lives. An old man gave out leaflets, an auntie cleared the tables of indifferent teenagers, an elderly can collector explained how his earnings rarely exceeded $15 a day. This wasn't a few puppets to distract swarms of commuters. This was social protest masquerading as a public art exhibition, a reason to be cheerful.

Whistling Billy Bragg's "Waiting for the Great Leap Forwards", I marched purposefully through the Esplanade Mall and found a bench roughly halfway along Marina Promenade. On my right, I picked out The Fullerton Hotel and what was once the iconic Clifford Pier. I had sat at the pier in 2006 and peered through the darkness at the twinkling lights of the cranes that were laying the foundations for Marina Barrage, which was going to create a new metropolis, girdled by a freshwater bay. In *Final Notes from a Great Island*, I wrote: "Singapore has to get the Marina Bay project right and it will. It has no choice. The government now accepts that a five-roomed flat, decent education and pristine trains that always run on time no longer impress younger, restless Singaporeans. They need to have some bloody fun in their own country …"

On my left was the "fun". The packaging was certainly alluring. From the close vantage point of Marina Promenade between the Esplanade and the floating platform, possibly the best place in the bay to see two worlds collide, Marina Bay Sands took my breath away. On first viewing, it doesn't look of this earth, but rather the childlike imagination of James Cameron running around the CGI department with his 3D specs on. Championed as the world's most expensive hotel at $8 billion, the three towers are home to 2,561 hotel rooms. On their own, they are just three tower blocks that might match the surrounds of an East London housing estate. It is the Kubrickian sky park that knits the trio together and gives the complex its surreal celluloid sheen. From where I sat, the sky park resembled a hoverboard awaiting the giant Nike-covered foot of Michael J. Fox to descend from the clouds.

An elderly Chinese couple arrived to take photographs of their grandson with the Sands as a backdrop. The kid looked up and said, "Wow." Nothing else. Just wow. I knew how he felt, of course. I can still recall the day we first spotted the new railings around our primary school.

I had planned to reach the resort by crossing The Helix pedestrian bridge but found myself thwarted by the Singapore Grand Prix. The Formula 1 race was a few days away and parts of the Marina Bay street circuit were in the process of being fenced off and blocked out, much to the inconvenience of those to whom Formula 1 racing means very little (if one were being cynical, one might say that's the majority of Singaporeans or anyone who cannot afford bottles of champagne that cost $1,000, but that's only if one were being cynical). Marina Promenade was closed off around its floating platform. I had no access to The Helix.

"Just go through, lah," I heard a voice say. The elderly Chinese grandparents were waving me through.

"There are construction workers inside," I replied, peering through a crack in the temporary fence. "I don't think I can go inside."

"Eh, never mind," the grandmother continued. "Just go through and bluff. Take shortcut. They will think you are an *ang moh* with the F1."

She was right. I snuck through a gap in the fence and immediately found myself in the path of a couple of concerned construction workers heading my way. With hands placed authoritatively behind my back, I nodded. They nodded back. I started to enjoy myself. Clearly, I was an *ang moh* foreman acting on behalf of mad F1 chief Bernie Ecclestone. Clearly, such foremen always examine F1 tracks dressed in Abbey Road T-shirts and khaki shorts. By the time I had reached the Helix, I was nodding, winking, waving and giving the thumbs-up to any workers in my eye line.

Now I love a good bridge. I always have. As a child, I would take regular day trips "up London" with my best friend Ross just to marvel at Tower Bridge (well, I admired the bascule mechanics of the English icon while Ross admired busty women). From Sydney Harbour Bridge to the Golden Gate Bridge and Brooklyn Bridge, I've been infatuated with them all but you never forget your first love. Tower Bridge stands tallest not only for its timeless bascules and elegant Cornish granite and Portland stone towers decorated in that Victorian Gothic style that is so quintessentially London but because I once found five quid there. My mum says this is the only reason why I remain fixated with bridges.

Still, The Helix did not disappoint. The world's first double curved helix bridge (although I seriously doubt engineers had previously been compelled to shout, "Quick, let's go and build the world's first double curved helix bridge."), the 280-metre-long pedestrian walkway provided a pleasant, sea breezy jaunt. Steel tubes form the minor and major helixes and I later discovered that the bridge actually begins at the Youth Olympic Park. But I am embarrassed to say that the Youth Olympic Park completely passed me by. But then, many Singaporeans might say the same about the Youth Olympics.

As I meandered across The Helix, I found myself humming, "Da da da da, da da da, da, da da." It was "The Imperial March", Darth Vader's main theme from the *Star Wars* movies. The ArtScience Museum presented itself on the right side of The Helix and somehow plugged into my internal jukebox. The lotus-inspired architecture is meant to represent "the welcoming hand of Singapore". No, it doesn't. It represents Darth Vader's sleeping capsule. I stared at the museum for several moments, waiting for its 10 white extensions, supposedly representing fingers, to open a little further and turn to reveal dear old Darth sitting on his black throne in *The Empire Strikes Back* and waiting for his helmet to cover his scarred head. Acclaimed architect Moshe Safdie designed the ArtScience Museum and he should confess now that when he was standing over his drawing book desperate for inspiration, he started humming, "Da da da da, da da da, da, da da."

I walked around the ArtScience Museum, along the boardwalk and rested on a bench that was part of an open-air theatre called

Event Plaza. The theatre was bookended by two floating crystal pavilions. One housed a couple of nightclubs, the other was preparing to open the world's largest Louis Vuitton boutique, which seemed incongruous. The glassy, Louvre pyramid-like facade belonged in a Dan Brown novel, possibly called *The Lost Tai Tai's Handbag*. More than two dozen foreign construction workers toiled under a humid sky, presumably to meet some insane deadline, while a plump *ang moh* stood around with his hands on his hips and pointed a bit.

As I scribbled away on the bench, a young Filipino woman appeared at my shoulder. She squatted to get a better view of my notepad and tried to decipher my handwriting. It was a futile exercise. I gave up trying years ago.

"Ooh," she said, smiling far too widely as she scanned the page.

"Er, good morning," I ventured cautiously.

"Mmm, yes," she said, continuing to read over my shoulder, her face almost pressed against my ear.

"Can I help you?" I asked, more assertively this time.

"No, no, I'm fine," she said, waving me away like a mildly irritating fly.

"Are you sure I can't help you with anything?"

"No, really, I'm fine," she said decisively, annoyed by my constant interruptions as she read my notepad.

"Well, I'll be off then," I muttered, rising quickly before she had a chance to pinch my notepad, and headed for the air-conditioned comfort of The Shoppes.

Marina Bay Sands might trumpet its leviathan of luxury outlets, its 1,000,000 square feet of retail space and more than 300 stores, but its greatest achievement is having the silliest, most pretentious name.

What the hell are The Shoppes? Was Singapore's shiniest shopping mall named by a three-year-old? Did he one day squeak, "Can we have some sweeties, some drinkies and some biccies at the shoppes?" and the name stuck? The name has that medieval, ye olde English pubbe, whiff of a Deep England, full of idealised, pre-industrial rural villages found in children's fairy tales. Anything prefixed by *ye* in England usually sells postcards, twee tea towels and shortbread biscuit tins for women with white hair in tartan skirts. Anything affixed with an extra *e* usually sells expensive lattes and has gone overboard with the Laura Ashley. With the quaint, jocular spelling of The Shoppes, I expected woodlands, pixies, toadstools and a troll beneath the food court.

Instead I stepped into a hybrid, an eccentric cross between the Gothic curved ceilings of St Pancras railway station in London and the bland functionality of an aircraft hangar, with an anomalous canal carving its way through the middle. Cavernous, curved and contemporary, The Shoppes have been called a modern shopping mecca (by the writers of the Marina Bay Sands brochure I picked up at an information counter) offering every ostentatious brand worth handing to the maid to stick in the car boot. All the names were there under one roof. From one spot, I picked out Gucci, Chanel, Hublot and Salvatore Ferragamo. I had never seen so many designer labels in such close proximity since last visiting a Toa Payoh *pasar malam*. And this was the first time that all the brand names had been spelt correctly. Never have there been so many products in one mall that I could not afford. I peered into the Cartier window and nearly required a lie-down. I was struck by the same question that occurred to me as I bluffed my way through the Formula 1 racetrack. Who, exactly, are The Shoppes for?

Bored within milliseconds, I decided to play a game: find a shop I could afford. I made it harder for myself by sticking to the higher levels. The layout of The Shoppes was not unlike that of the *Titanic*, with the lower levels being more financially accessible with a pharmacy, a supermarket and a food court (offering a standard plate of chicken rice for an eye-watering $6.80. For almost seven bucks, I'd expect Chicken Little on a plate.). Hidden among the Fendi and Ferrari boutiques, I chanced upon a shop within my price range: 7-Eleven. With chest inflated proudly, I yanked open one of the drinks fridges. A can of Coke Zero was $2.20.

So I couldn't really afford 7-Eleven either.

But The Shoppes did offer hidden gems along its walls in the form of an imposing series of blown-up black-and-white photographs of old Singapore stretched across giant canvases. I recognised the more obvious images of Fort Canning, Boat Quay and North Bridge Road but one or two grainier portraits were more ambiguous. After checking for information panels, I made a misguided attempt to flirt with the petite, attractive Chinese girl behind the info counter nearby.

"Hi there, I'm just wondering if there is any information on those photos," I enquired. "Are there any information panels anywhere?"

"I don't think so, sir," she replied cheerily.

"Please, call me Neil."

"I don't think so, Neil, sir."

"That's such a shame because the images are great, aren't they?" I gushed, with far too much enthusiasm.

"Yes, I suppose."

"You see that one up there is clearly Boat Quay. I'm sure you recognise the sampans and the shophouses and that one over there is Fort Canning. Do you know what Fort Canning's original Malay name was?"

She struggled with her indifference.

"I'll tell you. It was Bukit Larangan. Did you know that?"

She did not know that. She did not care. There was a pause. This was awkward.

"Oh well ... Hey, do you know when that Louis Vuitton store opens in that glass pyramid thingy?"

The girl's pretty eyes widened, sparkled. Suddenly, she was a mask of concentration, focused and energised.

"Yes, sir, Neil, it opens on 17 September. It's going to be the largest LV store in Asia."

It did. And it is.

"But it's not the only LV store in Singapore, sir, Neil," she continued breathlessly. "There is another LV store at ION in Orchard Road and a third store in ..."

I think she was punishing me for the Bukit Larangan stuff. We had different priorities. It was time to go swimming in the sky.

Two

I WAS sidetracked by a sampan. I had headed down to the basement to take the underpass beneath Bayfront Avenue that connected The Shoppes with the hotel towers when I spotted a muscle-bound Malay chap guiding two giggling Japanese women and their shopping bags down a canal. This is not an everyday occurrence for me in a shopping mall. Growing up in Dagenham, our modern shopping mecca (to quote Marina Bay Sands) was Lakeside, which skirted the borders of both Essex and Kent. The Shoppes has Hermès, BALLY and MIU MIU. Lakeside had a Hammers shop, Boots the chemist and hoodies. So riding a Chinese wooden boat through the middle of a shopping mall had an impudence that appealed.

I wandered across to the canal, which had a strange blue-green hue suggesting it had been filled with Listerine. The Singaporean gondolier (technically, if he's an oarsman in a sampan, he's not a gondolier, is he?) helped the Japanese ladies alight and handed them the shopping bags containing enough garments to clothe an impoverished village in Prada for a week. I waited for them to totter off before approaching a counter filled with the usual tourist tat.

"Good morning," I said brightly. "I see this is the counter for the sampan rides. How's your day been? Up and down?"

She didn't laugh either.

"How much is the sampan ride?" I asked, desperately hoping it might be free with every purchase in The Shoppes (I had relented and finally bought a banana from 7-Eleven and kept the receipt).

"It's $10, sir," replied the petite, attractive Chinese twenty-something. A theme was developing here. Did Marina Bay Sands ban fat, ugly people from everywhere but the casino?

"It's only for me," I pointed out. "I'm not bringing a family of six."

I craned my head and peered down the canal. The Listerine lake was less than 50 metres and five minutes long. Money is just not expected to be an issue to the type of visitor attracted to Marina Bay Sands. Opposite the canal was an art gallery selling photo collages for up to $50,000.

Toto, we're not in Toa Payoh anymore.

"But when you get to the end of the canal, you will go around the Rain Oculus," the counter girl continued brightly.

"There's a rhinoceros down there?"

"No, no, the Rain ... Oculus. It's like a water attraction. Every hour, swirling water is released through the hole, from two storeys above."

Unique, perhaps, but I passed on the sampan ride. It really wasn't the money in the end. It was the sight of the expectant gondolier (I'm sticking with gondolier now, we're almost done) smiling back at me and holding up his oar. Suddenly, the thought of me lying back on a luxury sampan while a grinning gondolier stood over me working up a sweat was rather disconcerting. Instead, the wonderfully helpful and courteous counter girl guided me through the underpass, across the hotel's ridiculously extravagant lobby and directed me towards the Sands SkyPark.

I had high expectations as I handed over $20 for a ticket. The Sands SkyPark defies logic, common sense and even the naked eye. Do you remember when you were at kindergarten drawing your first houses? The windows floated inside the square unsupported, the door was slanted and the roof was a circle. The teacher would give you a patronising pat on the head, privately giggle at your drawing and leave you in the reading corner eating the pages of some *Biff and Kipper* books. Well, that irreverent, rebellious, anarchic, nonconformist drawing is the Sands SkyPark. There is nothing sensible, rational, practical, mundane or clinical (adjectives so often associated with old Singapore) about the alien architecture.

Picture yourself again as that wide-eyed kindergarten kid explaining the fanciful features of his latest dysfunctional design to his jaded teacher as you consider the modern engineering marvel. The observation deck, designed to resemble a ship, is above three 55-storey towers, some 200 metres above the sea. Thanks to one of the largest and most daring cantilevers in the world, the park stretches 66.5 metres beyond one of the towers, making the platform longer than the Eiffel Tower lying down. (I've never fully understood such cocky proclamations. Who wants to see the Eiffel Tower lying down?) Hundreds of trees traverse the perimeter to provide shelter from the wind for visitors, joggers, hotel guests and swimmers, all of whom can number almost 4,000. It is a garden city poking out beneath the clouds and peering down at that slightly older, more established garden city below. I was thoroughly excited to see one from the other.

The glass doors parted on the 56th floor and an oppressive gust of blistering hot air battered me about the face. I tiptoed outside but could only squint towards the ground. The heat was intolerable and the sun's glare inescapable. I had neglected to bring sunglasses. Do not make the same mistake. It took my cowering eyeballs, fearful of being scorched, several minutes to adjust before being able to peek out from my scrunched-up eyelids. As I took a slow, tentative step towards the fence, a sticky wind decided to roar across the observation deck. I retreated and readjusted my underwear. The relentless sweat had trickled mercilessly down my back and made its way to my buttocks. The heat from 56 floors produces perspiration in unfortunate places. The vertigo almost produces something else entirely.

Heights are rarely an issue. I once climbed to the top of Sydney Harbour Bridge without hesitation, my only concern was being dressed in a billowing blue boiler suit that left me looking like Barney the Dinosaur's brother. But standing on a suspended cantilever that juts out from a hotel tower is difficult for the brain to compute. There is something in the subconscious constantly grasping around for the comforting familiarity of terra firma. I foolishly placed my hand and arm through the bars on the fence to get an unblocked panoramic phone camera shot of Singapore's skyline. The breeze tugged at my arm and loosened my sphincter at the same time. I did not shove my arm through the fence again. I noticed that most of the other visitors were also keeping a respectable distance from the deck's edge. There was a shared, unsaid experience among the majority of Sands SkyPark observers that day. We were all slightly shitting ourselves.

The view from the top is heady (and even hedonistic from the swimming pool) but overly familiar. I listened to the unbridled enthusiasm of an Italian family and actually envied their sense of awe. For the first-time visitor, the Sands SkyPark offers an intoxicating, unique 360-degree vista of glittering business and residential skyscrapers that is surely unrivalled by any other metropolis on the planet. A futuristic panorama that is always going to be more *Blade Runner* than Bishan. For many Singaporeans, it's their workplace. I picked out Clifford Centre, where I had once worked when the old, dowdy building (compared to its loftier neighbours) still housed newspaper offices, and thought about Egypt. I recalled an Egyptian mate from university who told us how he used to travel to work every morning and never look up from his magazine when the bus passed the Pyramids. I'm not suggesting the Sands SkyPark qualifies as one of the modern wonders of the world but the sentiment is the same. Overseas visitors scan the horizon and see a series of picture postcards. Singaporeans see their workplaces and favourite makan spots.

Ironically, the real pleasure from atop a sky bridge that defines new Singapore is outlining the map of old Singapore. Forget the high-rises. They can be spotted from beach barbecues along the East Coast. From its vantage point south of Singapore's business and colonial district, the observation deck allows the onlooker to block out the modern and trace the historic by following the Singapore River as it snakes its way through the city. The Fullerton, Boat Quay, Raffles' landing site, Clarke Quay, North Bridge Road, the former Supreme Court and parliament buildings, Chinatown and Fort Canning Park are all easily discernible from such a dizzying height. Like an archaeologist digging with a shovel 56 storeys deep, the 21st-century Sands SkyPark has managed to carve out 19th-century Singapore for all to appreciate.

I tried to locate the rough spot where my wife and I had sat on the rocks back in 1996 and posed for daft photographs at the (old) water's edge. The traditional fishing haunt had long since been swallowed by one of the Esplanade's theatres. Peering down at the Esplanade on my right, the Sands SkyPark also allowed me to put a stubborn argument to bed. The Theatres on the Bay are known locally and affectionately as the durians but I have always harboured misgivings over the nickname. From the observation deck, there is no debate. The two theatres are the bulbous eyes of a bluebottle fly.

I climbed to the highest point of the observation deck on the 57th storey, which houses the inevitable exclusive rooftop nightclub called KU DÉ TA (Get it? Cool right?), and heard the distant splashing of rich people. My timing was perfect. The midday sun offered no respite and a refreshing dip 200 metres above the sea in a pool beneath the heavens seemed very much the cut of my jib. I picked up the pace along the tree-lined path, with the Singapore Straits on my left and the city skyline on my right, and followed the splashing.

And there it was, the sexiest swimming pool on the planet—desirable, captivatingly curvy and, ultimately, unobtainable.

Being an infinity pool, the water gives the impression that it extends to the horizon, trickles over the side and falls 57 storeys below. Of course, the water is gathered in a catchment area and then pumped back into the main pool. My sister and I managed to replicate the effects of an infinity pool when we were kids in our Dagenham back garden. Whenever we sought to create the illusion of the water running off the horizon, we sat on the walls of our blow-up paddling pool. On more than one occasion, we underestimated the basic laws of physics and weight distribution and the paddling pool would ping up from the other side and bury my sister.

No chance of that happening at Marina Bay Sands. At 150 metres in length, the pool is the longest infinity swimming pool in the world, affording unrivalled views to the north and cooling breezes (for Singapore) from the south. It was a credit to my self-restraint that I refrained from stripping off right there in front of security staff and taking the plunge. I waved my SkyPark admission ticket pompously in the air and approached the pool counter. I was dazzled by a blinding array of gleaming white teeth. The counter girl was ridiculously pretty. She was Malay this time. Same Marina Bay Sands rule, different race.

"Good afternoon, I'd like to go swimming, please," I said, with an air of confidence I felt befitted the surroundings. "Where are the changing rooms?"

"Hello, sir, are you a hotel guest?" she enquired gently, in a measured, rehearsed voice that hinted that this was not her first time asking the question.

"Er, no, but I've got my ticket right here," I continued, still upbeat.

"Yes, sir, but that's only for the Sands SkyPark."

"But we're on the Sands SkyPark. It's a bit hard to pop anywhere else right now," I reasoned, still jovial, but wavering ever so slightly.

"I understand, sir, but the ticket only gives you access to the SkyPark's observation deck. The pool is reserved for hotel guests."

"But I've got my ticket," I pleaded, and held it aloft like Charlie and his Wonka bar. "And I've brought my towel. Look."

I produced my Beatles towel from my rucksack to somehow prove that I wasn't a liar. I still cannot believe that I brandished my Beatles towel and displayed it under the nose of the pretty girl.

"I can see that, sir, but the pool is only reserved for hotel guests," she reiterated, steadfastly professional and reasonable throughout. "If you booked a room, you could use the pool."

"How much are the rooms then?"

"Well, we're usually fully booked over the weekends but during the week, if it's off-peak, you might be able to get a room for $400."

The world's sexiest swimming pool is also one of the most expensive. I did not have $400 to hand. At that particular moment, I did not have 400 cents to hand in cash (the 7-Eleven banana had cleared me out). I had one weapon left in my armoury—desperation.

"You see, the thing is, I'm trying to write a book about new, sexy Singapore," I rambled. "You know, how the city-state, particularly the Marina Bay area, has been transformed in the last five years and what could be newer or sexier than an infinity swimming pool on top of the world?"

The sexy reference piqued her interest. At least, I thought it did. I covered my eyes from the glare as she smiled at me again and then offered me a positively Dickensian crumb of comfort.

"You can watch if you like, sir," she said.

"I'm sorry?"

"You can watch the hotel guests swim for a while if you want."

On that observation deck, the temperature exceeded 35 degrees, the southerly breeze felt like volcanic ash splattering against the back of my neck, the sweat was making my genitalia behave like a couple of hard-boiled eggs in a simmering saucepan and I had been cordially invited to watch wealthy tourists sip Singapore slings and grope each other on poolside sunloungers. How could I possibly refuse?

Feeling like a Victorian manservant invited up from the scullery to watch the aristocratic feast, I slumped on a bench and peered through a gap in a sunshade (the real function of which, I believe, was to separate the hotel guests from the SkyPark gawkers) and reminded myself that I had paid $20 for the privilege.

There is something disturbingly voyeuristic about ogling holidaymakers at a swimming pool. I thought of the British holiday camp swimming pools back in the 1980s when it had been briefly fashionable to build colossal windows along pool walls that faced into a restaurant or bar. The original, quaintly naive idea for such viewing windows was so that young swimmers got to perform forward rolls and back flips for their gushing grandparents and restaurant patrons were entertained by the balletic images of athletic breaststroking bodies gliding effortlessly through the water. Of course, what they usually ended up seeing was a couple of teenage boys dropping their shorts and jiggling their spotty arses from side to side while diners chomped on their sausages.

I fixed upon a plump Caucasian guy carving a trench through the middle of the rooftop pool. He had plenty of room to manoeuvre, not so much because of the pool's exclusivity but because his attempts to show off his butterfly looked more like a fat caterpillar flailing around in a puddle. Judging from the other SkyPark ticket holders who had gathered around me, he had drawn quite a crowd and treated us to a bit of a butterfly show. Our respective positions were clearly delineated. He was rich. We were not. He was cool. We were not.

For an encore, he picked up his cocktail, waded across the water, stretched out across the edge of the infinity pool, took a sip and threw his head back, the world literally beneath his feet. As the water poured around him, he reigned ... until a young Singaporean lifeguard came over and told him to take his glass out of the pool. The guy turned as puce as his back. Even in sexy Singapore, there are still rules.

And three weeks after I visited, Marina Bay Sands introduced another one. SkyPark visitors are no longer allowed to view the swimming pool independently. Three guided tours a day, which offer a brief stop at the pool, are now available to observation deck guests. The area where I had sat and watched butterfly boy do his thing is now closed off to the public. Apparently, hotel guests had complained of a lack of privacy and crowds watching them while they swam.

In my defence, I hadn't laughed too loudly when the *ang moh* got told off.

Three

WHEN I grow up, I want to be Alice Tan. Even allowing for the indomitable, resilient reputation of the Singapore Auntie, Ms Tan is one extraordinary woman. The retiree somehow managed to gamble for six days straight without once changing her clothes or taking a shower. On the eve of Chinese New Year in February 2011, the mother of four was informed by a fortune teller that her "fortune star" was at its brightest. With not a moment to lose, she dashed to Singapore's Resorts World Casino on Sentosa and set up home at the baccarat tables for the marathon six-day session. To underscore an obvious point, as I write this, Singapore's temperature is hovering around the 30-degree mark with the humidity at 70 per cent. I cannot sit at a desk for six hours without getting an uncomfortable undercarriage.

But Ms Tan did not wash for fear of scrubbing away her "fortune star". She did not change her clothes for the same reason. She claimed in the Singapore media that there was "no need" for clean clothes as a wet towel and deodorant had sufficed during her baccarat binge (but her croupiers had needed asbestos gloves and gas masks).

I retain a soft spot for Ms Tan because she reminds me of my grandmother in her prime. Her East London bathroom belonged in a show home, not because she polished regularly but because she had "a good stand-up wash in the kitchen sink" every morning. Why waste water and begrime the bath? My grandmother was conserving natural resources long before it became fashionable and Ms Tan did her bit at the casino. For six days, she had the smallest carbon footprint in Asia. And most certainly, the smelliest.

The 64-year-old lived on coffee and Milo, slept in her car outside the casino for no more than four hours at a time, used panty-liners to save on underwear, played among the smokers to conceal her body odour, bet between $500 and $1,000 a hand and switched from the gaming tables to the jackpot machines when tiredness took its toll because they substituted brain power for mere luck, which she had in spades, remember, according to the fortune teller.

She lost $12,000 and went home with a smell that will outlast religion.

Her story made the newspapers in Australia, where I originally read about the feisty Ms Tan. Singaporean stories of this nature are popular fodder for the print press Down Under as part of a reciprocal agreement between the two countries. Australian tabloids report on money-obsessed gambling Asians, draconian government rulings and Caucasian clowns getting caned for vandalising MRT trains to reinforce archaic stereotypes while Singapore gives media oxygen to the Southeast Asian Satan Pauline Hanson, incidences of racial intolerance and any suggestion that the property market is on a downward spiral to hint strongly that Australia remains a racist, economic backwater rather than a green, spacious, stress-free haven to retire to with Central Provident Fund (CPF) savings. (Neither side is entirely right nor entirely wrong, of course, but the tabloid tennis between the territories has been thoroughly entertaining for the last five years.)

As for the indefatigable Ms Tan, she is but a rookie in the

ongoing gambling games of endurance currently being played out in the city. In the same month that Ms Tan was felling her fellow gamblers with a single waft of her armpit, South Korean national Dr Lee Pan Seop disappeared. He was last spotted at the Marina Bay Sands casino at 3 a.m. on 22 February. He failed to turn up for work. He did not answer his phone. His fearful friends then lodged a missing person's report. Police attempted in vain to track Lee down. His vanishing act made the national newspapers. The 35-year-old with a PhD in international business was long gone.

And then he emerged 16 days later from the Marina Bay Sands casino.

He had not once stepped foot outside the casino during those 16 days.

He should never have been allowed in the casino in the first place. He clearly does not play with a full deck.

The longest I had ever spent in an Asian casino was around 16 minutes. In September 2001, I had spent three interminable weeks covering the Southeast Asian (SEA) Games in Kuala Lumpur. As a reward, apparently, the journalists were driven to the dreary, grubby, nicotine-stained casino in the Genting Highlands, north of Kuala Lumpur. I took pity on a lonely croupier at an otherwise deserted black jack table. I sat down and handed over a 50-ringgit note. She took it, dealt me a 17, revealed her two-card 19 and the game was over and my money lost faster than the time it took me to type this sentence. I did not get it. And I still do not get it. But with a casino deliberately secreted away inside Marina Bay Sands quietly going about its business of funding the entire resort and fuelling Singapore's economy, I was eager to at least try and grasp its magnetic pull. A pull so powerful, it cost a South Korean national his university research job and forced a retiree to wear panty-liners for almost a week.

But first, I took my seat in the outdoor Event Plaza for the largest light, laser and water show in Southeast Asia. Situated between the two crystal pavilions with downtown Singapore as a backdrop, the Wonder Full fancy fountains extravaganza had an enviable location. From the Bellagio in Las Vegas to Marina Bay Sands, casinos cannot get enough of dancing water jets swaying to a stirring classical soundtrack. Someone had handed me a leaflet earlier in the day about the Wonder Full show and I was keen to take it in before venturing into the casino for two reasons. First, it was free. Second, the leaflet declared that—and I must quote verbatim here to do justice to the generosity—"Wonder Full is Marina Bay Sands' gift to Singapore." Dear me. Nothing like a bit of humility, is there? I wasn't sure whether I should collect donations and thank you notes from grateful spectators or hand out sick buckets.

The Event Plaza was eerily quiet for a free, family-friendly show (and one that was a gift to the people of Singapore, remember). Being 9.30 p.m. on a Monday night, a packed house was never likely but the fact that most of the families gathering around me were a mixture of Asian and Western tourists suggested, once again, that Singaporeans are yet to fully embrace Marina Bay Sands beyond its baccarat tables. (In the interests of objectivity, I returned again on a Friday night and was treated to both a second show and a superb live jazz band, neither of which was treated with the audiences that both performances deserved.) The resort's appeal has not filtered down to the heartlands in the way that Orchard Road or even VivoCity at HarbourFront has managed to do.

Still, the Singaporean skyline by night, surveyed from the south for the first time, is always appealing. I picked out the Merlion, just a white dribbling dot on the landscape from this distance, and found myself distracted, as usual, by the puerile rather than the profound. When admired from the angle of the Marina Bay Sands Event Plaza, the Esplanade's Theatres on the

Bay can be found in the northeast corner. From here, the Swissôtel The Stamford hotel stood resolutely and most erect between the two round theatre domes. I will say nothing further, other than should you visit the Wonder Full light and water show in the near future, casually turn your head to your right and tell me you do not also see the most impressive phallic symbol in Asia.

Well, Marina Bay Sands' free gift to the masses was always going to be something of an anticlimax after that. But I was pleased to discover that Wonder Full had followed the well-trodden path of its predecessors by creating a light, laser and water show seemingly influenced by copious amounts of hallucinogenic substances. The narrative involved little more than a series of unhinged images being projected onto three water screens. First, a lotus leaf opened. I got that one, the imagery paid tribute to Darth Vader's sleeping chamber on the other side of the resort. But beyond the lotus leaf, I was lost in an assault on the senses involving giant eyeballs, green lasers and a disturbingly large baby with a humongous head straight out of *2001: A Space Odyssey* while Louis Armstrong thought to himself what a wonderful world it was. The only narrative that I could make out was the rather empathic banging of multicultural, multi-religious drums, with projected images of multiracial families hugging each other on the water screens. Backed by an uplifting symphony orchestra blaring through the stunning 7.1 surround sound system, Wonder Full felt like a National Day Parade rehearsal. All that was missing was Gurmit Singh jumping in the air and shouting, "Singapore! ... Are you ready to par-tee?"

Wonder Full was confusing, bombastic, nonsensical and, at times, bewildering. It was marvellous. With Louis Armstrong ringing in my eyes, I felt unexpectedly invigorated and bounded off to the money-pumping heart of new Singapore—a casino that for decades the country swore it would never build.

I joined a chirpy Chinese chap on the escalator. He wore jeans and a T-shirt. Neither was particularly smart. I peered down at my pressed trousers and collared shirt and felt distinctly overdressed.

"Excuse me, are you going to the casino?"

He smiled at me warmly.

"Of course," he replied. "Are you?"

"Yes, I am. I was wondering about your jeans. Isn't there a formal dress code here?"

"Please lah, they don't care about what you're wearing, only what's in your wallet," he laughed. "Hey, you're not Singaporean, right? Lucky for you, no need to pay an entrance fee, right?"

"So you're going to have to pay $100 then?"

"No way," he said decisively, producing a card. "I bought the annual membership instead. I will definitely go more than 20 times in one year. I can maybe go 20 times in one month."

And in he went, waving his membership card as he marched hurriedly towards another night with cold, stony-faced croupiers.

To appease anti-gambling campaigners and, yes, religious groups, the government imposed a casino entry levy on citizens and permanent residents. In a bid to dissuade gamblers from low-income backgrounds, the figure was set at $100 per day or $2,000 annually. Do Singaporeans across the socio-economic spectrum still visit the casino? Do Singaporeans like to play blackjack over Chinese New Year? Does a bear shit in the woods?

I found myself sandwiched in the queue between four *ah bengs* from Hong Kong talking baccarat tactics and a short Filipino in cowboy boots and a terrific white Stetson. The humourless security guard ordered him to remove his hat.

"Why can't he keep his hat on?" I enquired over Roy Rogers' shoulder. "It's a terrific hat."

"For security reasons, sir," the security guard said in a firm, flat tone.

"It's not as if he's going to put casino chips in the hat," I persisted, compelled to defend any short man happy to wear an oversized Stetson in public.

"No, he won't be putting any chips under his hat, sir."

Of course not. How silly of me to suggest otherwise.

Interestingly, the lack of humour permeated the casino. After showing my passport, I ventured into the main floor. There was red carpet everywhere, naturally, and ostentatious horseshoe-shaped curves above the gaming tables. I counted four floors: two for gaming and jackpot machines, a third floor comprising celebrity chef restaurants and a top floor of what appeared to be private rooms. The upper floors were clearly designated for the gambling whales, who could probably throw Stetsons on the heads of 20 hookers as long as their credit lines were good.

No one smiled. From table to table and through row upon endless, monotonous row of slot machines, the casino appeared utterly devoid of joy. Whether they were sitting around tables, hovering overhead, counting cards under their breath or scrutinising the impassive croupiers, the gamblers, the overwhelming majority of whom were Chinese, exchanged little in the way of conversation. Simple pleasantries, greetings or even simple expressions of gratitude were exceedingly hard to come by. Hunched backs slumped in stools as glazed eyes followed reel after reel while zombies shuffled from one jackpot machine to another, kept awake only by the free caffeine the casino graciously supplied to keep the comatose alert enough to find the nearest ATM, to keep withdrawing, to keep spending. The repetitive, ticking drone of the jackpot machines was occasionally punctuated by the squeal of ecstasy, but such exclamations of victory were all too rare. Otherwise the sound of silence prevailed over the casino floor—the sound of losing.

Las Vegas, for all its obvious faults, has a certain endearing tackiness, a kitschy quality that if not exactly charming is certainly entertaining enough to while away a couple of days laughing at the Elvis entertainers and ruddy-faced Americans in Hawaiian shirts. The end goal for both destinations is the same, but Las Vegas keeps the tongue in the cheek and plays up on the campiness. For many, Las Vegas is a pleasure. Marina Bay Sands feels too much like a business. If a film crew tried to shoot *The Hangover in Singapore*, taciturn punters would tell them to keep the noise down. Marina Bay Sands is closer to Genting or Star Cruises in tone and ambience, plusher perhaps, but the clientele is essentially the same—serious souls throwing down the Housing Development Board (HDB) mortgage on a hand of baccarat.

A casino floor supervisor type hurried past me pushing a wheelchair. With all the discretion that a 1.93-metre-tall Caucasian wielding a notepad in an almost all-Chinese casino can muster, I followed from a suitable distance. I need not have bothered. The smell led me to the commotion. Six casino employees busied themselves around a jackpot machine that emitted a stench fouler than Alice Tan's used panty-liners. Peeking out from a bank of machines opposite, I glimpsed the cause of their consternation. A scruffy, unkempt thirty-something Chinese guy (who must have seriously stretched the boundaries of the establishment's dress code) was slumped in a stool, his head resting on the jackpot machine. He was covered in vomit. So was the jackpot machine. So was the carpet. He turned slightly and the vomit dribbled down his chin and across the machine's buttons. Whether he was exhausted, unwell, pissed or a combination of all three was impossible to tell, but he was certainly delirious.

With an efficiency that was as effective as it was rehearsed (clearly, this was not their first time), the staff had lifted him into the wheelchair, whisked him through an emergency side door, cleaned the machine, washed and vacuumed the carpet (even though the carrot blended in well with the "lucky" red colour scheme) and disinfected and deodorised in less than three minutes.

Two Chinese aunties playing on the jackpot machines nearby didn't bother to look up. They were busily feeding $10 notes into their games from a distance of less than three metres away and were not about to allow a comatose gambler to disrupt their momentum. They reminded me of my mother, my mother-in-law, my grandmother and my late great-grandmother, all of whom adhered to the same money maxim: never mess with a woman when there's gambling involved.

Singaporeans may recall the shuffling, tapping sounds of mahjong tiles from their childhood as their aunties played in a room next door. I remember torturous afternoons sitting in British caravan sites staring at bingo cards. As any British working-class woman will tell you, there are only two rules in prize bingo. Rule number one: the first player to complete a straight, vertical or diagonal line (or four corners) wins. The second, and probably the most important, rule is this: don't even think about interrupting a woman when she's playing prize bingo. Children may pee their pants before they are allowed to ask their mothers where the toilet is during a game of prize bingo. Husbands may keel over with heart attacks but they must never, ever, cause a disturbance if their wives are only one number away from a full house. As a child, I was always expected to sit silently while my mother marked off the numbers of her bingo card, desperate to win a tea towel worth less than the cost of five games of bingo.

"Stop talking," she'd hiss, glaring at the bingo caller for not uttering the right numbers. "This is for a full house."

"I'm not talking, I'm just sitting on the chair," I'd plead truthfully.

"Well stop breathing so loudly then. I'm playing two bingo cards at once here."

"They cost you 10 pence each, mum."

"That's not the point. I want to win that Stonehenge tea towel."

"But we've never been to Stonehenge."

"Right, that's it. Here's 10p. Don't spend it all at once. Go and share it with your sister."

My mother was in the Marina Bay Sands casino. She was everywhere. She was hunched in front of a computer screen for electronic roulette (which was as dull as it sounded), hushing family members around the blackjack tables, checking her change, counting losses and privately cursing the winners.

I inadvertently wandered across to the smoking area of the casino floor and soon felt nauseous. The croupiers, some of whom were only in their early twenties, stood helplessly exposed, lost in a fog of nicotine, their lungs presumably at risk from the omnipresent second-hand smoke. Regardless of whatever tips they received—and from the nature of the chain-smoking, complaining, *ah-beng*ish clientele in their smoking dens, I'm thinking they weren't getting enough to retire—no employee should be threatened by such harmful levels of passive smoking in the workplace in 2011, should they? Or should the casino staff join hands and express their gratitude at being part of the Marina Bay moneymaker? The resort is projected to stimulate around $2.7 billion, or 0.8 per cent of Singapore's gross domestic product, by 2015. Thanks to the casino and the industry around Marina Bay Sands, more than 10,000 people will be employed directly, with another 20,000 jobs created indirectly, as those 600 gaming tables and 2,500 slot machines and electronic table games need to be serviced and maintained. What's a little lung damage among such financial figures?

The projected revenues have been measured, but the real cost has yet to be determined. Opposition to both casinos has been vocal ever since they were approved by the government in 2006 (even within the government, key ministers initially disapproved of the idea) and careful, calculated steps have been taken throughout to distinguish Singapore from all that hedonism and sleazy debauchery often associated with Las Vegas, Macau and Orchard Towers. Marina Bay Sands is touted primarily as a business conference and shopping destination (The Shoppes!) and the well-worn line that the casino covers only 3 per cent of the floor space has been trotted out on numerous occasions.

Yet in the week that I visited, newspapers reported on a second-hand car dealer who died after setting himself on fire in March 2011. He had lost more than $120,000 at the casinos so he parked his car along the East Coast Parkway (ECP), called his girlfriend to say goodbye and killed himself. Maybe he would have accumulated similar debts after visiting Genting Highlands or the casinos on Star Cruises, maybe not. Perhaps unsurprisingly, One Hope Centre, which organises weekly support sessions for gamblers, has seen its attendance figures double. According to the *Straits Times*, six voluntary welfare organisations witnessed an increase in gamblers seeking help in the last year, with seven in ten claiming the casinos had caused their financial downfall.

Ironically, these gamblers are not even the resort's main target audience. The average Singaporean is on the periphery of Marina Bay Sands in every sense (even allowing for the free laser show and jazz concerts). If Wonder Full is a gift for all Singaporeans, then the casino is a gift for the elusive VIPs I failed to find on the upper floors. They account for about 70 per cent of the casino's revenue. Marina Bay Sands is really for them. Like The Shoppes and the rooftop infinity swimming pool, the complex is Captain Ahab, interested only in harpooning whales.

After a couple of hours sniffing vomit, inhaling cigarette smoke and spotting my mother everywhere, I went a little stir crazy. In truth, I went mad. I gambled the contents of my wallet—a grand total of $12, to be precise. I had earlier spied some Wizard of Oz slot machines and as it is the lifelong favourite movie of my little sister, I succumbed to temptation and followed the yellow brick road to financial ruin. It was part sibling sentimentality and part stinginess. The Wizard of Oz slots were only 5 cents a go. The munchkins gobbled up my $2 bill and some buttons flashed at me, I pressed one and my $2 vanished in a single spin.

"Woah, woah, woah! What happened there?" I cried, far too loudly and painfully for a $2 loss.

"You pressed the maximum bet button," a voice replied.

I thought it was God. I turned to my right and realised it wasn't God, but a slim, squinting elderly Chinese auntie who was so short-sighted that her nose almost touched the machine screen as she watched the reels spin. She didn't look at me once.

"What did I do?"

"You press maximum. Next time press minimum, then can spend 5 cents each time."

She giggled. She was laughing at my parsimony. Right, I'll show you, you blind old bat, I thought. It was time for the big notes. Well, it was time for the only note left in my wallet—a $10 bill.

A dozen or so spins later, the $10 had gone but there was credit in the wonderful wizard's bank. I pushed the collect button, ripped off the cash voucher, poked blind old bat in the eye and waltzed over to the cashier.

"I'd like to cash this voucher, please," I declared.

The cashier stared at the voucher.

"It's for 60 cents," she muttered.

"Yes, it's been a very productive evening," I boomed. "May I have it all in cash, please?"

I laughed all the way to Marina Bay MRT Station. And then I realised I had missed the last train home.

Four

MARINA South used to be about the shagging. That remains one of my earliest and fondest memories of Singapore with my old mate Scott. We were not shagging each other. In fact, we were quite possibly the only people within running distance not having sex. Having been in Singapore for just a few weeks back in 1996, my old travelling partner Scott and I were taken by genial local host David, our best mate at university, for a game of bowling at Marina South. Driving along what I think must have been Marina Boulevard, there were more balls bouncing around in car parks than there were at any bowling alley. I have never quite ascertained why young Singaporean courting couples are compelled to drive to the farthest-flung corners of the island—Mount Faber, Sembawang Park and Marina South—before getting naked, other than an irrepressible urge to get as far away as possible from their omnipresent parents. I admired the self-restraint. When I was overcome with an irrepressible urge at 18, I struggled to reach the back door of my house.

Developments in and around Marina Bay Sands led to most operations and businesses in and around Marina South closing down by 2008. Intriguingly, Singapore's dwindling birth rate continues to be cause for concern. The government may want to consider reopening those old Marina South car parks.

I recalled the halcyon days of Marina South as I struggled along Marina Street. I had impulsively decided to walk from Marina Bay MRT Station to Marina Barrage, a brisk 20-minute stroll, thanks to archaic memories of peaceful greenery, open spaces, minimal traffic, crickets chirruping, exotic fauna, families kite-flying and cars rocking. That was the Marina South of yesteryear. Today's Marina South is a dusty, grimy, noisy, sweaty building site, a combination of rumbling cement trucks, cranes busily burrowing their way through to the earth's core and bored construction workers dozing at their security posts.

Turning left into Marina Place, I was confronted by hundreds of trees on the kerbside, still in wooden boxes but destined to decorate the Gardens by the Bay. The three waterfront gardens will skirt the reservoir like a green necklace. Just the sheer scale—more than 100 hectares—and the diversity, with their conservatories and themed gardens, will be the final aesthetic piece of the puzzle for this man-made southern haven. In the future, Gardens by the Bay will offer visitors one of the most arresting walks in the region. Currently, it offers one of the most unpleasant. I stood before a sign for the gardens that promised flowers as far as the eye could see. I could only see exhausted foreign construction workers sleeping in the street. They were taking lunchtime naps under the street's tree-lined canopy, evidently not expecting an idiot to ramble along such inhospitable, untidy roads. It was uncomfortable, but not as uncomfortable as the sticky heat scratching at my scrotum.

Finally, I turned into what I humbly believe might be Singapore's greatest achievement and provides an ecological template for much of the lackadaisical planet to follow. Marina Barrage is more than just a dam and a lifestyle attraction (although it accomplishes both with minimal effort), it is a pumping artery for a country dependent upon the oxygen of green technology for its survival. I'm all for the Prada handbags on sale at The Shoppes but they soon lose their lustre when you can't wipe them because there's no water in the bloody tap.

My former Australian town was, at one stage, less than 15 per cent away from that becoming a reality. At the height of the merciless drought of 2006 to 2008 that leached the soil, decimated agriculture, left some farmers suicidal and facilitated the deadly Victorian bushfires of February 2009, Geelong's water storages had reached critically low levels. Residents were just a handful of rain-free months away from turning on the tap and nothing coming out. There was talk of desalination plants, recycling plants, dam building, rerouting dying rivers and buying water by the truckload from interstate. There was so much talking. Delegations from resource-rich Australia were sent to resource-poor Singapore to learn how to manage a declining water supply. How PUB officials managed to refrain from blowing raspberries whilst singing "You're not singing anymore", I'll never know.

In the end, Geelong was rescued not by desalination plants or new dams but by residents showing initiative through various water-saving measures (such as my infamous tanks) and Mother Nature herself. The heavens opened. Regional water supplies rose quickly, gardens could be watered again, treasured rose bushes bloomed once more and order was restored in the suburbs. Sceptical Australians were right after all about those ridiculous recycling plants in places like Singapore. Who wants to drink their own wee wee? It's so much easier, cheaper and cleaner to wait for the rains to fall. Singapore does not think this way. The city favours self-reliance and innovation rather than rely on the whims and fancies of Mother Nature. Marina Barrage will prove more dependable.

From the outside, Marina Barrage has all the allure of the former Queenstown Remand Prison. The low, grey, drab entrance did not bode well, nor did the inescapable presence of armed security (understandable considering they protect the country's most valuable resource, but hardly inviting). I had a quick pee in one of the waterless urinals—naturally—and ventured onto the barrage itself. To the casual visitor, Marina Barrage is Pamela Anderson. There is little going on up top, it's what's going on underneath that counts. Built across the 350-metre-wide channel, the dam connects Marina South with Marina East, blocks out seawater and creates a freshwater reservoir (the country's 15th). (There are 17 at the time of writing and more will follow. This is Singapore.) Five rivers now feed into Marina Bay (Singapore River, Stamford Canal, Rochor Canal, Kallang River and Geylang River if you are taking notes) ensuring that storm water collected as far away as Bishan and Ang Mo Kio is eventually stored in Marina Bay. In Geelong, I couldn't find a way to store the water in my front garden.

And as for those snobby visitors who bewail the unsightly *longkangs*, or open drains, beside cafes and condos, they are not the result of neglectful sanitation or inferior Asian standards of hygiene (I overheard this once on a bus). No *longkangs*, no water and a humiliating dependence upon a gloating neighbour. You choose.

I had the barrage to myself, despite it being the Saturday afternoon of the Singapore Grand Prix weekend, which was remarkable because it's the only location that joins all the dots on the horizon. The SkyPark Observation Deck gives a bird's eye view but it cannot reveal Marina Bay Sands. (If it did suddenly, you might want to hold on.) The Singapore Flyer shows off everything from the comfort of an air-conditioned cocoon with the exception of the Singapore Flyer itself and some of the skyscrapers provide a coastal panorama but nothing of the city itself. Only Marina Barrage showcases the best of Singapore.

Standing in the middle of the dam, the future Gardens by the Bay were on my left, the bulbous bluebottle buzzed around beside the floating platform and the Grand Prix grandstand, the dominant Singapore Flyer occupied centre stage and kayakers dotted the Kallang Basin on the right. Only a handful of engineers building the Marina Coastal Expressway (MCE) on a sea pontoon behind me were further south of the Central Business District (CBD) than I was. I stood at the foot of the city. I had the best view of the city and it cost nothing. Why are visitors not flooding the barrage at weekends?

I noticed a Chinese construction worker in a hard hat heading my way. I stopped him to enquire about visitor numbers. He did not speak English. He was from China and very much a member of new Singapore. Sitting in my glasshouse, I would have some difficulty throwing stones labelled "foreign workers", but the language barrier is proving to be as effective as the one upon which I was standing. My Chinese is woefully deficient and my Hokkien never really got past *chee* and *bye*, but the increasing prevalence of the mainland Chinese language is causing no little public disquiet. I went to Giant supermarket recently to buy a singlet (the neighbours had clearly had enough of my man boobs through the front door grilles) and the first two employees I encountered were from China and spoke no English. Who am I to behave like an indignant imperialist and go all Somerset Maughan, demanding only English be spoken in all supermarkets? I can only be inconvenienced, rather than slighted. But if I were a Singaporean Malay, Indian or Eurasian struggling to be understood in a Singaporean supermarket, despite speaking the country's first language of business, I might be inclined to feel slighted, rather than merely inconvenienced.

At the Marina East side of the dam, a Police Coast Guard craft dangled in the air. A blue rectangular boat hoist was lifting the vessel from the open sea and into the reservoir. Half a dozen Police Coast Guard officers had gathered as their workplace craft was loaded onto the contraption. I sidled up to the youngest, most impressionable-looking of all the men in uniform.

"What's that blue thing on wheels for?" I asked.

"That lifts the boat from the sea and into the reservoir," he said, as the boat was indeed lifted into the air by the hoist, which rolled gently across the dam before lowering the vessel into the reservoir on the other side.

"Why would you be worried about the reservoir? Surely any illegal immigrants will be on that side of the dam," I reasoned, pointing to the sea.

"Cannot say."

"Have you guys caught anyone today?"

"Cannot say."

"Can I at least take some photos of the boat being hoisted into the air?"

"Cannot."

"Well, thank you. You've been very helpful."

I obeyed the officer of the law's instructions and did not take any photographs from the water's edge. I retreated 5 metres to one of the dam gates and joined a couple of visitors snapping away like the paparazzi. Taking photos of an innocuous boat-lifting exercise from a further 5 metres away will surely keep Singapore's borders safe for the foreseeable future.

Standing above the gate, I was joined by an energetic security guy, who was jabbering away into a walkie-talkie.

"Excuse me, can I ask you a question?" I began slowly, more tentative this time. "Why does the Police Coast Guard need to patrol a closed-in reservoir?"

"No lah, this one not for illegals," he said excitedly. "This one for Formula 1 over there. Must protect, right or not? Got many big shots in town. We must keep law and order, put on a good show. Cannot let F1 see any trouble."

He beamed with unmistakable pride as the sleek patrol craft was lowered into the reservoir. He smiled and jabbed his walkie-talkie aerial towards the boat and then out to sea.

"This one ah, illegal immigrants got no chance," he stressed. "They try to come in with one silly, small sampan. You know sampan?"

"Yeah, I know sampan," I replied, but he ignored me, preferring instead to mime someone sitting at the back of a sampan and steering.

"Sampan is a small, small wooden boat with that little putt-putt engine," he continued, still miming. "How to escape? ... Putt-putt-putt ... Sure get caught one ... Putt-putt-putt ... We pick them up, kena stroke, and then we send them back. How to escape in Singapore?"

"Er, well Mas Selamat managed to escape," I interjected, referring to Singapore's most infamous fugitive.

"Ah, yeah, that one did escape," the security guy mumbled, visibly deflated.

He perked up suddenly.

"But we catch him already, right? We catch him in the end, right?"

"In Malaysia though, right?"

"Yeah lah, I suppose Malaysia police help us a little bit there."

His gaze drifted out to sea, where engineers were digging and drilling their way towards connecting the Kallang-Paya Lebar Expressway (KPE), the ECP and the Ayer Rajah Expressway (AYE), linking east and west via a tunnel behind Marina Barrage. The MCE is scheduled to open by the end of 2013 and it had better. Or else.

"This one ah, you see them all working, must build correctly, the 'gahmen' watching them closely," he stressed, eager for a distraction after my impudent Mas Selamat interruption. I regretted letting that one sneak out, but then so does the government.

"It's a massive engineering project for Singapore, I imagine," I agreed.

"No lah, bigger than that. Look where it is. Look where we are. Look over there."

I was getting dizzy.

"One small, small mistake and that's it, we got a tsunami already," the security guy insisted. "Look where the tsunami will go. If that happen, the 'gahmen' will hammer the engineering company."

I wished my "gahmen"-fearing friend well and, with considerable hesitation, stepped into the Sustainable Singapore Gallery, which is an early contender for the most boring exhibition name (we're only four chapters in so I'm expecting stiff competition). The Sustainable Singapore Gallery does not inspire awe and expectation, at best it offered an air-conditioned respite from the humidity. But, as the saying goes, you can't judge a book by a shit title. The gallery was thoroughly uplifting. Singapore's water story is miraculous, easily one of the country's most groundbreaking (and soon to be oft-copied) achievements. And cynics please take note. I'm not the naive victim of a "gahmen" brainwashing exercise. The PAP didn't inculcate my abiding admiration for the city's transformation into a global hydrohub. Living in Australia for five years and enduring draconian water restrictions did that.

Back in 1977, if someone tumbled into the Kallang River, the race was on to see which killed the victim first: drowning or drinking a drop of the water. In those days, both Kallang and Singapore rivers were little more than open sewers. Lee Kuan Yew instigated a clean-up operation that took 10 years to complete.

By 1987, Lee envisioned a dam enclosing Marina Bay to create a freshwater reservoir to alleviate the dependence upon Malaysia. This was 1987. I have no idea what Britain was doing in 1987, other than trying to grow Rick Astley quiffs and emulate his swizzling leg moves to "Never Gonna Give You Up". Meanwhile Australians were focusing on male tight perms, moustaches and cricket scores (they still fixate far too much on the last two). Neither country was concerning itself on the national stage with the natural resources left at its disposal in 2012.

The centrepiece of the exhibition was a working scale model of Marina Barrage, demonstrating how each of the nine crest gates opened sequentially at low tide during heavy downpours to release excess water and prevent CBD flooding. The model even showed how the water was released slowly through drainage pumps at high tide, complete with a miniature Orchard Road shopping district being submerged because the water didn't clear fast enough. I'm kidding, I'm kidding. As I write this, an international panel of drainage experts concluded that Marina Barrage did not cause the Orchard Road flash floods. For two consecutive years, the shopping belt has been washed out and the coincidence was too much for many. Pre-Marina Barrage, such flash flooding was rare. Post-barrage, Orchard Road went under twice in two years. But computer models attributed the shopping soakings to increasing rain frequency and an inadequate drainage system. I am still tickled by those images of soaked designer handbags floating in shop windows. Mother Nature hasn't lost her sense of humour.

She is, of course, the large elephant in the room. Marina Barrage has two primary, and very public, purposes: to increase Singapore's fresh water supply and reduce periodic flooding. But there is a third reason. The United Nations Intergovernmental Panel on Climate Change has projected sea levels will rise up to

59 centimetres by the end of the 21st century, but this figure did not take into account the melting of the Greenland or Antarctic ice sheets. Singapore is a tropical, low-lying densely-populated dot on the landscape. I don't need to paint you a picture. Singapore has built all reclamation projects since 1991 at 125 centimetres above the highest recorded tide level. Marina Barrage cannot hold back the tides of climate change but it will buy time as our grandchildren run for Bukit Timah Hill. Their soggy iPhones won't save them but Marina Barrage might.

On a positive note, the government has got really rather revolutionary (and it wasn't that long ago when the mere juxtaposition of "government" and "revolutionary" would have had civil servant letter writers needing a lie-down) with the Active, Beautiful, Clean Waters (ABC Waters) Programme. Launched in 2006, water catchment areas were to become lifestyle attractions: recreational destinations for families to swim, kayak and generally splash around in. It really was safe to get back in the water. In old Singapore, reservoirs had all the aesthetic qualities of a safety deposit box, with security protecting the environmental crown jewels. I know because I once went skinny-dipping in MacRitchie Reservoir with a couple of Canadians at 4 a.m. I'd like to say they were Canadian women but, alas, they were Canadian men, one skinnier than a twig, the other a more deranged version of Kramer from *Seinfeld*. The twilight paddle under a moonlit night was delightful, but why my Canadian male friends insisted on us being naked remains a mystery. When we spotted the torch of a security guard on the shore, we ducked under the water and held our breath (and that's all we held, I can assure you). It's not the rebelliousness that disturbs me, but the homoeroticism. Why didn't we just keep our underpants on?

No need to resort to such antics now in order to get wet in

a reservoir. The PUB wants the public to take stewardship of its water supply, to grab a paddle or a snorkel and dive into a local ABC Waters project (there are currently 15 but there are plans for more than 100 within 15 years). Skinny-dipping with skinny Canadians is not an option at this stage.

Five

MY sister made me play with dolls. That's my story and I'm sticking to it. I had Star Wars figures. She had Sindy dolls. (The British version of Barbie, I seem to recall. Rather than hang out at pool parties with Ken, Sindy made cups of tea, watched soap operas and moaned about the weather.) My Star Wars figures were housed in a rusty Rover biscuit tin. My sister's Sindy dolls resided in a three-storey penthouse furnished with lift and hot tub. Naturally, little Luke Skywalker was often found hanging out with Sindy's mates in the third-floor spa. The trouble was those original Star Wars figures were half the size of the average doll. Even Chewbacca only came up to Sindy's groin. When they stood face to face, quite frankly, the image was disturbing. When the rebels surrounded Sindy's bikini-clad beauties in the hot tub, the scene belonged in that veritable pornographic classic *Snow White and the Seven Inches* (I've never seen the film, I just Googled funny porn titles involving dwarves and I'm still laughing).

During the summer school holidays in England, we regularly visited the Bethnal Green Museum of Childhood in East London to gaze at more dolls and action figures inside glass display cases. We followed the nostalgic path of our mother, who had grown up in Bethnal Green and had frequented the museum as a child.

It was a generation thing. We were both skint and the museum was free. When my mother accompanied as tour guide, we were obedient. When my sister and I made the trip from Dagenham to Bethnal Green alone, we were bloody murder. We'd leave home at 9.30 a.m. and she'd complain that I had eaten all the sandwiches on the station platform by 9.45 a.m. Then I would moan that I was hungry by 10 a.m. When we arrived at the museum, she'd run off to look at Sindy dolls and anything from *The Wizard of Oz* while I dashed off in the opposite direction to find the Star Wars figures. We would both get lost and I'd find her in the arms of an elderly volunteer sobbing quietly by the rocking horses. It was embarrassing. This only happened last summer.

They were happy days. Years later, I found myself standing in the Smithsonian National Museum of American History and staring transfixed at an original pair of Dorothy's ruby slippers from *The Wizard of Oz*, the movie that provided the soundtrack to my sister's childhood (and, therefore, much of mine). Without a moment's hesitation, I called her on my mobile from Washington and described the iconic shoes in excruciatingly microscopic detail. I thought she was going to cry down the phone. I nearly did when I got the phone bill.

That's what beloved pop culture artefacts can do to you. They are Dr Who's TARDIS, transporting us to wherever our memories allow us to go. Imagine my unbridled joy then when I discovered that Singapore had opened such a treasure trove of prepubescent nostalgia in my absence.

I walked briskly along North Bridge Street, turned into the narrow Seah Street and almost missed it. Squeezed between the usual eateries, the MINT Museum of Toys was not the most obvious attraction and might be glossed over by the casual observer. The museum, which also includes a rooftop bar and a toy-themed restaurant called Mr Punch, is housed in a graceful, slender, wavy-lined, contemporary grey building. In the mangled syntax of Yoda, who was inside, find it you must.

I followed the cartoon panels of Popeye and Superman along the entrance slope, bought a ticket (discounted with a POSB card) and headed straight to the fifth floor. The Peter Rabbit collection was interesting but I hurried on after a polite glance. I knew what I was looking for. I didn't notice any other toys as I dashed across the floor with callow carelessness to gaze upon my childhood. And there they were, on a high shelf in the opposite corner—a row of original Star Wars figures, the Barbie-sized ones from 1977, still boxed, unopened and complete with price tags. The lower shelf was filled with the traditional regular Star Wars figures, untouched in their boxes. Seeing them in such pristine condition, in their original blisters, took me away to my childhood. I was back in 1983, wandering aimlessly around the biggest toyshop in Romford, riffling through the Return of the Jedi racks, checking which figures I had, which ones I needed, which ones I could afford and which ones would match the ambience of Sindy's hot tub. I had taken leave of my senses. They had gone time travelling. I could smell the plastic of the Star Wars figure blisters, peer down at my old school uniform, hear Billy bloody Joel whining on about his "Uptown Girl" in the background and my mother's voice shouting, "For fuck's sake, Neil, how much longer are you gonna be? I've got to buy a shower cap and peroxide Sylvie's hair."

As I took my time in the Moment of Imagination and Nostalgia with Toys Museum (to give the exhibition its full—and fully deserving—title), I enjoyed the reaction of other visitors: their smiles of recognition, eyes widening as a stored memory file suddenly got rebooted. A Chinese uncle stared at a bust of Dan Dare, Britain's first intergalactic space hero and more than 50 years old. The bust was one of only ten ever made. Younger

Asian couples examined the Green Hornet vehicles, Bruce Lee's star still retaining its enigmatic allure over the continent. Grandparents giggled when they saw the Japanese-produced Robby the Robot toys while their grandchildren pointed at original Mickey Mouse models. I took little notice of the life-size Darth Maul statue, despite him being one of the better villains in *Star Wars*, and yet I almost wet myself when I spotted a Buck Rogers in the 25th Century pocket watch (I did when I saw its US$25,000 price tag). Buck Rogers was part of my growing up, Darth Maul wasn't. He belongs to my youngest brother. And that's what the MINT Museum is for. The admission fee does not grant permission to peer at old (albeit extremely valuable) toys; it's a unique ticket to ride back to our childhoods. Now that's priceless.

The MINT Museum ranks as the world's finest collection of toys simply because it isn't a collection of toys, but a collection of collections. Whatever the cultural or geographical background, every visitor will unearth a childhood gem from their past among the diverse range of international artefacts. I loved the Batman items, including a tinplate Commissioner Gordon car model that is the only example on the planet. Circus figures and performers, so crucial in the evolution of the toy, also form another magnificent collection, with a pair of German tumbling acrobat toys made in 1840. The female acrobat, like Gordon's car, is assumed to be the only one around. There are teddy bears; Matchbox, Corgi and Dinky cars; London buses (a personal favourite); classic enamel signs and even lunchboxes. (The Incredible Hulk lunchbox took me back to Saturday nights in the living room watching through teary eyes as poor Bill Bixby tried to thumb a lift at the end of every episode accompanied by that haunting piano theme.) No generation in the last 150 years has been neglected.

As parents are the gatekeepers of our toy collections, I kept thinking of my mother. As I took photographs of an original 1977 Star Wars poster (worth a small fortune!), I remembered a bizarre long-distance phone call that we'd had several years ago.

"Here, guess what I found in the loft?" my mother asked, taking a break from packing up and moving away from our old Dagenham home.

"I don't know," I wondered. "The cat?"

"No, we got him out this time. I must remember to close the hatch when we're not up there ... No, I found some Star Wars wallpaper from when you were a kid. A whole roll of it, in decent condition."

My voice trembled.

"You mean the one I had on my wall when I was four years old?" I enquired, the anticipation rising. "That's the original Star Wars wallpaper from around 1978, with the beautiful hand-painted images of key scenes in the film?"

"Yeah, that's the one. I'm holding it now. Got almost a roll of it here, still in the cellophane."

She was holding a rare artefact. She was also holding a family heirloom.

"That is amazing, mum. Just amazing. I can't believe it. I don't know what to say."

"Well, yeah, anyway, Christmas is coming so I thought I'd wrap all your presents in the stuff."

I dropped the phone.

We exchanged a few words and the rare Star Wars wallpaper ended up in a frame rather than as wrapping paper and currently sits in storage as I determine its permanent home.

Prudent toy choices can be a profitable enterprise. The MINT Museum had more cameras on each floor than the average bank. The Buck Rogers pocket watch was one of many expensive gems, including a Robby the Robot and a Green Hornet car (both worth US$15,000) and a collection of Beatles memorabilia worth many times that figure (there were items with John, Paul, George and Ringo's signatures scribbled across the front, which immediately add a couple of zeroes to their value). By the time I had reached the James Bond Aston Martins and the still-boxed Sean Connery figures from *Thunderball*, I was ready to steal the lot. At a conservative estimate, the collective value of the artefacts runs into the tens of millions. So forget the Rolex watches, save Buzz and Woody when the kids are done.

There was one particular display that was provocative, emotive and, to some, distasteful, but necessary for those very reasons. It was a golliwog collection. As a toy, the golliwog has every reason to be in the museum, being a popular rag doll in children's books dating to the 19th century. Whether it's a cultural artefact that deserves preservation or a racist caricature depends on your point of view. One can lead to the other. The Darkie toothpaste, the Alabama Coon board game (promising a "jolly game for the players") and salt and pepper shakers in the form of mammy figures, or black domestic workers, were appalling. That is why they should be chronicled. The dolls and the "nigger" games and toys are uncomfortable reminders of past ignorance and intolerance. Hopefully they will not pander to persistent prejudices. We must be repulsed. But I saw a couple of visitors snigger.

After spending far more time in the museum than expected, I headed for the warmth of the exit. Here's an invaluable tip. Dress warm for the museum's air conditioning. Some of the fragile tin-made playthings have survived two world wars and Singapore's humidity, so the older the toys, the cooler the floor. Rather fortuitously, I bumped into the museum's owner, the endearingly passionate Chang Yang Fa. An engineer by trade, Chang opened the museum in 2007, originally to provide a public showcase for his personal collection. Astonishingly, the five floors provide him space for around 5,000 items at any one time—he rotates the displays—which make up only 10 per cent of his entire collection (he stores the rest in Ang Mo Kio). He paid for the entire building, including the interior fittings, the rooftop bar and the enamel sign-filled restaurant, out of his own pocket. The MINT Museum is not a moneymaking exercise; it is about philanthropy. Chang's only ambition is to establish the world's finest collection of international toys in Singapore and encourage as many people as possible to visit. A self-made Singaporean, Chang has essentially given his collection to the country (the admission fee barely covers costs). He's preoccupied with preserving childhood memories rather than profits. It's not a bad legacy, is it?

Inspired by the altruistic toy collector, I embarked on a bit of preservation myself. I lazily took the MRT from City Hall to Raffles Place to go to The Fullerton Hotel. I had two reasons to visit Singapore's iconic hotel. The Fullerton Heritage Precinct has attempted to amplify, rather than airbrush, the waterfront's history by incorporating retail and dining outlets in and around its classic buildings. I was curious to see if it had been tastefully done or was a schizophrenic architectural hybrid. In other words, neither historic nor contemporary, just a mess. Most of all, though, I wanted to visit the exact location where Saint Jack told the shrink from *The Sopranos* to "fuck it".

In a bargain bin in Australia a couple of years ago, I was thrilled to discover a dusty DVD of *Saint Jack*. As I watched it, I sat open-mouthed as the Singapore of 1978 revealed itself. Writer-director-actor Peter Bogdanovich (the shrink to the shrink in *The Sopranos*) helmed *Saint Jack* and, in the penultimate scene in the movie, sits on a bench beside Collyer Quay when the titular character, Jack Flowers (played by Ben Gazzara), tells him where to go. In new Singapore, *Saint Jack* is no longer banned so it seemed apt to return to The Fullerton now.

Much to my disappointment, there was no bench anywhere near where Bogdanovich had once sat, probably because it would block the al fresco promenade of One Fullerton. But I stopped close by and recalled the dozens of sampans rocking gently behind Bogdanovich on what is now Marina Bay. The imposing Doric columns of The Fullerton Hotel, tastefully lit, rightfully diverted attention from the humdrum high-rises. From a certain angle, the view was no different to the one at the end of the movie when Jack emerges from the General Post Office.

I crossed Collyer Quay and wandered through The Fullerton Hotel's side entrance (the former main entrance to the post office). Framed black-and-white photographs depicted post office clerks serving customers on a counter 300 feet long (the longest in Southeast Asia according to one of the information panels, a curious claim to fame, but then it's where Singaporeans came to buy their lottery coupons so it's surprising the counter wasn't longer). From paintings to books, display cases and photographs showing the building's official opening in 1928, there was a conscious effort at every turn to tip the hat to the hotel's past.

A British red pillar box greeted me at the entrance of the Post Bar, built on part of the site of the former post office counter, which staged one of the funniest scenes in *Saint Jack*. When Jack Flowers hands a friend's ashes to a wonderfully no-nonsense Chinese counter girl (quite possibly a real GPO staff member back in 1978 as Bogdanovich preferred to use authentic locals), she asks if the parcel is fragile and then lobs the ashes over her shoulder. I tried to visualise the post office counter but its remarkable length was unfathomable. The counter at our local post office in Dagenham was only 5 metres long.

I stepped tentatively into the Post Bar but the slightly

supercilious looks of the well-heeled clientele suggested I was spreading dog shit across the tiled floor so I took my leave, continued along the splendid courtyard and poked my head into The Fullerton Heritage Gallery. Opened in July 2010, the gallery takes a glimpse into the hotel's history, with artworks, film clips on the adjacent Clifford Pier, Customs House and The Fullerton Waterboat House and photographs of the legendary lunchtime PAP rallies beside The Fullerton in the rain. (It always seemed to pour down at those PAP political rallies, didn't it? Was it for dramatic effect? Didn't anyone check the weather forecast beforehand?)

The gallery also contained another functioning red pillar box from the UK. I say functioning because it is one of only three in Singapore (the others being outside the Post Bar and the Singapore Philatelic Museum) in which letters can actually be posted. Was it cheesy? Undoubtedly. Did it lean towards pink gins, Noël Coward and closet colonialism? Most definitely. Did I spot British families gathering around the pillar box— something found on most street corners in their homeland—to pose for holiday snaps? Absolutely. Like Singaporeans flocking to Melbourne's Chinatown or Australians staggering into Aussie bars in Bali to watch the rugby, Brits abroad seem to have a need for a security blanket on the road, something I will never comprehend. If comfort comes only from what's reassuringly familiar, why not cut the middleman out and spend a two-week holiday in the living room?

Feeling rather facetious, I wondered if *Saint Jack* had a role to play in The Fullerton's heritage. I approached a Filipino bellboy and enquired about the General Post Office.

"Yes, sir, the old post office counter used to run right across there," he said brightly, pointing towards the Post Bar. "Did you see the red pillar box? Many of our guests like the red pillar box."

"Yeah, it's marvellous. But did you know a scene from a Hollywood movie was shot at that exact spot?" I said. "It's still the only Hollywood movie to be filmed in its entirety in Singapore."

"Really? What's it called?" the Filipino asked, genuinely interested.

"*Saint Jack*," I replied enthusiastically.

"Oh, I've never heard of that one," he said softly. He was hoping I was going to say *Transformers*.

"Er, you know *The Sopranos*, right? ... Well, the psychiatrist who the psychiatrist sees, the guy with the big glasses ... He directed *Saint Jack* and is in a key scene right in front of this building."

Commendably conscientious, the bellboy took out a Fullerton Hotel pen and jotted down some indecipherable notes on a Fullerton Hotel notepad.

"Wow, what's the film about?"

"Prostitution in Singapore," I said matter-of-factly.

His eyes widened.

"Prostitution, really?"

"Really ah? Prostitution?" repeated the Filipino's colleague, looking up suddenly from his desk computer. I hadn't noticed he was there. "Can I buy in Singapore?"

"Yah, can I buy this film in Singapore?" the Filipino echoed.

"You can now," I said. "I'm not sure if there are any DVD copies left but the movie isn't banned in Singapore anymore."

"People ask us about the hotel's history all the time," the young concierge said. "But I never knew they filmed a Hollywood movie here."

The Fullerton Hotel concierge promised to inform his upmarket clientele that a movie concerned with pimps and prostitutes was once filmed in their luxurious abode. Even those behind the Fullerton Heritage Precinct could never have possibly visualised old and new Singapore being pulled together by Bogdanovich's murky masterpiece. I was suddenly inspired to search for *Saint Jack*. I provided my Filipino friend with some additional movie trivia and took my leave.

"Hey, that film, ah," his colleague piped up again. "It's really about prostitution, ah?"

Six

I CRANED my head, peered up at the second floor of the New Taiwan Porridge Restaurant and recalled a Hollywood actor smirking down at me. The tastefully restored shophouse, standing at 110 Amoy Street and squeezed between the CBD and Chinatown, was evidently a popular lunchtime destination for the white-collar crowd. When I had seen the building the night before, it had housed a shipping chandler and the late American actor Ben Gazzara had been leaning against the window on the second floor, lazily watching the hawker stalls and the rickshaw drivers on the kerbside. In *Saint Jack*, just one skyscraper, the OCBC Building, loomed like a post-modern leviathan over the crumbling street. Today, the area is dwarfed by the encroaching high-rises creeping ever closer. Like a scene from *War of the Worlds*, old and new Singapore battle for supremacy around Amoy Street.

In 1979, of course, old Singapore still held sway over the city in every sense. On its international release, *Saint Jack* was immediately banned in its country of origin. Residents were not granted permission to study Peter Bogdanovich's portrayal of their neighbourhoods until a one-off screening at the Singapore International Film Festival in 1997. An entire generation missed the movie, which is a cultural travesty, not least because the making of the film is one of the most entertaining Singaporean stories—if not Hollywood stories—of all time.

Chronicled in Ben Slater's book, *Kinda Hot: The Making of Saint Jack in Singapore*, the movie's evolution in its homeland mirrored that of the city's cultural enlightenment. Despite government crackdowns (and official tourism brochures to the contrary), Singapore remained a breeding ground for gangsters, gambling, enterprising, productive pimps and rampant prostitution. Go to Bugis Street today and a spirited uncle will shove a leaflet advertising cheap Mandarin lessons into your hand. In 1978, the leaflet would more likely have been a dildo. Of course, that was all cleaned up in official crackdowns in the ensuing decades. (OK, none of the vices have been entirely cleaned up but the streets are very clean and very safe, even for the prostitutes and pimps.)

Knowing that Paul Theroux's original novel *Saint Jack* had been frowned upon by authorities, but not actually banned, director Bogdanovich assumed that permission to shoot the movie adaptation would be denied. Consequently, he pretended to shoot another movie instead, going so far as to write a treatment entitled *Jack of Hearts*, a gentle romantic comedy set in exotic Singapore, which he submitted to the Ministry of Culture. Astonishingly, *Jack of Hearts* was granted approval, even though many of the character names were the same as those in Theroux's novel. Clearly, no one at the Ministry of Culture had read *Saint Jack* (they had far too much porn to get through).

When the director arrived in Singapore to shoot *Saint Jack*, on a tourist visa, a customs officer enquired if he had any copies of *Playboy*. (Why have Singaporean civil servants been so long obsessed with porn? They must spend more time examining pornographic material than the most dangerous of perverts.) The American director confirmed that there were no copies of

Hugh Hefner's magazine in his suitcase but did not let on that he planned to make a movie on hookers that was partially financed by Hefner. That's often the trouble with the average civil servant. They miss the wood for the trees. Too much porn really must ruin the eyesight.

"So that was the window where Ben Gazzara looked from," said Ben enthusiastically. After my chat with the staff at The Fullerton, I had contacted the author and Asian film aficionado. He kindly agreed to give me a tour of the movie's remaining locations. There are not many left.

Still, I was like a kid let loose in a sweet shop all afternoon. We left Saint Jack's old employer and found a back alley between Amoy Street and Ann Siang Road. In one long take in *Saint Jack*, Ben Gazzara has a detailed conversation about his long-term ambitions with friend William Leigh (portrayed by the late Denholm Elliott, who went on to play Indiana Jones's sidekick Marcus Brody and the scene-stealing butler in *Trading Places*). The alley itself was unaltered. Apart from the inevitable high-rises hovering behind the trees, the disorderly lane had not changed since 1978. Scruffy and unkempt, there were the backs of shophouses on one side, with their slated roofs and elegant, art deco spiral staircases. On the other, bikes and plant pots were propped up against the paint-chipped wall, which was partially obscured by the overhanging trees from the charming, if incongruous, Ann Siang Hill. Watch the movie (or find the clip on YouTube) and then venture into this Chinatown back alley. Gazzara and Elliot could have filmed there yesterday.

We crossed Read Bridge at Clarke Quay and stopped near the point where Jack throws photographs of a naked US senator and a rent boy into the Singapore River in the movie's final scene. Jack then interacts casually with the locals before meandering along North Boat Quay towards the old police station (now the multicoloured MICA Building). Sampans swamped the Singapore River and ramshackle, crumbling shophouses hummed with the incessant loading and unloading of goods on the dock while merchants in grubby singlets climbed over pallets and boxes. The Clarke Quay of 1978 was abuzz with a vibrancy that the waterfront location has struggled to recreate ever since despite spending tens of millions along the way. Ben and I peered down at those otherworldly, already fading, white pod covers dotted along the riverbank to shelter diners from the equatorial elements. They looked like something ejected from an alien mothership.

Continuing along River Valley Road, we wandered towards Oxley Road in search of a brothel. That juxtaposition is shamefully puerile, I know, but the close proximity of the movie's major bordello on Institution Hill, where real prostitutes were hired as extras, to Oxley Road is a source of eternal amusement. As we crossed Oxley Road, I recalled the last time I had been in the street. In 2008, I returned to Singapore briefly for a book launch and stayed at the nearby Lloyd's Inn (if it's not the cheapest hotel in the Orchard shopping belt, then it does a damn good impression). In a sleepy search for supper one night, I left the hotel and stumbled down Oxley Road. As I passed a sizeable property, an armed officer stopped me. We were the only people in the street.

"Can you walk on the other side of the road, please, sir?" he said firmly.

His request was framed as a question, but the tone unambiguous. I had no choice in the matter.

"I'm just going for some supper," I reasoned.

"Walk on the other side of the street, please, sir."

The question had given way to an order. I noticed the street sign: Oxley Road. I examined the gloomy building behind the dense foliage that served as a screening. The cogs move slowly when I'm tired and hungry.

"Ah, this is Lee Kuan Yew's house," I exclaimed, genuinely intrigued. "Is he at home now?"

"On the other side of the road, please, sir."

Reluctantly, I did as I was told and trudged over to the other side. From the supposed safety of the opposite kerb, I faced off with the police officer. We were at least an impenetrable 5 metres apart. National security had been preserved for another day.

From my point of view, we looked ready for a game of "kerbsy". For those not familiar with kerbsy (which, in fairness, would probably include just about anyone who hasn't grown up on a British housing estate), the game consists of two players standing on opposite sides of a road who try to score points by accurately throwing a football at the opponent's kerb so it bounces back into their arms. Had I been handed a football at that moment, the temptation might have been impossible to resist—a game of kerbsy with Lee Kuan Yew's security officer is the stuff of dreams.

"Look, mate, I've got to ask. What do you think I can't do over here that I can do over there?" I wondered.

"Everyone must walk on that side of the road," he replied flatly. "There are no exceptions, sir."

"But I'm wearing a pair of shorts and a singlet. What could I possibly do in a pair of flip-flops? Click and clack all the way down the street? You could hear me coming a mile off."

He smiled, but didn't answer. I wanted to query the legality of asking a pedestrian to step off the pavement of a public road but thought better of it.

Passing Oxley Road, Ben and I sweated our way to the top of Institution Hill in pursuit of our brothel. Jack's Dunroamin' Club was filmed at the transformed 6B Institution Hill (the decaying, derelict, some say haunted, colonial house on the hill was barely standing before the film crew intervened). The house had long since been replaced by the swanky condo Aspen Heights, its residents oblivious to the fact that their apartments were built on the site of the swankiest Singaporean brothel ever seen on a cinema screen. Moving aside to allow a BMW to pass through the security barriers, I thought about those who frequented the fictional Dunroamin' Club and how much they had in common with those now living at Aspen Heights. With property prices exploding, they're still getting screwed on Institution Hill.

One legendary brothel still standing is the Goodwood Park Hotel. The Khoo family-owned landmark on Scotts Road is famous for three reasons. First, The Kinks played their only Singaporean gig there in 1965. Second, I was cast to play Stamford Raffles in *Talking Cock the Movie* there. And finally, the hotel served as *Saint Jack*'s military rest and recreation compound (where American troops were supplied with prostitutes while on leave from the Vietnam War). Admittedly, the first two are only famous to me. But a teenage Eric Khoo did hang around the set while Bogdanovich shot key scenes in his family's hotel. Despite extensive renovations in the ensuing years, the layout of Goodwood's swimming pool is little different to the one depicted in *Saint Jack*, minus the dozens of horny American servicemen slavishly dribbling over Asian prostitutes (you have to go to Orchard Towers to see that now).

After the Goodwood Park Hotel, we followed in the footsteps of James Bond. In *Saint Jack*'s final act, Gazzara's character finds himself embroiled in a seedy covert CIA plot. He must blackmail a bisexual American senator by taking photos of him in uncompromising positions. George Lazenby played the US senator. George Lazenby succeeded Sean Connery as 007 in *On Her Majesty's Secret Service*, one of the most unsettling Bond movies (and the only film in the franchise with a downbeat ending). The entire sequence took place, on foot, in real time, from the Shangri-La Hotel, along the winding Orange Grove

Road, down into Orchard Road and ended at the Singapore Hilton with Lazenby, complete with superb seventies moustache, propositioning a young Chinese chap. Behind them, a street poster promoted the retail wonders of the new Specialists' Shopping Centre, where I was gainfully employed for my first three years in Singapore. Specialists' Shopping Centre has since been bulldozed, despite being a relatively new mall when the film was made. A road in rapid transition, Orchard was a peculiar place in 1978. There were still green spaces between the malls. Crickets chirruping in the background betrayed the street's agricultural past. The Singapore Hilton was a glimpse of the future.

Saint Jack had inadvertently captured the country at a crossroads, halfway between third world and first. For this scene alone, Bogdanovich deserves a medal in the National Day Awards for documenting—and preserving—Singapore's most famous street while it was coming to grips with its metamorphosis.

Retracing the steps of Lazenby along Orchard Road, Ben and I discussed the legacy of *Saint Jack*. The banned film finally had a one-off screening in Singapore in 1997 at Chinatown's Majestic Cinema (also closed, although a rat once ran across my feet in that cinema so my suriphobia makes me less sympathetic to its demise).

"And the DVD was finally released, even in Singapore," Ben pointed out. "And it sold pretty well here, too. I don't think there are any copies left. The only place that I know of where *Saint Jack* is still on the shelves is Australia."

"But it belongs in a museum," I pleaded, channelling Indiana Jones in melodramatic fashion. "Every Singaporean should watch *Saint Jack*."

Ben eyed me sceptically.

"Well, all right, not every Singaporean. Every Singaporean adult at least," I corrected. "Even then, film clips could be played on a loop continuously at places like The Fullerton and in museums. That great 360-degree panoramic shot in the opening scene that captures the entire waterfront, the post office scenes, old Clarke Quay ... kids can see all that stuff."

"The National Museum did show the film in 2009. They even enquired about getting a print of *Saint Jack*," Ben added. "But there are issues over the film's rights. They did enquire though."

They must enquire again. Like the MINT Museum, *Saint Jack* liberates long suppressed memories, depicting a time and place so alien to new Singapore that it might as well have concluded with those awful alien pods at Clarke Quay usurping the city. Future generations will grow up ignorant of Singapore's original borders, unaware that Marina Bay Sands has not always been the southern tip of the country. It used to be Fullerton Road, marked by Bogdanovich sitting on an elaborate bench decorated with Chinese characters. *Saint Jack* can be for young Singaporeans what I thought *Made in Dagenham* was going to be for me. Set in my hometown in the 1960s, *Made in Dagenham* chronicled the world's first all-female industrial strike action at the town's Ford Motor Company's car plant. The 2010 movie was entertaining, but geographically inaccurate. Today's Dagenham bears only a passing resemblance to its swinging sixties' predecessor so a disused factory in the Welsh town of Merthyr Tydfil doubled for my old home. I cannot overemphasise my horror when I discovered this geographical travesty. Using a Welsh town to represent my childhood home constitutes a crime against humanity.

Nostalgia can be addictive. I suspect that is why I am uncontrollably attracted to the creaking British cop show *Dempsey and Makepeace*. Filmed on location in London in 1985, the programme looked dated by 1986, which was probably the last time I watched it. Then I returned to Singapore in 2011 and discovered a cable TV channel repeated episodes every Thursday night. For those unfamiliar with the programme, a rugged cop from New York (Dempsey) was partnered with an upper-class, private school-educated peroxide blonde detective (Makepeace) to take down organised crime in London (don't ask). At a time when no police officer carried a gun in the UK, Dempsey pulled his gun at the drop of a hat. If his mug of tea was served cold in an East London cafe, he pulled a gun and shot the bacon slicer. Despite sporting a startling range of knitwear not seen since Bing Crosby sang "Little Drummer Boy" with David Bowie, Dempsey bedded every woman in London except Princess Diana and, of course, Makepeace.

Surprisingly enough, the show does not hold up well. But London's locations, particularly in the East End not far from where I grew up, resurrected a town that had long ago been crushed by Canary Wharf. As a procedural cop drama, *Dempsey and Makepeace* makes a terrific comedy. The programme fairs much better in resuscitating a city that perished years ago.

The Singapore of Paul Theroux's novel has also long gone but it has been preserved by Bogdanovich's movie. New Singapore has determined that its people are now mature enough to watch *Saint Jack* (there's more than enough porno DVDs going around for censorship civil servants to earn their 13th month bonus).

The MINT Museum exhibits what the city once did during childhood. *Saint Jack* tells us what the adults got up to.

And we're all adults now.

Somewhere within the Warner Brothers' empire in Los Angeles, an original print of *Saint Jack* probably sits on a shelf. Perhaps it's the property of Roger Corman, producer, financier and king of the B-movie. Either way, the film should be the property of Singapore. Fullerton photographs of the old post office and pretty pillar boxes have their place in the hunt for heritage but *Saint Jack* is real. Its footage is priceless. The Fullerton precinct recognises the economic value of preserving its past as new Singapore flourishes. But old Singapore stays alive only as long as rare artefacts like *Saint Jack* remain accessible to all.

Seven

I FOUND myself lying on my back and thinking of England. I had spent the last five minutes walking up and down Cantonment Road asking strangers if they had any idea where Pinnacle@ Duxton was. They had each stared at me with a delightful mixture of bemusement and uncertainty, nodded towards the interconnected seven towers of 50 storeys that encircled much of the street and dominated the skyline in every direction and then wondered whether it was medication time. When the street was momentarily deserted of passers-by, I stretched out on the pavement and tried to reproduce a childhood memory.

My hometown of Dagenham and Duxton Plain Park are kindred spirits. One is home to the world's once biggest public housing estate, the other the tallest. Dagenham led the race to find homes fit for working-class heroes after World War I. Pinnacle@Duxton picked up the baton in the 21st century, designing a standard for public housing beyond the imagination of the flat-capped Cockney brickies who had laid the foundations almost 100 years earlier. Dagenham demonstrated to the world that comfortable, affordable homes could be built practically and prudently with public funds, Pinnacle@Duxton added the swagger. Singapore's most unique HDB development has been the recipient of numerous international design awards. Dagenham now has one of the highest teenage pregnancy rates in Europe. My childhood home craves the municipal foresight and ingenuity that made Pinnacle@Duxton a reality. Singapore wants Dagenham's fertility rates. It's comforting to know they still need each other.

Unexpectedly, Pinnacle@Duxton made me think of Parsloes Park. As a teenager, I would cut through Parsloes Park, a sizeable green public space at the heart of Dagenham's vast housing estate, to get to my future wife's house (I trudged along if her parents were home but moved like Usain Bolt if they were out). The red tiled slates of identical rooftops surrounded me. The view never changed, no matter which way I turned. Parsloes Park marked the centre of one of the world's biggest (and, for a while, the most famous) housing estates, surrounded by 27,000 homes and more than 100,000 people. The familiar vista was usually only altered on Friday evenings when second-hand Fords rocked gently in the car park while oblivious pensioners cleared up their dogs' poop. For the longest time, I thought that "dogging" was couples having sex in their cars while the elderly took their dogs for a walk nearby.

From the world's biggest to the world's tallest, I tried to find a position where Pinnacle@Duxton dominated the landscape in every direction. That's why I ended up lying down on the pavement of Cantonment Road.

"Bloody hell," I muttered.

Should you be passing or visiting Pinnacle@Duxton, do take the opportunity to lie down on the pavement in front of the housing complex's entrance on Cantonment Road. No other vantage point captures the intimidating immensity of this incongruous icon towering over Chinatown's cowering shophouses. My view was framed entirely by the soaring curves of the seven towers, their two gardens slicing through the buildings like layers of cream in a Black Forest gateau. Built on the Duxton Plain site to replace two of the oldest 10-storey HDB blocks in the country, Pinnacle@Duxton was first mooted by Lee Kuan Yew in 2001 to showcase the future of public housing and commemorate the historical significance of the location. The fact that Pinnacle@Duxton falls within Lee Kuan Yew's constituency of Tanjong Pagar was entirely coincidental, apparently. When Lee Kuan Yew says, "Jump", lots of buzzing civil servants standing around him in garish baseball caps at community events usually cry, "How high?" And the answer was 50 storeys high, across seven towers, with 1,848 housing units and two sky gardens, all of which must connect to the existing Tanjong Pagar Community Club whilst not disturbing the historical nutmeg trees below. Ten years later, I marvelled at the answer, dumbfounded. Where else would a building project running into the hundreds of millions have to incorporate a few historic nutmeg trees along a narrow strip of park?

I was content to stay longer lying on my back, snapping photographs from my unique worm's eye view but people were beginning to stare and one of those little shih-tzu-type dogs was trotting my way, sniffing the ground and preparing to cock a leg.

The grey tiled slope at the entrance led to an outdoor HDB museum built on the site of the original Duxton Plain blocks, which I wandered through quickly. We both know that story. Singapore needed houses overnight. The British-backed Singapore Improvement Trust proved to be about as useful as Michael Jackson's doctor so the HDB took up the challenge. Some residents were unwilling to move away from their wooden kampongs but the appalling—and purely coincidental, no, really—Bukit Ho Swee fire in 1961 forced them to accept the moral of the *Three Little Pigs*. The HDB housed a nation in a single generation, and the rest of the world has been a bit condescending about this socio-economic miracle ever since. When it opened in 2009, Pinnacle@Duxton was an unsubtle retort to the snide critics. Fuck 'em.

I followed the sheltered walkway that protects the thousands of residents from the sun, rain and killer litter, but mostly the killer litter. It's no joke. In Toa Payoh, I was once hit on the shoulder by a putrid fish head. I screamed. I defy anyone to peer down at their shoulder, notice a decapitated little Nemo staring back at them and not go ape shit.

I found a lift and sought out Pinnacle@Duxton's sexy bits. The seven towers are linked, both on the 26th and 50th storeys, by the world's longest, continuous sky gardens, which weave their way through each block. Quite rightly, the sky garden and jogging track on the 50th floor are open to the public, at a cost of $5, because they sit on the roof of an HDB building. Residents enjoy the exclusive use of the amenities on the 26th floor, which is equally fair. On the 50th floor, I was confronted by a sign. It was titled Sky Garden House Rules and provided a list of dos and don'ts. It was mostly don'ts. Everyone being ordered to leave during a thunderstorm seemed a rather obvious stipulation and I was tickled by the insistence of no gambling. Personally, I'd happily fork out $5 to watch a gaggle of aunties drag a mahjong table out of the lift and give the tiles a shuffle up in the clouds on the 50th floor. The sign also said that there was to be no soliciting or touting in the Sky Garden. Now who in their right mind is going to lug a suitcase full of cleaning products up to the 50th floor to flog bottles of washing-up liquid? There cannot be people queuing up for tea towels and dishcloths on a sky garden, surely.

As instructed, I tapped my ez-link card beside the turnstile. Nothing happened. I tapped it again. The turnstile refused to budge. A sign smaller than the rules and regulations sign stating "You cannot sell trays of eggs on the sky garden" indicated that the ez-link card had to be validated at a machine in Block 1G. I was in Block 1B. I poisoned the air with some well-chosen Hokkien expletives and suddenly stopped when the lift opened. A couple of European tourists waltzed past me, tapped their ez-link cards and spun through the turnstile. They were also treated to a quick burst of Hokkien invective. They were impressed. They thought I knew how to say "cheerio, bye" in a local dialect.

At ground level, I encountered a frazzled mother and her three lively children who were taking turns to cover their entire bodies in ice cream and kick each other in the shins.

"Excuse me, where do I go to get my ez-link card validated for the Sky Garden?" I asked, pointing towards the roof, just in case she didn't know where it was.

"Er, I'm not sure, ah," she replied, distracted by her three urchins practising their clothesline manoeuvres on each other.

"Aiyoh," one of the older boys said, momentarily releasing his blue brother from a chokehold. "It's 1G, Level 1, the office, OK? Go to the office, 1G, Level 1, OK?"

He shook his head resignedly. Residents must get asked this idiotic question from day trippers frequently. And then he went back to strangling his brother.

I found the office, where a teenager guided me through the simple procedure of tapping the machine to extract the $5 and validate my card. I returned to the summit of Pinnacle@ Duxton via the lift at 1G. The layout and floor plan for the 50th floor were identical to those in 1B, utterly indistinguishable. It was most alarming. The grey tiles, the gates and fences and even the position of that damned rules and regulations sign were in the same place, to the millimetre. Who measures these things? I cannot align three movie posters in my living room.

I nonchalantly tapped my ez-link card and beamed proudly as the little red light turned green—take that my European cousins and your first-time entry, if only your debt-ridden economies had been so forward-thinking—and pushed on the turnstile. I clicked forward, then stupidly clicked backwards to check that my rucksack was zipped up. Why I felt compelled to perform this trivial task in a turnstile is quite possibly a debate I need to have with myself at some point. Still, the turnstile had clicked twice and assumed I had departed. I was stuck.

"Er, help," I cried meekly. "Is anyone there?"

The entrance to the Sky Garden in Tower 1G was deserted and even if it wasn't, well, would you pay $5 to rescue me from a trapped turnstile? I'm not sure my wife would.

"Hello, if you can hear me, could you help me, please? I'm stuck in a turnstile," I shouted to an empty lift lobby, staring at the electronic numbers on the panel above, desperately hoping they would reach number 50.

"Hello again, can anyone hear me?" I called again, irritated now. "Actually, I really hope no one can hear me because if you can hear me stuck in this poxy turnstile and you're choosing to ignore me, then you are one selfish bastard."

After an age had passed (probably three minutes), I took matters into my own hands. I pushed myself up against the turnstile, removed my backpack and swivelled around. Taking out my ez-link card again, I stretched my orang-utan arm through the turnstile, managed to have enough limb left to bend it around the corner and fumbled for the card reader on the wall. Eventually, I heard a faint beep, spun around quickly and flung myself at the turnstile, which gleefully spat me out onto the sky garden.

Having learnt from the scorching observation deck at Marina Bay Sands, I donned cap and sunglasses and stepped onto the tiled walkway. There is nothing else quite like Pinnacle@Duxton's

Sky Garden in Singapore, or anywhere else for that matter. Unusually for a Sunday, there were only a handful of residents dotted around, doing all the things one might expect in a popular communal space within the HDB heartlands: jogging, stretching, reading a newspaper, taking their children out on tricycles, having a snooze on a bench, canoodling with a girlfriend away from parents, loosening limbs through tai chi, tapping a calculator to solve homework sums. But they did all this 156 metres in the air. It's a wonder flight stewards do not march across the sky bridges handing out packets of peanuts.

On the southern side of the Sky Garden, I marvelled at the breadth of the view, stretching from Labrador Park to beyond Marina Bay, incorporating Singapore's mini-archipelago of the Southern Islands. As I counted the dots that encompassed the city-state's empire, I noticed behind me that a courteous architect had thought to include some tables and chairs to allow visitors to sit and reflect high on the seaside. I dumped my bag and flopped down.

"Fuck me," I shouted, ripping my thighs from the sizzling seat and performing a leg wax that would be the envy of most Brazilians.

It was indeed thoughtful to provide chairs. It was bloody masochistic to use thick plastic and anchor the bastards 50 storeys high in direct sunlight with no shade. Visitors expect breezy climes when they reach Pinnacle@Duxton, not scorched testicles.

Different areas of the Sky Garden were conceptualised as distinct landscapes. I loved the tongue-in-cheek thinking behind the "Beach". Loungers and deckchairs had been placed around a boardwalk shaped like a beach and a shoreline, with blue rubberised flooring depicting the sea. Of course, beyond the sea is the real sea, on the other side of the fence. It was cheesy but charming. Other gardens included the "Lounge", with tables and chairs mercifully in the shade, a "Sky Gym", with an actual gym offering an unbeatable location, and a "Hillock", which was a grassy knoll. The only grassy knoll I know of apart from the one where JFK was shot.

Just about every iconic structure, building or national heritage sign within 15 kilometres was recognisable from the Sky Garden. Rather than search for them all, I picked a spot at random and tried to locate as many as possible with only a turn of my head. The Peranakan shophouses snaking through Neil Road (I will rent an office there one day), the Supreme Court, People's Park Centre, Chinatown, Clarke Quay, the MICA Building, the spire of the Armenian Church of St Gregory the Illuminator, Bugis's magnificent Parkview Square (possibly my favourite building in the city because of its discordant daftness. It could have been Eliot Ness's home address.), the Istana, that ugly office block in Novena shaped like a fat orange frankfurter, the flats in Lorong 1 Toa Payoh where I once lived and the housing estates of Bishan and Ang Mo Kio—all from the same position.

The roof housed vast water tanks, all secluded and screened of course. As I pondered the green technologies and water harvesting capabilities of the tanks above my head, I was struck by the most obvious of ironies. There were no public toilets on the Sky Garden. Or if there were, I certainly couldn't find them. I dashed along the jogging track frantically searching for a toilet, gazing up only briefly at the green tip of Bukit Timah Summit in the distance. I passed the different (but same) towers, peered into the lift lobbies and checked that the rules sign was in the same position beside each lift (it was), but my search was futile. There was no toilet. And yet the monolithic water tanks loomed large overheard, flushing and feeding every one of the 1,848 apartments beneath my feet. Perturbed, I pondered climbing the ladder to piss in one of the tanks.

I had to leave.

As I waddled cross-legged towards my original turnstile at Tower 1G, I glimpsed something down on my right: a swanky yachting marina. It was Sentosa Cove. I had not seen Singapore's exclusive playground for international oil magnates and Asian money launderers before. Yes, all right, I'm kidding, aren't I? Another development built on reclaimed land, Sentosa Cove was nothing but sea when I last lived in Singapore and it occurred to me that Pinnacle@Duxton was one of the few places in the country where one could spy on the rich and infamous. From the top of Singapore's most illustrious public housing development, I could see its private parts. I liked the symmetry. By definition and deliberate design, Pinnacle@Duxton was built to be as inclusive as possible. Shared communal spaces, online forums and residents' Facebook pages underline how the kampong spirit of the early Duxton Plain blocks lives on at the Pinnacle. Sentosa Cove, on the other hand, was created to be the most exclusive address in Singapore, the most private of properties.

It was time to do a little trespassing.

Eight

VIVOCITY is a paradox. Singapore's largest shopping mall has really tried to be something more aesthetic and less soulless than a number of little retail boxes jockeying for attention inside one big box. The funky wavy design is appropriate for its harbour setting and the wading pool, water features and playground are entertaining diversions for children while their parents replace their hand phones because the new model has a shinier keypad. HarbourFront MRT Station and the air-conditioned Sentosa Express provide easy access for the day trippers on either side and there is even a surreal resident marching band that likes to creep up and scare the shit out of you with a bombastic bang of their drums. How I refrained from chasing that giggling little drummer boy and shoving a drumstick up somewhere sore I'll never know.

The problem with VivoCity isn't the shops, the breezy al fresco dining or Sgt. Pepper's bloody cast-offs terrifying daydreamers, it's the people. Not the calibre, but the sheer quantity. Within the first month of the mall opening in late 2006, VivoCity pulled 4.2 million visitors through its doors. That's a staggering figure, practically the entire population of the country. If 60 million shoppers visited the Heathway mall of my Dagenham childhood, there would not be the time for pickpockets to get to every handbag. VivoCity isn't a shopping destination, it's a game of Space Invaders: constantly avoiding moving targets, sidestepping to avoid a headbutt in the groin from a kid running towards Toys "R" Us and resisting the temptation to poke a shopper in the eye for confusing her pointy Giant bags for a cat and my legs for a scratching post.

Eager to escape that damn marching band of drummers who appeared to be following me, I crossed VivoCity's promenade and stepped on to something that Singapore has incontestably got right. For the tentative day tripper or the seasoned traveller, it's always the little things. Our memories, opinions and judgements are formed by the little things. The glitzy, expensive hardware is soon forgotten if the software has been neglected. For example, I once stayed in a delightful five-star hotel in California thanks to a movie junket (where a journalist gets paid to fly overseas, write a couple of preferably gushing features whilst conveniently forgetting that the said journalist had to stab himself in the leg with his pen during the movie to stay awake). The hotel's opulence was beyond my comprehension (and my salary) until I broke that little paper seal on the toilet seat that indicated the facilities had been cleaned. They hadn't. Or if they had, the cleaner had failed to spot an object last seen being skippered by Sean Connery in *The Hunt for Red October*. When you come across a turd large enough to be used by police on riot control, it becomes exceedingly difficult to remember anything positive about the hotel. And I haven't seen *The Hunt for Red October* again either.

So let's get back to the little things. Little things like the Sentosa Boardwalk. When I first visited Singapore's signature tourist attraction in 1997, the task of navigating one's way from the small island to the even smaller one was protracted and uncomfortable. There was no MRT at HarbourFront back then, so it was either on a bus, in a taxi, on foot or up above via a creaking cable car from the then deserted Mount Faber. Taxi drivers preferred trips to a syphilis clinic than Sentosa, knowing that there was little chance of collecting a customer for the return leg. There was a shuttle bus from the terminal on the other side of West Coast Highway but the queues were always long and the buses always packed. But all of the above were preferable to stumbling across Sentosa Gateway. With little respite from the sun, causeway walkers were treated to the picturesque splendour of the port shifting containers around on Pulau Brani and clouds of dust blown up by irate taxi drivers pissed off that they were going over in the first place.

Thank God then for the Sentosa Boardwalk. Opened in January 2011, the two-way, canopy-covered travelators cost $70 million (for a boardwalk? Are the timber planks filled with gold nuggets?). Green screenings alongside the travelators featured indigenous tropical landscapes. There was nothing but green on my left and the dancing spangles of Keppel Harbour on my right. Knowing that I had a bit of a hike ahead of me to get to Sentosa Cove, I was happy to let the travelator do most of the walking. In 15 years, Sentosa had never been more welcoming, literally pulling me towards the island. I arrived invigorated and raring to find the rich kids' playground.

I found the Sentosa Visitor Centre, picked up a map and a few leaflets and sat down to savour some air con. No one else was in the centre and my body momentarily considered a nap. The sofa was most accommodating and I realised my eyes were closing.

"Yes sir, can I help you, sir?"

I opened my eyes. A smiling auntie stood over me waving a walkie-talkie around.

"Er, sorry, yes. I'm er, going to go to the ..." I stammered, still rather dazed.

"Yes sir, can I help you, sir ... Yes?"

I was being interrogated by a female Basil Fawlty. I cleared my throat and sat up straight.

"Er, yes, right, sorry. I'm trying to get to, er, the bus. Yes, I want to take one of the buses around the island, please."

I didn't mention Sentosa Cove. I didn't look like someone who should be going to Sentosa Cove. I looked like an old dosser nodding off in the Sentosa Visitor Centre. In a benign but transparent manner, Walkie-Talkie Woman was trying to get rid of me. Clearly, she was rushed off her feet with all the other visitors not in her centre.

"Yes, yes, you come this way, please sir," she said, ushering me to my feet and handing me my notepad. Short of poking me with a porcelain statue of the Merlion, it's difficult to see how she could have got me to move any faster.

"OK, I was just wondering if ..." I began.

"This way please, sir," she interrupted, pointing towards the exit. "You go through the door, please sir. That's it. You go through the cave, got buses after the escalator. Thank you, sir."

She opened the door and pointed towards the street, just in case I wasn't sure. With a nod to Charlie Chaplin and Universal Studios Singapore next door, I'm surprised she didn't deliver a comical kick up the arse to help me on my way.

Following her instructions, I found the fake cave, weaved through the fake stalactites and stalagmites, admired the fake, albeit pleasant, waterfall and made my way down the escalators. At least the escalators were real. I failed to locate the bus stop and got lost in the underground car park.

If hell exists, then it must lie within the depths of a Singaporean underground car park. Steamy, uncomfortable, grimy, dusty buildings with the stale air trapped within, the car park's pollutants index is boosted by the fetid, choking fumes of vehicles performing more laps than Sebastian Vettel in the futile hunt for an empty space. There is more screeching than a Hitchcock movie and more honking than a frog chorus. Sentosa's car park failings are compounded by the presence of The Singapore Car Park Attendant. In the words of Plato: never employ a car park attendant who actually wants to be one. And for God's sake, never give these buggers a whistle. There are certain attendants whom I won't name (two words: Lucky Plaza) who appear intellectually incapable of not blowing their whistles. Drivers are unaware of what the blowing means. Pedestrians waiting by the kerb are equally clueless. Does the incessant whistling mean stop, go, slow down, speed up, hold your position, turn left, turn right, pedestrians cross, pedestrians wait, none of the above or all of the above? Even the car park attendant doesn't know. But he's been given a uniform, a smidgen of authority and a whistle and he's going to bloody well enjoy himself.

Sentosa car park attendants not only had whistles, they also had those rectangular flashing disco lightsabre pointy things. Whistles were emitting indecipherable instructions in one direction, arms were flailing about in the other, while the flashing disco lights overhead seemed not to say "Park on the left" but rather "I came to get down, I came to get down ... So get out your seats and jump around ... Jump around ... Jump up, jump up and get down."

Of course, frazzled coach drivers with Chinese tour parties threatening to smash through the emergency windows if they were not sitting at a baccarat table within the next five minutes did what all drivers do in such situations, they ignored the car park attendants. For all the blue-faced whistling and frantic light flashing, the attendants were largely bypassed. I was tempted to wait and see what they lost first—their patience or an eyeball from all that exhaling—but I spotted a yellow Sentosa bus across the car park and dashed past the tour buses.

For the most obvious of reasons, Sentosa Cove is not meant to be accessible to the proletariat. There was going to be some walking involved. I took the bus towards Allanbrooke Road, which has long confused because it splits at the roundabout and heads off in opposite directions with Bukit Manis Road sandwiched in-between. I got off beside a swanky restaurant hosting a wedding party in the northwest and ventured south and then west with only cicadas for company. As I watched the lizards poke their heads around tree trunks, I stopped for a breather. I dumped my bag on the ground, rummaged around for a bottle of water and took a swig just as a shiny speedster raced past, kindly blowing a smattering of grit in my general direction, much of which stuck to my damp, tacky face. There was little time to determine the vehicle's manufacturer, but it was one of those convertible-phallic-fast-car-small-knob types; the car equivalent of the yapping Yorkshire Terrier that constantly snarls at your feet, demonstrating its aggressive hardness, while you sigh indifferently before drop-kicking the little bastard. The car roared past a speed-reading box on the other side of the road, clocking more than 80 km/h, which I presumed exceeded the speed limit for Allanbrooke Road. I also presumed the Sentosa Cove-bound driver didn't give a shit.

Wiping the grime from my face, I heard another convertible tearing towards me. This one was a white open-top BMW. With the exception of taxis, are cheap cars banned from using Allanbrooke Road? Four blondes, hair dancing around like candyfloss in a hurricane, shot past me and I turned away for fear of being struck by globs of peroxide. The jaunty Caucasian women giggled as they thundered along. I know because I heard every snippet of their conversation. Chatting in an open-top car, at speed, must be like making a phone call in a wind tunnel. How do you sit beside someone in the back seat and take them seriously when their big, blowy hair makes them look like Marge Simpson?

Finally, I reached the double archway entrance to Sentosa Cove. A Malay security guard stepped down from his post. He was the first Singaporean I had seen in half an hour. He eyed my sweaty demeanour, bright purple rucksack and scruffy T-shirt and shorts cautiously. My presence was unexpected. No one walks in and out of Sentosa Cove.

"Hello there, I was just going in to have a wander around Sentosa Cove," I opened brightly. "I've heard so much about it and, would you believe, I've just seen it from the top of Pinnacle@ Duxton and thought I'd nip down and have a look at it."

"Ah, it's private property, sir," he replied evenly. "They are private residences here."

"I understand that but this road cannot be private, can it? It's a public road, right? I can just have a stroll down the road."

"You see that shelter there behind the little roundabout? That's the Sentosa Cove Arrival Plaza. You can go over there and have a look, but then you must not go any further."

And with such a warm welcome, I ventured into what has been called the world's most exclusive address (by the people behind Sentosa Cove).

Built on reclaimed land, Sentosa Cove defines new Singapore: its aspirations, its direction and its desire to reposition itself on the global stage. A cost-effective manufacturing hub no more, Singapore has long coveted the pharmaceutical and technology titans. With that skills base now on board, Sentosa Cove's role is to provide a play base. If Marina Bay Sands represents a desire to be the Monaco of Asia, Sentosa Cove is a very deliberate attempt to be the Switzerland of Asia. (If Singaporeans were just occasionally permitted to live in the "Singapore of Asia", then there might not be such a crisis of conscience concerning national identity.) Declining birth rates require an injection of people and the nation will only accept the best: wealthy investors seeking attractive tax incentives, banking stability and—that most priceless of commodities in a dense metropolis—a private playground. The banks on the mainland take care of the former while Sentosa Cove takes care of the latter. For the discreet businessman, what's not to like about this arrangement? An apartment downtown, dinner designed by one of the many chef hats at Marina Bay and a weekend hang-out at Sentosa Cove to pick up the yacht for jaunts around the South China Sea. With a stable government, the absence of corruption so systemic elsewhere in the region, *kiasu* civil servants, dependable infrastructure and every English Premier League game live on cable TV, Singapore ticks every box for the wealthiest of the wealthy seeking somewhere to dump sackfuls of cash. And how do Singaporeans benefit? Well, someone's got to drive those Sentosa buses and man the security posts, haven't they?

I stopped at a promenade platform overlooking Sentosa Cove and surveyed the marina. Bordered by gleaming, glassy low-rise apartments, the marina was filled with yacht masts gently swaying in the breeze. I peered down to my left and spotted, of course, the ubiquitous Harry's Bar. Do expats and Western tourists drink anywhere else in Singapore? I've got nothing against the Harry's Bar chain but moving from one outlet to another in the franchise must get repetitive. There can be only so many rugby repeats one can watch on TV whilst being surrounded by the "diddly dee" Irish tat that expat pubs so often favour. In Harry's Bar, a decent crowd had gathered to watch one of the Rugby World Cup semi-finals. There was plenty of cheering from men constantly toasting the TV while their partners whooped in all the right places. I cannot recall the teams, other than they were two of those countries that expats will usually support in a foreign land but seldom give a shit about once they return home.

I spotted my second Singaporean. His Singlish gave him away. The young Malay guy had given a European couple a lift to Harry's Bar—in a golf buggy. He had transported them from their Sentosa Cove apartment to the pub, a distance of no more than a couple of hundred metres, in a golf buggy. Well, you get what you pay for. And someone paid $17.9 million for a bungalow on Cove Drive, which faces the waterway, not long before I visited in September 2011. When Sentosa Cove Pte Ltd completes the complex in 2014, there will be 1,766 condominium units and 394 bungalows. There will be no further apartments added. Exclusivity comes at the highest price and foreigners, who make up at least half the buyers, are willing to pay it. Sentosa Cove is the only place in Singapore where foreigners can own land, and land that comes with a chauffeur-driven golf buggy, too.

Unexpectedly dejected, I trudged back to the sheltered bus stop beside the Sentosa Cove Arrival Plaza. A luxurious private coach was parked in the bay with the slogan "the world's most desirable address" slapped along the side. Sentosa Cove might do exclusive but it doesn't do subtle. There were only two Caucasians on board waiting for the bus to depart. The Singaporean driver stood chatting and smoking with other local drivers near me. An elevated four-wheel drive with tinted windows pulled up behind the coach and dropped off a couple of tanned Caucasians. Some weary Indian workers were sitting on the ground beneath the shelter, sharing a bottle of water and resting after presumably spending all day—a Sunday—building a new billionaire's bolt-hole. Another bus parked up behind the fancy private one.

It was a Sentosa bus. I was furious.

I hadn't noticed this bus in the underground car park, nor had I read about it in the tourist leaflet nor on the website. I hadn't even known that it existed. That bus could have spared me a sweat soaking along Allanbrooke Road an hour earlier. Why would the ultimate seaside haven for the haves tolerate a public bus full of the have-nots? Its route was displayed on a window: a shuttle service running directly between HarbourFront MRT Station and Sentosa Cove. The bus had the potential to carry those pesky peasants directly from public transport and drop them into the very private laps of the landowners. It made no sense until the doors opened and the penny dropped. The bus was packed with Singaporeans and Southeast Asians. They were all there—cleaners, sweepers, waiters, labourers—all going to work. Sentosa Cove really was for them after all.

I was suddenly conscious of my skin colour.

Whether they were table wipers, security guards, bus drivers, construction labourers or bloody golf buggy drivers, the only Singaporeans I encountered at Sentosa Cove were blue-collar workers performing largely menial jobs. As I waited in line with them, I caught a glimpse of Pinnacle@Duxton in the northeast and was just able to make out the Sky Garden. Towering above Chinatown's history, the very public and very accessible building pointed the way forward. Pinnacle@Duxton is a Singaporean building for Singaporeans (perhaps of a certain financial means, but Singaporeans nonetheless). But who is Sentosa Cove for?

It's for the Lycra lady who ran towards the bus stop at that particular moment. She was a Caucasian in her late forties with expensively coiffured, dyed hair and immaculately presented in head-to-toe black Lycra. Jogging stylishly towards the queue, she wore black sunglasses that had something ridiculously expensive written down their arms, her trainers appeared to be 20 minutes old and my mischievous memory is adamant that her miniscule iPod was gold-plated. Her earrings contained a pair of diamonds last seen in *The Pink Panther*. She was that manicured, thoroughly manufactured, vision of natural perfection that only obscene wealth can provide. Even her beads of sweat had been trained to trickle away from her face to avoid an unsightly complexion.

She trotted towards the bus queue and performed that annoying jogging-on-the-spot routine until the crowd parted slightly so she could continue on her way. And we did. Lycra lady swaggered along the street like she owned it, which in a way she did. The coach drivers smirked. A Chinese auntie muttered something. I stared at my shoes, embarrassed.

Like everyone else in Singapore, I've been well drilled. I can parrot the immigration mantra. I understand the fundamental economics behind foreign talent and the desire to attract the wealthiest elite to dump their fortunes here, no questions asked. But at that moment, I didn't care. I saw only the foreign haves and the local have-nots and was struck by just one objective, rational question.

How the hell do Singaporeans put up with us?

Nine

I WAS once packed off to California to meet Han Solo. Just typing that sentence sends a tingling frisson of excitement through my fingers, indicating what a thoroughly sad man I am. Nevertheless, I gleefully accepted the media junket offer without checking flight times or interview schedules. I spent more time in the air than I did in California. I fell asleep during the media screening of Harrison Ford's new movie on Hollywood Boulevard. When I woke up, a lovely American film critic beside me kindly pointed out that I had dribbled down my chin. But then Ford's thriller *Firewall* could do that to a viewer.

The brief trip to the home of American cinema was spent in that hazy, zombie fog of jet lag. I was there, without ever actually being there. I know I asked Ford if the proliferation of home computers and social media had the potential to corrupt young minds. He retorted with a convoluted analogy that involved smashing my head into a piano. I stared at his earring. I peered down at his waist, half expecting to see a bullwhip hanging from his belt. He caught me glimpsing beneath the table. He thought I was looking at his crotch. I asked him if he planned to make another Indiana Jones movie. He yawned. I yawned. My eyes were closing. I was falling asleep interviewing my childhood idol.

"Right, that's all we have time for."

It was a tall, leggy blonde PR girl calling time on the interview. I shook my head and did that eye-widening thing to stave off the droopiness. Unfortunately, I was offering Ford my hand to shake at the time and turned into an eye-bulging Roger Rabbit. I was trying to be alert, but it came off as alarming. Indiana Jones wisely left the room without shaking my hand.

Less than an hour later, I was lining up for the Back to the Future simulator ride at Universal Studios in Los Angeles. My malfunctioning body was threatening to go on strike, but my movie-mad mind was aware that this was the only opportunity I had to fulfil a boyhood fantasy of flying a DeLorean. Being on a media trip however, I went to Universal Studios alone. Men who visit movie theme parks alone often spend their weekends dressed as imperial stormtroopers running through shopping malls and shouting, "It's them! Blast them!"

Beyond exhaustion, my sleep-starved brain had moved into a higher plane of giddy, giggly euphoria, thanks to that final burst of adrenaline which fuels aching limbs before everything shuts down entirely. I found myself climbing into the DeLorean simulator with a group of teenage girls and muttering, "Roads? Where we're going we don't need ... roads."

The girls stared at me.

"Have you been on this ride before, girls?" I shouted over the ride's narrator.

They shook their heads.

"It's gonna be great. I hope we can get this baby up to 88 miles an hour."

I laughed. They didn't.

"Der, de de de de, de de de de!"

I was singing the bloody theme tune. I was rocking from side to side and singing the *Back to the Future* theme tune. I had gone through the wall. I no longer needed sleep. I needed a sedative. The American girl beside me leant towards her friend.

"Look at him," she said. "What's wrong with the old guy?"

The old guy loved Universal Studios. Plucking the maudlin strings of a violin, Universal Studios was my babysitter growing up. After my parents divorced, my mother went to work and I was tasked with looking after my little sister with the help of *The Incredible Hulk*. Old Bill Bixby kept us company through the school holidays as he travelled through small-town America seeking to reverse the damage done by the gamma rays. He was also an extremely *kaypoh* busybody, second only to Angela Lansbury in *Murder, She Wrote*. David Banner, Bixby's character, was always acutely aware that you wouldn't like him if you made him angry. But did he head for a peace commune or a mountaintop monastery? No, he washed dishes in a Chinatown diner owned by Triads. He knew how to keep his head down did David Banner. And he never left Universal Studios. That was the best part. Every episode was filmed on Universal's backlot. He travelled the entire country, but every diner was always the diner in *Back to the Future*, and the same diner where Robert Shaw met Robert Redford in *The Sting*. Every street led to the Hill Valley courthouse, where lightning struck the clock tower to send Marty McFly Back to the Future. These were also the same streets that Austin Powers danced along in the opening scenes of his first movie.

So I revered Universal Studios. I was making a pilgrimage. It was a chance to express my gratitude for the childhood companionship. Being jet-lagged and having met Han Solo earlier in the morning only added to the day's dreaminess. I just regret falling asleep in my French fries at the Jurassic Park cafe.

Still, I hope you can appreciate my unadulterated joy when I lifted my daughter and posed in front of the iconic revolving planet logo of Universal Studios Singapore inside Resorts World Sentosa. If ever a small single structure symbolised new Singapore, it would have to be this one. The little red dot really is a centre of the universe. Its evolution as an entertainment destination in such a short period is beyond breathtaking when you consider what had been there before.

More than 10 years earlier, we had taken my wife's parents to the generously-titled Volcanoland, which was once situated not far from where I now stood with my daughter outside Universal Studios. Volcanoland was quaint. Some might say crap. Volcanoland promised visitors an "active" volcano with terrifying earth tremors, belligerent bursts of blistering air and horrifying hissing sounds shooting from its fissures.

It was a fibreglass model that shook a bit.

Young Singaporeans were employed to portray indigenous Mayan people, an image that confounded the senses to begin with, and their primary role was to scare the crowd by shouting, "Ooh, look it's really shaking ... I think the plastic volcano is going to explode any second ... We better run for cover ... Wait! Pose for your photos first."

That's what Sentosa offered visitors until Universal Studios turned its world around.

We bought our theme park tickets and the race was on between my three-year-old daughter and me to see who could reach the delightfully tacky Hollywood main street first. I won, but only by a gentle pulling of her pigtails when she was distracted by the presence of Woody Woodpecker. While she ran off to join the queue for a photo with Woody, I noticed that the Universal Studios crowd was decidedly different to that of its Californian cousin. There were hardly any obese people. And anyone who thinks I'm taking an easy cheap shot here has obviously never been to Universal Studios or Disneyland in California. I'm not referring to regular folks carrying a bit of holiday weight. I'm taking about a rare group so large that they still wear flared trousers because they haven't been able to reach below their waists since the 1970s. The morbidly obese do not go to weight-loss programmes in the United States. They are given motorised carts and sent to the nearest theme park with explicit instructions to ram the buggers into everyone's ankles from behind with one hand whilst holding a bucket-sized soda in the other.

Such people were hard to find. Instead, we were surrounded by tour parties from China. On these overseas collectives, the tour guides must be under incalculable pressure not to lose anyone on their watch so the tourists are usually labelled to make identification easier, perhaps with a discreet sticker on the chest. Not the mainland Chinese tour parties. They took no chances. They covered themselves in luminous yellow T-shirts that made the retina recoil. And the laughably loud shirts were topped off by matching yellow baseball caps. The group looked like they'd all been showered in vomit. No tour guide could mislay these guys. How do you lose 25 giant corn on the cobs?

Like most visitors, we turned left at Hollywood and made our way around the park in a clockwise fashion towards Madagascar, the second of seven themed zones. We joined the queue for Madagascar: A Crate Adventure, based on the animated movie by DreamWorks. We lined up for no more than 15 minutes under a covered queuing area complete with fans and water coolers. At most theme parks, water coolers require a compass and a seasoned cartographer to track them down. They are everywhere at Universal Studios Singapore. My daughter adored the riverboat adventure, pointing and waving at the animatronic characters, waterfalls and jet sprays. The ride lasted 10 minutes. My daughter sang "I Like to Move It, Move It" for the next 10 days.

We next joined a queue for the hairiest, scariest attraction in any theme park—the queue for a photo with a cartoon character. If there is one thing that fatherhood has taught me, it is never mess with a parent lining up to get a photo with a cartoon character. Something happens in the brain; a chemical imbalance occurs and a parental instinct kicks in to shield, protect and enhance one's offspring. We once strolled through an Australian wildlife reserve in Tower Hill, Victoria, and stumbled across some emu chicks crossing the footpath. Then we encountered the mother bringing up the rear. She looked down at me. I'm 1.93 metres tall and she looked down at me. Then she peered at her exposed chicks, examined the distance between us and determined that we were too close. She gave chase. I took off like I'd sat on a spike. Her fixed maternal gaze sent an unequivocal message between the species: do not come between me and my babies. I hadn't since seen such a steely-eyed desire to protect at any cost until I joined that photo-taking queue. The message was the same: do not come between me and my babies' chance to take a photo with Gloria the Hippo or I will fucking kill you.

Women grabbed their children and jostled for space while fathers primed their cameras, taking photos of random kids with Gloria just to calculate the correct lens and focus (at least I hope that's what they were doing). Anyone who accidentally joined the queue from the wrong end (invariably one of the corn on the cobs from mainland China) was picked up by the baseball cap and thrown out by irate mothers. Oblivious passers-by who wandered across the shot just as the camera clicked were swiftly chased away to avoid a public lynching. And throughout all of this, the young, exasperated theme park guides tried to usher impatient parents into a single line only to be told, "Bollocks! I've paid over $70 for this ticket so you're gonna let me get a cute shot with Gloria and my little girl or I'm going to kick you in the nuts."

And that was just my wife.

Honestly, we loved chasing after the men and women in suits. Camp, kitschy and cheesy have always entertained and titillated more than the refined and sophisticated. I happily pursued Marilyn Monroe past the marvellous New York Library facade and insisted on a photo in front of a sidewalk stoop, or front door steps, complete with fake steam coming through the pavement grate. I cannot get enough of the celluloid Americana. Is it artificial and cynically manufactured for corporate gain? Does it reflect the reality of life in New York? Who cares? I didn't grow up in New York. I grew up in small-screen New York, as presented to me by Universal Studios. I was in heaven. Dashing from one cinematic hero to another, however, I did spot one unusual trend. There were a number of young men queuing up to have their photos taken with Woody Woodpecker, Alex the Lion from *Madagascar* and other cartoon characters. Now it's one thing to line up beside the lovely Marilyn or even Betty Boop, but seeing a single man putting his arm around another man dressed as Woody Woodpecker and beaming like a lottery winner was unsettling. Should these men be allowed in public places unsupervised?

Having cornered Beetlejuice in New York, I spotted a park guide beckoning me towards a show called Lights, Camera, Action! The lame title almost dissuaded me but I picked up my daughter and joined the pleasingly short queue. (In fact, we didn't line up for more than 15 minutes for any attraction the entire day. Hint: Follow the theme park rules and go on a Tuesday or a Wednesday during the low season and avoid weekends.) Well, the special effects show was just wonderful. Hosted by Steven Spielberg, Lights, Camera, Action! supposedly gave kids a basic insight into how sound effects and sound stages work but, really, this one was for the kids inside the grown-ups. The opening montage of classic Universal Studios movies, everything from

Back to the Future to *Jaws*, *E.T.* and *Backdraft*, was worth the admission fee alone. Like the MINT Museum, I was taken back to my Dagenham living room when I was a wide-eyed, open-mouthed, cross-legged kid trying to focus on Marty getting up to 88 miles an hour and ignoring my sister's pleas to play *Grease* again.

After the sequence of film clips, Spielberg ushered the group onto the main sound stage, modelled on the interior of an NYC boathouse, and that's all I'm going to say. I prefer to keep the man behind the curtain and focus on the wizard. Besides, I came out rather relieved that the special effects show wasn't a fully interactive show. When we visited Warner Bros. Movie World in 1997, the studio tour host pulled me out of the audience to play Superman on the grounds that I made a decent Clark Kent: bespectacled, tall, dark and drippy. To the merriment of the masses, they stretched me out on a plank, wearing an ill-fitting Superman costume in front of a cheap back projection screen. I thought I was a passable Man of Steel until we shuffled out later and I overheard an elderly Australian chap mutter to his wife, "That's the first time I've seen Superman played by a skinny Pommy bastard."

When we lined up for the brilliant Battlestar Galactica duelling roller coasters, we attracted some uncomfortable glares from a group of fidgeting teenagers. We had played our child swap card. For the benefit of those who do not have children, the child swap system allows couples to both go on an adult-only ride without queuing twice. The first parent lines up as normal while the other minds the children, refraining from leaving them outside Lost Property, and then they swap over at a designated location. My wife waited at the Battlestar Galactica entrance for me to return, then she hurried down the express lane (a separate line for VIPs wishing to pay a small fortune to avoid lengthy queues).

When she jogged past the impatient teenagers waiting in the regular queue, they tutted and shook their heads with that familiar combination of adolescent aggression and world weariness. If any of those guys happen to read this and believe we were somehow cutting the queue that day, I can only say that I would happily and unreservedly grant you our places in the express lane. But in return, you would have to spend a day carrying around a sweaty, jiggling child constantly poking you in the face and shouting, "I want to play with Woody's pecker. I want to play with Woody's pecker." That's only fair.

Unknowingly, we saved the best to last. After the carousel, Shrek in 4D, the interactive Donkey dancing and the 15-year-old WaterWorld stunt show (come on guys, I watched the same performance in California more than a decade ago and the plane worked in that one), we took full advantage of the child swap system for the Revenge of the Mummy roller coaster. The ride was everything a theme park attraction should be: thrilling, relevant, interactive and fully immersive. Like Terminator 2: 3D in California's Universal Studios, Revenge of the Mummy has a clear narrative that complements its source material. It's not just a roller coaster with a couple of dusty bandage-covered mannequins beside the track but an entire movie experience that begins the moment guests join the queue inside an enormous Egyptian tomb. We were ushered into mine cars and swiftly sent hurtling through the tomb's darkness in every conceivable direction, with flames licking the ceiling and scarab beetles scurrying across the walls. In movie-related theme parks, the most memorable attraction always pays clear homage to its cinematic origins to engage not only the thrill-seeker, but also the film buff. Revenge of the Mummy achieved both with aplomb. Direct film references were plentiful and I shit myself. It is quite possibly the perfect theme park ride.

But for the *kiasu* types, that's still not enough. The Revenge of the Mummy ride was budgeted at more than US$20 million and Singaporeans have lamented that the queue is too long. Universal Studios Singapore is the only theme park of its kind in Southeast Asia, its owners promising not to build another in the region for the next 30 years. Some Singaporeans say there are not enough rides. Aware of the energy-sapping humidity and unpredictable monsoonal weather patterns, Universal Studios Singapore maximises every square inch of its layout. All seven themed zones are connected around a central lake. Most of the streets are sheltered from both the sun and the rain and fans are provided in most queuing areas to minimise discomfort. Some Singaporeans say the theme park is too small. Universal Studios Singapore is smaller than its American counterpart, but it's also slightly cheaper. Some Singaporeans say, "Wah, still so expensive." These are the same Singaporeans, incidentally, who once laughed sarcastically when I informed them of weekend plans to visit Sentosa. To them, the island was a perennial source of national embarrassment, with a creaking monorail, dilapidated attractions and a decaying infrastructure. Sentosa served only regional tourists and *ang mohs* who didn't know any better. Singaporeans knew better.

As I sat in Mel's Drive-in, based loosely on *American Graffiti* (one of my favourite movies from the 1970s), I thought, Sod the cynics. Just be grateful that the theme park overcame the economic downturn and is actually here. Universal Studios Dubailand broke ground in July 2008. Universal Studios Singapore also broke ground in 2008. Dubailand was supposed to open in 2010 but became a direct victim of the global financial crisis. The money ran out and the project was put on hold. Apart from a gate bearing the Universal Studios logo, no work has been carried out in Dubai since 2009. Singapore welcomed more than two million visitors through its Universal Studios gate within nine months of opening in 2010. I know where I'd rather be, sitting in Mel's Drive-in, slurping shakes and watching my daughter dance along to Mel's Dinettes singing "It's My Party (and I'll Cry if I Want to)".

Resorts World Sentosa won the bid to build Singapore's second integrated resort shortly after I left in 2006 because the consortium promised to deliver Universal Studios. Unlike Marina Bay Sands' emphasis on high-end retail, conferences and museums, Resorts World Sentosa's focus was family entertainment. It had to do it for the kids. Speaking as the biggest of them, I can only say that Universal Studios Singapore is an unqualified success. I hope they keep the kids in and the *kiasu* out for many years to come. Besides, the *kiasu* have already got their theme park next door.

And so, with a heavy heart, I kissed my family goodbye and trudged towards the casino.

Apparently, this is the place for proper grown-ups.

Ten

AROUND the middle of 2008, some Australian friends and I were sitting in my house and lampooning the latest farcical fallout from the unfinished local swimming pool. The Leisurelink Aquatic & Recreation Centre, to give the pool its full mouthful, was going to be the jewel in Geelong's municipal crown. The town planners of my former Victorian home promised a 50-metre pool to go with a learn-to-swim pool, spa, toddlers' pool, hydro pool, gymnasium and a couple of water slides for the kids. My daughter was due in June 2008. The aquatic complex was also due to be delivered in 2008. The swimming serendipity appropriately synchronised. However, there was a delay. There were many delays, with the deadline constantly pushed back by increasingly castigated councillors. So with my friends sitting comfortably in my living room, I regaled them with the Singapore story. No, not that Singapore story. The shorter one, the one about the even smaller island.

I explained that there was an island off the southern coast of Singapore called Sentosa. A former military garrison turned tourist destination, the green isle was an escape from the encroaching urban sprawl on the other side, so much so that most Singaporeans had forgotten about it. Sentosa had gone stale.

An entire makeover was needed to resurrect the faded funhouse, pull visitors away from Hong Kong and Macau and bring the roar back to the Merlion. So around the time that the City of Greater Geelong unveiled the blueprints for an all-under-one-roof aquatic complex, the island's radical transformation began under the stewardship of the Sentosa Development Corporation and Resorts World Sentosa.

And that night I made the boldest—and daftest—of bets. In many respects, I was the first person in the world to place a bet on the Sentosa casino. I had a friendly wager with those present in my living room that Resorts World Sentosa would be topped off and opened before the public swimming pool in Geelong.

At that time, the prediction seemed preposterous. Geelong's swimming pool was only a year away from opening. In contrast, Resorts World Sentosa had to knock up several themed hotels, including Crockfords Tower, Hard Rock Hotel Singapore, the Festive Hotel and Hotel Michael; dig a couple of lakes; add some state-of-the-art productions and animatronics shows and build a galleria with more than 20 high-end boutiques and fashion labels. Oh and throw up Universal Studios Singapore, too, if they could possibly spare the time.

Resorts World broke ground on its Sentosa site on 16 April 2007. Resorts World Sentosa celebrated its soft opening on 20 January 2010, just 34 months later. Whatever one's thoughts are on gaming, such productivity throughout a global economic downtown is bewildering.

Meanwhile on 4 August 2010, the *Geelong Advertiser* reported that Victoria's second-biggest city was still waiting for its aquatic complex to open after another deadline had passed. Originally scheduled to open in 2008, D-Day was moved back to late 2009, then again to April 2010, and again to August 2010, before finally opening in September 2010. The Geelong council insisted that the coordination of such a vast project (a public swimming pool, remember), the weather and transporting equipment from overseas had affected all the deadlines (and those council shovels cannot lean on themselves).

I know, I know. This is a mischievous, facetious comparison. Resorts World Sentosa was built with private funding, using building materials purchased from much closer to home and employing (and exploiting) the cheapest non-unionised foreign labour around the clock. Geelong's terrific aquatic complex (where my daughter eventually took her first swimming lessons) relied upon tax payers coughing up A$31 million for a public development so every design feature, alteration and modification had to be voted on before being able to move forward. The swimming pool was built by a committee. Resorts World Sentosa was built by a casino. Had Geelong filled the complex with roulette wheels rather than rubber rings, councillors might have met their deadlines.

Still, I won my bet. Only a fool would bet against Singaporean efficiency. But then, only a fool would bet against a Singaporean casino.

I stepped off the escalator and thought about a recent chat with a taxi driver. Before embarking on this second journey around Singapore, I had been discreetly pumping taxi drivers for information about the two casinos. They are a better barometer than any government survey. Through their daily trips to both Marina Bay Sands and Resorts World over a long period, they have an instinctive gut feel for how each of the casinos is faring and whether visitor numbers are up or down, simply because they are always there. Sometimes they drop off passengers, too. One taxi driver told me that he can make up to six trips a day to the casino but hadn't once dropped a local family off at Universal Studios Singapore. That single anecdote says more about a national mindset and a country's priorities than any number of tedious government statistics.

"I always go to Resorts World," the taxi driver told me, when I enquired where his favoured baccarat tables were. "I tried Marina Bay, don't like it. Not my kind of people. You wanna go casino, go Sentosa. Sentosa got more people like me, you know, got more my kind of people."

I wasn't entirely sure whom he was referring to. Who was his kind of people? Singaporeans? Chinese? Taxi drivers? Or did he specifically mean Singaporean Chinese taxi drivers? I envisioned a packed gaming floor of Chinese guys forever bemoaning long airport queues and who abruptly disappeared between the hours of 7 a.m. and 9.30 a.m. and from 6 p.m. to 8 p.m. every day. In truth, I had little interest in visiting a second Singapore casino—there's only so much passive smoking and coughing one can tolerate around blackjack tables—but decided to pop into Resorts World's cash cow to meet the taxi driver's people.

Asian casinos like red. No other colour quite says prosperity (or chintzy) in a casino the way red does, with a splash of gold in its gaudy bits. I took in the vast, curved entrance, which was far more conspicuous than that of Marina Bay Sands, and was dazzled by the reds and golds competing for attention on the walls, pillars, carpets and mosaic floors. I was struck by the vision of an interior designer, standing where I stood now, hands on the back of his hips, very light on the loafers, theatrically effeminate and shouting, "More red, darling, we just can't have enough red. We need to make these poor sods feel as lucky as possible ... Wait, is that black? Tarquin? Where's Tarquin? Can I see something black there, Tarquin? You know how I feel about black. Tarquin, fetch my poodle. I need to lie down."

Have you pictured the interior designer yet? Now imagine he was given a design project, in which the colour scheme was vibrant red with splashes of gold, taste and subtlety were optional and money was no object. That's the entrance of the casino at Resorts World Sentosa.

Inside the casino, the red walls and carpets will soon be diluted by a hint of nicotine yellow. The gaming floor stank. Clouds of second-hand smoke hung in the air at every turn, allowing more than 7,000 chemicals—70 of which can cause cancer—to really permeate the lungs of unfortunate, non-smoking croupiers. Halos encircled the tables, suggesting their occupants were either obliterating their vital organs or Simon Templar had popped in (a pop culture reference for the aunties and uncles, that one).

Even though I visited both casinos at similar times, Sentosa was much quieter. Perhaps this was not surprising. Having opened first, the casino enjoyed a brief monopoly until Marina Bay Sands started to claw at its clientele. In its first full non-monopoly reporting period after MBS opened, Resorts World's revenue fell 15 per cent. The government also intervened. In September 2010, the resort's free shuttle buses within Singapore were banned (except for hotel guests coming from the airport) after the service was sneakily extended into the heartlands. Of course, no one should get their hanky out for Resorts World Sentosa. At the time of writing, the island's casino business was expected to earn in the region of $2 billion in 2011 alone. The entire costs of knocking up the entire 49-hectare site will probably be paid off by the time you finish this sentence. That's why they were in such a hurry to finish the project, just in case you had assumed the corporate suits had rushed completion so they could all ride the Revenge of the Mummy roller coaster. (The Geelong swimming complex needs the population of Australia to visit before it dreams of generating such revenues. Still, that's no excuse to charge an adult A$5.60 to swim. Swimming pool staff wear City of Greater Geelong shirts but they should wear ski masks and carry shotguns.)

The well heeled were not well represented on Sentosa's gaming floor. Indeed I was hard pressed to find someone not wearing shorts. I joined a small, appreciative crowd to watch a bizarre musical performance. Before an audience of no more than twenty, a rocking band enthusiastically backed the Chinese version of Celine Dion. Her name, I was later told, was Cui Xia and she is apparently well known within the Mandarin ballad community. Indeed, she belted out the tunes with astonishing gusto. She was in the middle of a Chinese cha cha cha and, not content with her perfect pitch, performed little dance routines in a slinky black number, spinning around like one of the Spice Girls. She closed her eyes, smiled broadly and raised her hand aloft as she nailed the big notes. She had lost herself in the moment. She was gone. She was in residence in Vegas, singing for another full house at Caesars Palace. It's a shame she had to open her eyes again really and see an old guy dozing at the bar, his head bobbing up and down on his arms, several over-aged *ah bengs* counting out their chips, a white Lamborghini parked beside her at the side of the stage that was being offered as a jackpot prize and a couple of Chinese mainlanders with rusty-nail dyed hair dancing drunkenly with all the rhythm of Robocop.

I kept waiting for the gentle shudder and the slight clinking of shaking glasses that always signalled the ship pulling out of Keppel Harbour. I was on Star Cruises again, surrounded by men and women in shorts and flip-flops impatiently waiting to reach their favourite regional destination known as "international waters". No need to buy a cruise ticket and shuffle along in those interminable queues for the buffet any more. Genting has brought its casino and its clientele to dry land. If Marina Bay Sands at least made an attempt to maintain a facade of international glamour and respectability, Sentosa barely bothered. Like its Genting predecessor in Malaysia, the new casino already felt jaded and old. This was the gaming home of the housing estates, and the casino was more than content to throw a few free Fantas their way as they dropped a day's salary with every hand. From housewives to hawkers, taxi drivers to technicians, blue-collar punters were the bread and butter here. I was the only Caucasian on the gaming floor. My conspicuous demeanour cannot be overstated. When the notepad came out for some furious scribbling, even the croupiers and pit bosses paid attention. As for the punters, I might as well have been naked. They only ever had their eyes on the prize.

I lost $10 in less than a minute on a jackpot machine and drank three cups of Fanta orange in a pitiful attempt to get my money back (a pointless exercise, I will now acknowledge, because I didn't have enough money left for a taxi home and later belched all the way to Bedok on the MRT). Before leaving, I stopped at a three pictures table, only because I had no idea what the card game of three pictures involved. Unfortunately, the table was situated in yet another smoking area so it was some time before the fog cleared to reveal that everyone seated at the table was wearing shorts, including two aunties. I was beginning to think trousers and dresses had been outlawed. I was drawn towards a chunky Chinese auntie sitting at the corner of the table. A picture of concentration, she squinted at the croupier while her legs jigged up and down under the table. She wore shorts and flip-flops and held a cigarette in one hand and a can of Guinness in the other.

It is an image that will never leave me.

In search of something less grubby, I left the casino and took my place in a waterfront amphitheatre along the new FestiveWalk. While I waited for the free Crane Dance show, I realised everything had gone: the old Sentosa arrival centre, the crappy gift shops and the quirky cafe with the fluffiest omelettes.

Everything had been torn down since my previous visit and replaced by a fancy seafood restaurant with presumably other swanky eateries to follow. Even Sentosa's famous bird stand, from which exotic parrots and macaws once welcomed visitors with squawks and mimicked phrases, had gone. That particular loss hit me pretty hard. The bird stand was where a macaw once bit my mother-in-law as she posed for a photo. Sentosa staff refused to let me adopt the macaw. I loved that bird.

But most of old Sentosa has gone and not before time. The bits that were worth saving—Images of Singapore, Fort Siloso, the nature walks and all the World War II sites—have been preserved. I'm still not sure about Butterfly Kingdom though. In fairness, my jaundiced view can be attributed to once visiting the attraction with my wife, who had convinced herself that every butterfly species had a life cycle of only 24 hours. Whenever a butterfly fluttered nearby, she nodded knowingly, smiled empathetically and said, "I wonder how many hours he's got left."

"Look, we've had this conversation a million times before," I replied. "Butterflies do not all live and die in a single day."

"They do, you know. I read it in a magazine."

"What magazine? The one with the cover story about the fat woman from Leeds left heartbroken after her Egyptian husband ran off once he got his British passport?"

"I know, it was terrible, wasn't it? Yeah, that one."

"It's not true."

"It is true. Every butterfly in this place will be dead by the time they close tonight."

"So there'll be a carpet of butterfly bodies at closing time, will there?"

"Yep, and then there'll be a whole new lot of butterflies in the morning ... Ah, look, I reckon he's on his way out."

She now acknowledges that some butterfly species do get to

see Tuesday if they emerge from their chrysalises on Monday, but remains adamant that they are very much in the minority. Unlike her daft theories, however, Butterfly Kingdom has survived the islandwide makeover. Old Sentosa endures only in fragments, dotted around the place like its camouflaged gun posts. But the perennial favourites are still there, maintaining a sentimental peephole into the quirky and certainly quieter island I first visited in 1997.

But new Sentosa soars on the mechanical wings of the astounding Crane Dance. In a valiant stab at verisimilitude, I thought I had better hang around for the free water show. To be honest, the prospect of looking at projected images of national pride stretched across a wall of water for the umpteenth time did not appeal. I had already seen them all: strobe lights, fire plumes, animated characters, dancing fountains, even green lasers shooting from the Merlion's eyes. As the sweat melded my buttocks together, I shifted uneasily and expected more of the same set to an eclectic classical soundtrack.

I could not have been more wrong.

The Crane Dance was such a groundbreaking, original marvel of technological innovation that I am not going to reveal anything other than it is a love story between two birds. To deny you the opportunity to sit there as I did, transfixed and spellbound, with all my weary cynicism immediately dispelled by childlike wonder, would be unfair. Just watch it and hopefully succumb to its audacious size and scale like I did.

The beautiful balletic images were indelible, following me along the Sentosa Boardwalk and onto the MRT. And then I lost them. They were gone. I spotted a rotund woman at HarbourFront Station and my memory played a vicious trick. The crane birds vanished, leaving me with a chain-smoking, Guinness-swigging, gambling auntie getting jiggy with it under the table.

Eleven

I STOOD in front of a padlocked rusty gate and peered down the murky tunnel, stretching my arm through the bars and running my hand along the algae-stained brick walls. With bottom lip firmly pushed out, the sad countenance gave the game away. I was thoroughly pissed off. Still, that's no excuse for off-colour bomb jokes.

The secret tunnels of Labrador Nature Reserve, or Labrador Park, had slipped beneath my radar during my previous sojourn in Singapore. Built by the British underneath what was then Fort Pasir Panjang in 1886, the subterranean walkways led to storerooms that served the gun emplacements above ground. Shortly before the British surrendered to the Japanese, they invoked the scorched-earth policy and destroyed much of their coastal artillery. After World War II, the rise of air defence systems made Britain's 19th-century coastal forts about as reliable as their military intelligence on the Japanese in 1942. Labrador Park's lush jungle soon enveloped the tunnels. They disappeared and were largely forgotten about until 2001 when they were rediscovered and opened to the public. During my Antipodean adventure, Labrador Park was expanded, historical sites became more accessible and more interactive and more sections of the tunnels were opened to the public, making it a popular historical location for visitors.

So I performed Riverdance all the way along Port Road as I was French kissed by every mosquito in the Berlayar Creek, only to find the tunnels were bloody closed. I was not amused. With my itchy, rapidly swelling shins and ankles looking like I'd covered them with a tin of diced carrots, I grabbed the bars of the padlocked gate and shook them violently, just like they do in the movies. It never works in the movies either.

I spotted a phone number for the National Parks Board, or NParks to be precise, and that just fuelled my irritation. The marketing guru who originally suggested that the secret to a fab and groovy name for a company or a civil service department is to randomly throw in capital letters in the word is right up there with the relative who gets drunk at a family wedding, knots his tie around his forehead like Rambo and plays air guitar to "Hotel California". Those inane capital letters are the marketing equivalent of playing air guitar—all wind and no substance.

The padlocked gate and the capital letter thing sent me over the edge. I rested my head between the bars and called the NParks hotline.

"Hello, NParks, how can I assist you?" the woman asked cheerily.

"Yes, hi there, I'm standing outside the gate of the underground military tunnels inside Labrador Nature Reserve," I replied gruffly.

"Yes. They're closed."

"I can see that. The padlocked gate gave me a bit of a clue. How long have they been closed?"

"Ooh, quite some time already, sir."

"But I've read online articles about the tunnels written as recently as 2011 by visitors to the tunnels."

"Ah, well, I'm afraid they are closed now. I cannot say when they will reopen. We are carrying out some maintenance. Maybe next year."

With regard to such small-scale buildings, maintenance is carried out in a matter of weeks or months in Singapore. Years are only required to reclaim land from the sea and stick a trio of towers and a sprinkling of roulette tables on top.

"You haven't found some live ammo in there, have you," I asked sarcastically. "Are there any unexploded World War II bombs in there?"

"That I'm not so sure."

I stepped back suddenly from the tunnel's gate. She had thrown me off-kilter. What a reply. I was now most anxious to pursue the conversation further, but I also remembered that most hotline phone calls to government departments are recorded (purely for training purposes) and I had frivolously deployed the word "bomb". Not in a threatening or belligerent sense, but out of curiosity. Still, the b-word had been dropped nonetheless. I was alone, too. There's never a loud American tourist in knee-high socks when you want one to point the finger at, is there? Besides, red ants were devouring my forearms with militaristic precision, displaying a level of organisation unheard of for an army at Fort Pasir Panjang.

It's true. The British military history of the area in the 19th century reads like a rejected script for *Carry on Camping*. In 1887, a concerned Vice Admiral Hamilton reported to Governor Frank Weld that he had landed at the nearby Fort Siloso and the only security that he encountered were a few rickshaw drivers eating supper. Quite understandably, they took more interest in their rice as this unidentified European wandered around the fort, examining mounted guns, magazines and casemates, without once being stopped and asked for identification. Best of all, a

Russian officer was found in one of the coastal forts, lying back and leisurely sketching Singapore's entire military operation. He was later fined $10 and told never to do it again. It's impossible to sneak into Fort Siloso now without a young Sentosa employee chasing you up the hill shouting, "Sir, mus' pay first, ah, mus' pay first."

In many respects, the underground tunnels are little different to Labrador Nature Reserve. No longer secret, they remain somewhat hidden and cut off from public view. Labrador is a little tranquil gem. As well as the war relics, with improved information panels and interactive displays from what I remember, the quiet coastal corner boasts the only rocky sea-cliff on the mainland, offering corals, sea grasses, horseshoe crabs and the common hairy crab. I spotted a monitor lizard, my first since returning to Singapore. It was like catching up with an old friend. About 1 metre in length, it dipped in and out of the sea, making the most of the high tide to navigate its way along the shoreline (and mostly to get away from me following it).

Dragon's Teeth Gate (or Long Ya Men) was another pleasant discovery. The craggy granite outcrop, along with another outcrop, once stood imperiously at the entrance to Keppel Harbour. Dragon's Teeth Gate was a geological signpost for travellers, with ancient mariners documenting the rocks in the 1300s. I was awed by the presence of such an imposing, historical, natural Asian landmark, until I read the small print. Sadly, like many of Singapore's heritage sites, it was artificial, a replica of the original Dragon's Teeth Gate. But modern Singapore cannot take the hit for this one. Blame the British. Straits Settlements Surveyor John Thomson had the rock outcrops blown up in August 1848 to widen the entrance to the new harbour. A joint collaboration in July 2005 led to the high stone replica of Long Ya Men, which is better than nothing.

I continued through Comchest Green, which was opened in 2008 to provide a comely seafront garden location for retirees to hang out and ponder their 4D numbers, and headed for the Bukit Chermin View Harbour Walk, which follows the shoreline along Keppel Bay. It was also closed. A theme was developing. Construction workers were applying the final touches to the flooring so the harbour walk will be open by the time you read this sentence. Go visit. Keppel Harbour and the Southern Islands had never looked better from an entirely new vantage point and I should know. I was hanging off the construction site fence and clinging to a Keep Out sign at the time. I had to jump down. A foreman in a hard hat had spotted me and I really needed to pee.

Among its many accolades, new Singapore has the world's best toilet within its borders. I had never serviced the planet's most luxurious lavatory before. I might have once made use of the world's worst—a dustbin on the deserted platform of Wanstead Park Station (and in a pitiful plea for forgiveness, I was 13 years old, stricken with gastroenteritis, and as my nan's house was too far away, I might have left an incriminating trail to the poor woman's property). Indeed, my enthusiasm was matched only by my bladder. I had prepared meticulously for the world's best toilet, drinking continuously around Labrador Park and resisting the urge to relieve myself through the gate leading to the underground tunnel. No one samples the delights of a five-star restaurant on a full stomach. I intended to fully savour the experience.

Five years on the Aussie long drop can do that to a man. Having been a regular trekker around the splendid offerings of Parks Victoria (and few public authorities in the world manage their flora and fauna better than Victoria), I grew accustomed to their long drop toilets. The clue is in the title. The toilet is nothing more than a long drop. Australians do no-nonsense common nouns better than anyone else. The drinking receptacle for beer is shaped like a pot. So Aussies go with "pot". When my daughter was born, she was chauffeured around in a buggy, pram or pushchair, depending on where we were or who we were with. My Australian aunties called it a "pusher". They have no time for any of those fancy nouns like buggy or pram. When a stranger once asked if my daughter needed a "pusher", I nearly throttled him for trying to sell her drugs.

Getting back to the Aussie long drop, it was a wonder of plumbing and environmental sensitivity. Rather than bulldoze forests to create an elaborate sewage and drainage system so a foreign tourist had somewhere pleasant to blow her nose after a five-minute stroll along a boardwalk, a single hole was dug and the long drop went in. Sometimes the actual toilets were made from stainless steel, or they were nothing more elaborate than wide plastic tubes, but the end result was the same—down the tunnel and onto the mound deep beneath the toilet block to be disposed of or treated and recycled later. So if you plan to visit Australia's great outdoors, be prepared. There is nothing more disconcerting than emptying your bowels and not hearing the comforting plop afterwards. That plop is the crashing cymbal at the end of a rousing performance from a symphony orchestra, an empathic conclusion to proceedings. Without that reassuring splash of water, you're not quite sure if you've finished. At times, you're not even sure that you've started.

So I intended to hear every tinkle inside The Jewel Box.

Located at the summit of Mount Faber, The Jewel Box replaced the old cable car station, which was always the most pointless of buildings. Apart from offering cable car travellers a bird's eye view of Keppel Harbour as they made their way across the skyline, Mount Faber Station was nothing more than a bit of a joke. It was a hilltop ghost town offering tourists little else than the chance to spot a randy couple getting it on in a nearby car park. On the few occasions that I made it to Mount Faber Park, I used to get a perverse kick out of watching overseas visitors step out from their cable cars and take cursory looks around the empty, gloomy summit with confused, slightly cross expressions that always said, "What the fuck are we doing here?"

Well, they now have The Jewel Box. With several upmarket eateries and the obligatory retail shop for any miniature Merlions missed on the other side, Mount Faber offers more creative outlets for the credit card while being fixated with being first in the most bizarre categories. Among the more surreal successes were the world's tallest artificial Christmas trees (at 61 metres), the first Santa sleigh ride by air and the first company to be presented with the world's only life-size cable car cabin by LEGO. I do not wish to mock these achievements. Indeed, I spent several fruitless minutes trying to find the LEGO cable car. I just struggle to imagine many other CEOs haranguing their subordinates for failing to get hold of a cable car made out of LEGO.

But everyone wants a clean toilet and The Jewel Box was awarded "Best Toilet in The World" by a French International Website. A strangely vague accolade, in all honesty, with details a little sketchy. The capital letters of the French website were provided not by me, but by The Jewel Box. I presumed that was the proper name of the site. If it was, then I failed to track it down. If it wasn't, why be so secretive? The lovely woman working for The Jewel Box was certainly not secretive about the toilet. Bearing in mind the lavatory was the property of a premium establishment, and my sweat-soaked *ah pek* attire suggested I had little intention of dining there, she might have been forgiven for any reticence. Yet she was most accommodating about her comely commodious commodes.

"Yes, the toilets are this way," she replied, gesturing towards a tinted glass door that automatically slid open as we approached.

"And is it true they were chosen as the world's best toilets?" I asked.

"Yes, that is true. It was according to a French website. It's just down that corridor. Will there be anything else, sir?"

An unusual query from a young woman when being led to a toilet but I declined the unexpected offer of assistance and followed her directions.

There are multi-million-dollar show flats in Singapore that are less inviting than The Jewel Box's bogs. I followed a narrow carpet-lined corridor, which gave the impression of being wider thanks to the floor-to-ceiling mirror on my right. Such elaborate mirrors in a toilet usually say pervert, rather than panache, but the sheer grandiosity of The Jewel Box overcompensated and, I hope, prevented curious men from shaking off any drips in front of the mirror. The temptation was certainly there. I turned left and another sensor-operated tinted glass door opened. I was half expecting to find Captain Kirk sitting on the throne of the Starship Enterprise. Instead there were cable cars, dozens of cable cars. The extraordinary floor-to-ceiling window at the far side of the toilets framed much of Keppel Harbour. Sentosa, Fort Siloso, Universal Studios, Labrador Park, a docking cruise ship and the Southern Islands were all captured in one unforgettable living picture frame from inside a public lavatory. Visitors hand over a few bucks for a similar view, albeit a revolving one, on Sentosa's Sky Tower, but at The Jewel Box, it comes free with every pee.

I stood in front of three individual, elegantly mounted marble wash basins and stared at the encroaching cable cars as they carried families of tourists towards me. I could see their faces. I started giggling childishly. My puerile streak momentarily contemplated whipping out the little fella and shouting, "Never mind your cable cars, how about this for a cable? You didn't know they had a sky tower at Mount Faber, did you eh?"

But I refrained. Besides, from that distance, there really would have been nothing to see. Being alone in the lavatory, I peered into each of the cubicles. The toilet bowels were marble and sculpted like white eggs, the artistic symbolism of which seemed ironic. When I grew up, my mother always referred to constipation as being "egg-bound".

"He's having trouble going again," she'd tell my classmates' parents. "He's egg-bound. The turtle's head keeps popping out to say 'hello', then it goes back in again. Definitely egg-bound."

Beside the cubicles was the soothing presence of a built-in fish tank. Fortunately, the tank was entirely enclosed. Otherwise, drunks might have been inclined to add to its water level on Saturday nights. I toyed with the idea of crowning one of the eggs, but the strategic location of the urinals offered greater appeal. Standing over the first urinal, I tilted my head to the left and savoured the sights of Keppel Harbour. Ordinarily, the only distractions offered by a Singaporean urinal are stained tiles and hilariously broken English graffiti saying things like "Cheng Hong suck you, give $10".

Holding various limbs and appendages, I carefully pulled out my smartphone with my left hand and captured a picture postcard of the cable cars dotted along Keppel Harbour whilst taking care of business with my right. I concentrated on not swapping hands and confusing the two.

In all honesty, I was in no hurry to leave. The view from the toilet was quite intoxicating. But there is only so long a man should loiter in a public lavatory holding a phone camera.

Twelve

WHEN I left Singapore in 2006, the island was a garden city. Within days of returning in August 2011, the nation declared its intentions of becoming a city in a garden. NParks tried to sell the vision of a seamless green infrastructure within an urban landscape, with parks, connectors, nature reserves and gardens tended by volunteers all knitted together. There was talk of a green road map, a 10-year development plan to cultivate an islandwide garden allowing residents to step beyond the concrete confines and into more natural surroundings.

Letter writers complained that a city in a garden might attract more snakes and frogs.

Who would handle all these malignant mammals and repugnant reptiles was the common concern. I strongly suspect the answer will be the same poor sods who currently maintain the public gardens and lawns in the heartlands. The invisible people who also sweep up leaflets and junk mail because residents, probably those same letter writers, had earlier succumbed to the strain of carrying a flyer to the nearest void deck dustbin.

Bloggers suggested that the green concept was the latest cynical government initiative to draw attention away from its poorest showing yet in the 2011 general election, the "gahmen" naively hoping a cluster of garden beds and some pretty bird-singing trees might somehow pacify the restless masses seeking political change. Even if such conspiracy theories were true (and they're not), so what? Would you rather live in a society that aspires to create a city in a garden or a shit hole? I've lived in shit holes. Gardens smell better.

Surrounding a country's citizenry with such biodiversity is no mean feat. I struggled for five years to surround my Australian house with the relevant greenery. When I was handed the keys to my Geelong home, I was also presented with a stunning garden, a dazzling array of seasonal colour, fruit trees and rose bushes.

I killed the lot in six months.

Planted, raised and nurtured by the loving hands of a full-time gardening pensioner, her horticultural highlights stood no chance once I got hold of a pair of clippers. Between the soil-leaching drought and my incompetence, our garden withered and perished. For the next five years, I swapped every dead tree and shrub with indigenous flora, many of which also failed to make the cut. There wasn't a hardy, resilient drought-tolerant native in Australia that I could not kill.

With every frustrating weekend that was spent digging, watering, pruning, weeding, mulching and replacing the natives, my deep admiration for dedicated, committed gardeners grew. Anyone willing to spend time successfully covering a space with something green, pretty and living deserves respect and gratitude. Singapore plans to fill and link every nook and cranny in the future and the Southern Ridges provides a glimpse of what a city in a garden might eventually look like.

So I strode rather energetically through Mount Faber Park on the first leg of a 9-kilometre walk through lush rolling hills that did not exist when I last lived in Singapore. Thanks to eight trails, three parks and two bridges, the Southern Ridges join the green dots between Mount Faber and Kent Ridge Park in the southwest (and it's not too much of a diversion to continue on to West Coast Park). To satisfy my bridge fetish, I was particularly keen to surf the Henderson Waves, which opened in May 2008 and completed the unification of the Southern Ridges.

After admiring some old, decommissioned cable cars being used as forest furniture (a terrifically daft idea), I reached Henderson Waves. As I was reading the information panel, thunderclaps announced that a downpour was imminent. Of course it was. I was about to walk across the exposed, unsheltered and heighest pedestrian bridge in Singapore. Rain was never in doubt. God was about to start crying. That was a popular one when I was growing up in England. Rain was Mother Nature's way of informing sinners that God was sad, his tears falling on us all. Of course England made him sad. It was always pissing down.

Feeling a bit like Bear Grylls, I sought cover beneath an overhanging tree above the information panel. It worked for five minutes. That was when the absence of raindrops gave way to giant globs of water that had accumulated and joined forces as they fell through the layers of leaves before smacking me on the head. At that moment, I noticed a Chinese couple pointing at me animatedly beneath a shelter on the other side of the bridge's entrance. I dashed over to beat the deluge.

"Why you wait under tree?" the husband asked.

They were tourists from China. The accent and clothes gave them away. They were attired for the Arctic but still didn't think to bring an umbrella.

"I thought I was covered from the rain," I replied, shaking my damp clothes.

"We wonder why you wait under tree," he continued, "when it is raining."

"Well, like I said, I didn't realise it was going to get so heavy."

"Yeah, we wonder why you wait under tree when there is shelter here."

Yes, all right, mate. I needed this guy like I needed damp underpants. At that moment, I was eager to get rid of both. Thankfully, the monsoonal clouds parted with typical seasonal speed, and I had the cool Henderson Waves all to myself. I left the Chinese couple to point out the bleeding obvious to the next passing stranger.

Websites and guidebooks mention that Henderson Waves is the tallest pedestrian bridge in Singapore, but that means very little until you stand on the bloody thing. The stylish structure soars. Designed, I am chuffed to say, by architects in both London and Singapore, the unique crossing is 274 metres long and 36 metres above Henderson Road. Peering over the edge, the vehicles passing below appeared awfully small. The post-storm breeze was a trifle unnerving. And that's when I realised that new Singapore, just like its predecessor, is still "heightist". Unless you are a victim of heightism, you have no idea the prejudice that one suffers daily at the hands of ignorant town planners, engineers and designers. When I leant ever so slightly over the bridge, I noticed that the guard rail stopped at my groin. More of my gangly frame was unprotected above than protected below. Ponder if you will the position of your groin. Have a quick peek below the waist and picture standing on viewing platforms, hilltops, balconies, sky gardens, in HDB corridors and the like and imagine that that's where all the safety fences and walls stopped. That was me on Henderson Waves, 36 metres above the cars and leaning over just above the groin. One gusty blow and my groin would have been a goner.

For anyone who does struggle with acrophobia, the bridge designers kindly remind visitors how high they are at regular intervals, having carved the height above sea level into yellow *balau* timber boards. (To give an indication of its size, there are said to be 5,000 timber boards placed across the bridge.) The highest point that I registered was 77 metres above sea level, at a spot where Henderson Waves looked down grandly at the neighbouring HDB blocks.

The bridge's name derives from its splendid architecture—a waveform of seven curved steel ribs that are lit up after 7 p.m. Each of the ribs provides an alcove that serves as a shelter. There are seats inside each rib, but the ribs provide better shelter from the sun than they do the rain. And even then, I suspect that if anyone sat for long enough beneath one of the ribs in the midday sun, they might leave Henderson Waves looking like a zebra. Take a hat or an umbrella when visiting Singapore's curviest bridge.

Henderson Waves provides a literal link to old and new Singapore. The sparkly Jewel Box and Sentosa-bound cable cars are now a short, direct walk away from the colonial past of Telok Blangah Hill Park. Popular with trading communities in the 19th century, Telok Blangah has a history that is represented by the restored bungalow of Alkaff Mansion. But the park is preoccupied with its future. I appreciated the foresight of the Sembcorp Forest of Giants as I wandered among its saplings. A simple but effective initiative, the arboretum, a living collection of trees for education and research, comprised 600 trees that had once dominated the island before old Stamford popped in. Called emergents, these jolly green giants, such as the *tualang* and the *jelutong*, will eventually reach heights of 80 metres. Planted in early 2010, they will take 50 years to mature. My mother has always said the same about me.

As I continued through Telok Blangah Hill Park, I realised I was slightly out of step with the forest. I had been away too long. I jumped at everything. Every rustle made me retreat. A squirrel scurried across the path and I made a noise that a mouse might make if it were inflated by a bicycle pump. I spent five years in Australia and found kangaroos, wallabies, possums, koalas, echidnas, platypuses, emus, dingos, snakes, dolphins, manta rays, seals, sharks and whales in their natural habitats. Not many Australians could say that. They probably wouldn't want to. Still, I once swam over a basking shark in Port Philip Bay, tracked southern right whales along the Southern Ocean, watched a seal swim through my legs, followed a tiger snake as it slithered in front of my daughter's pushchair and narrowly missed hitting a kangaroo in the bush three times (and no one wants to hit any animal in the bush three times).

And here I was in Telok Blangah Hill Park shitting myself over a squirrel.

I had spent too much time in casinos and theme parks and needed to get back to nature. NParks, however, made my attempt a little difficult. I reached the Forest Walk, only to find sections of the Earth Trail closed for slope stabilisation (they reopened in early 2012). The repair work was unfortunate because the restricted access that was still available was an easy meander through the secondary forest canopy via a steel structure that reached 18 metres. As the usual, more enjoyable route to Alexandra Arch was not an option, I retraced my steps and found Depot Road and the incongruous HDB block of 106B. There was nothing wrong with this particular block. On the contrary, I rather envied its setting, backing directly onto the forest. But I found the sudden transformation most peculiar. One moment I was alone in the forest with only squirrels and raptors for company, the next I was in a FairPrice queue behind an uncle buying 16 jars of bailing mushrooms. Standing in line with an uncle buying 16 jars of bailing mushrooms is disorienting at the best of times, doing so only two minutes after trekking through a deserted forest was mind-blowing.

I had stumbled upon the fascinatingly eerie Depot Heights Shopping Centre, a quiet retail centre at the foot of the hill dwarfed by the encroaching jungle. I noticed a FairPrice employee preparing a display of Christmas decorations. She needed a rocking chair and a duelling banjo. It was *The Hills Have Eyes* up there.

I rejoined the superb Forest Walk at Preston Road, having passed some wonderfully scruffy black-and-white bungalows, and crossed Alexandra Arch. Well, Marble Arch has nothing to worry about. Alexandra Arch was always going to be something of an anticlimax after the curvy lines of Henderson Waves, which was shortlisted for the World Architecture Festival Awards under the transport category in 2008. Crossing both bridges in the Southern Ridges was like going on a single, spectacular date with the high school heart-throb, only to end up with the slightly shorter, dumpier cousin the following week. Measuring 80 metres long and 4 metres across, Alexandra Arch's steel and granite design resembled an open fig leaf and provided a pleasant stroll between Telok Blangah and HortPark, but my heart belongs to Henderson Waves.

I had high hopes for HortPark (crap capital letter in the middle of the name aside). I even ignored the unfortunate jargon that such well-meaning initiatives are always lumbered with in Singapore, with HortPark touting itself as a one-stop gardening hub, i.e. a gardening centre. (I cannot recall having to visit one garden centre in Geelong to buy a shovel and then needing to drive to another for a pitchfork. Most garden-related tools, books and equipment tended to be under the one roof. Really, it's not that remarkable an achievement.) But I was intrigued by HortPark's emphasis on communal gardening. I expected to return to the allotments of my childhood that were populated by glue-sniffing skinheads.

In the UK, allotments are small parcels of land rented out by local councils to provide a quiet corner for residents to grow crops. Or, in the cases of some of the allotments along the District Line between Dagenham and Barking, provide a place to hide stolen electrical goods in ramshackle sheds. Allotments have long been the domain of the working class. Indeed, the modern allotment really took off in the 19th century as an attempt to calm civil unrest by giving the landless poor a "field garden" to potter around in. After the unexpected results in Singapore's general election of 2011, perhaps every HDB estate in the country will soon end up with its own HortPark, complete with silly capital letter in the middle.

Growing up in Dagenham, my best mate Ross and I often hung out at the local allotments that ran alongside the London Underground tube lines. Not because we had any interest in growing anything or had a penchant for hanging out with old-timers reminiscing about the Blitz whilst spilling tea from battered thermos flasks onto their tartan blankets, but because we were busy being Stig from *Stig of the Dump*. Clive King's modern children's classic was turned into a TV series in 1981 and, for a brief period, kids were often found running wild around allotments and rubbish dumps with dirty faces and matted hair, substituting tea towels for loin cloths. In truth, Ross and I looked like Stig of the Dump all year round so an extreme makeover wasn't required.

Using corrugated iron scraps, dumped council house windows and doors and some old curtains, we recreated Stig's dump, constructing a fine den, which served us well until a gang of skinheads sniffed too much glue one afternoon and indulged in a demolition derby with their Dr. Martens boots. The camp was destroyed and we stopped going to the allotments after that, much to my mother's relief who thought our dog was eating her tea towels.

I expected a more sedate, sanitised environment at HortPark and it certainly was, to the point of being a bit dull. Once I'd had a polite look around the themed gardens (I lost count after 10, but enjoyed the cheeky Car Park Garden), I was half hoping the skinheads might pop in to liven the place up a bit. HortPark has noble intentions, encouraging all Singaporeans to maximise their gardening potential by showcasing how green spaces can be utilised in any abode, be it a balcony, a hallway or inside an apartment. There were some terrific parks for children and a butterfly garden, outside which I called my wife who confirmed again that they would all be dead in the morning. But the six glasshouses, which provided prototypes for the Gardens by the Bay, neatly summed up HortPark. They were educational research centres, but the science had obscured the fun.

HortPark was almost at odds with nature. There was no anarchy, no real Darwinist wildness at work. Like the gardens of a typical HDB estate, every showcase was perfectly groomed, pruned and manicured, not a plant leaf or flower petal was out of place. Despite its truly admirable attempts to bring green-fingered gangs together for some communal digging and planting, the one-stop gardening hub bore little resemblance to the scruffy allotments of my childhood. A controlling hand was still at work, a stubborn reluctance to really allow residents to be let loose on the project, cultivate their own plots independently and take ownership of the land. Instead, the park had the feel of any other government hub, albeit a pretty one. HortPark was closer to a gardening museum than a living, evolving green space.

By the time I had zigzagged my way up the steady ascent from HortPark to Kent Ridge Park, I was done. My first gentle stroll across the southern hills of Singapore had been an exhilarating one, but my sore hamstring was contemplating industrial action.

I nodded to some construction workers carrying out some repairs (probably slope stabilising) and stopped for a drink.

And that's when I heard the bird.

I knew the bugger was coming before I saw it. The faint swoosh of its wings indicated that it was close and it was big. Indeed the raptor flew so close that I instinctively ducked, which was probably just as well as a rather confused lizard, still very much alive, was trapped between its talons, the reptile's whip-like tail slashing through the air in a futile protest against its capture. The raptor swooped effortlessly despite the persistent wriggling of its prey and landed on an almost horizontal branch not 10 metres from where I was standing. No doubt the laborious hunt beforehand had left the lethargic raptor less fussy about where he stopped to make the kill. The bird of prey, possibly a sparrowhawk but difficult to determine in the dusky forest, glared at me, calculated the distance and his lofty position and figured its dinner was not about to be disturbed.

I heard the flesh being ripped from the lizard's neck as its tail continued to thrash around pathetically. The sparrowhawk (I'm going with sparrowhawk, no one else was there to contradict me) pecked away with its bloody beak at the back of the dying reptile's neck in a methodical, clinical fashion that was utterly engrossing despite its obvious brutality. No one puts on a bloodier, more macabre show than Mother Nature. The distinct sound of skin and gristle being torn from the bone was reassuringly familiar, sharing the aural qualities of a plate of chicken wings being devoured at a coffee shop table. Pinned to the trunk beneath the sparrowhawk's vicelike talons, the half-eaten lizard refused to succumb. The mortally wounded creature's pointless efforts to cling to life were almost humbling. Eventually, its tail fell and hung limply over the side of the trunk. The merciless sparrowhawk continued to feast.

And I watched the raptor's 10-minute audition for *National Geographic* from the front row, thoroughly enraptured. With a cast of thousands and the greenest of set designs, the Southern Ridges puts on one hell of a show. But the flamboyant fauna had definitely saved its best for last. For the first time, I felt like I was truly back in Singapore. My Singapore at least. Marina Bay Sands and Sentosa have unquestionably elevated the island's entertainment value, but they will never be able to put on a production as authentic as that one.

Thirteen

THE voice on the other end of the telephone line provided the clearest indication yet of Singapore's newfound sexiness. It wasn't one of those phone services. No matter how desperate, I have always refrained from calling sex chat lines. Not because I am a moral, upstanding citizen who refuses to wallow in a filthy pit of parasitic perverts but because I am a tight-arse. Have you seen how much those phone calls cost per minute? Half an hour is more expensive than a night in Geylang. No, I was aroused by three otherwise nondescript words that highlighted how bright the little red dot now shines.

"Hello, Lucasfilm Singapore."

It doesn't take much to get me going.

But the idea of dialling the local telephone number of a rented Changi office and speaking to a Singaporean auntie who works for someone, who works for someone, who works for someone who once bumped into the bearded guy who made *Star Wars* in his office toilet is about as sexy as it gets. Incidentally, I referred to the telephone receptionist as a Singaporean auntie for no other reason than she sounded like one: polite, friendly and jovial but always to the point. In my head, I pictured Mon Mothma in *Return of the Jedi* (which I appreciate is a reference that could lose many readers and scare one or two others).

"Er, hello, yes, have I really gotten through to Lucasfilm?" I replied to Mon Mothma, surprised that the most perfunctory of online searches had come up trumps first time.

"Yes, this is Lucasfilm Singapore. How can I help?"

How could she help? How about by sending an email to George Lucas expressing my deepest gratitude for fundamentally shaping my childhood? Or by simply telling me where I can get one of those stormtrooper costumes tailored so I can spend weekends tapping on taxi drivers' windows at Changi Airport and ordering them to move along.

"Er, yes, right, well, I'm looking for the Star Wars Sandcrawler," I finally sputtered.

"I'm sorry. What are you looking for?"

I pictured a red light marked "nerd alert" suddenly blinking on her office phone as her pointed finger hovered over the receiver.

"No, no, it's not what you think," I insisted, desperately distancing myself from the grown men who collect Star Wars toys, watch the films endlessly, attend conventions and live with their mothers.

I no longer live with my mother.

"I'm interested in seeing the Sandcrawler Building, the new offices for Lucasfilm Singapore that will be shaped like the sandcrawler from *Star Wars*. I'm standing here right now at one-north, you know, Fusionopolis, trying to find it."

"Oh, I see," a relieved Mon Mothma sighed, realising I wasn't standing outside her Changi office in a hooded robe. "You're in Buona Vista."

"That's right. I'm in the middle of Fusionopolis and there's construction at two building sites."

"Yes, one of those is ours."

I was crestfallen. I had read reports that the future permanent home of Lucasfilm Animation Singapore, to be modelled on the Jawa sandcrawler from the first *Star Wars* movie, was scheduled to open its doors to the world's most talented artists in 2012. So I had expected to be confronted with a near completed glassy sandcrawler and, at the very least, a stone statue of Yoda or something.

"No, I don't think the building will open now until very late 2012 or early 2013," Mon Mothma pointed out. "But thank you for showing an interest."

I was initially rather flattered by her closing remark, a sincere gesture of gratitude from a colossal corporation that still recognises where its power derives. But then I thought the line was too quick, too rehearsed. It was more like a cynical crumb of comfort to pacify the anoraks and dissuade them from turning up at Lucasfilm offices, waving Toys "R" Us lightsabres and shouting, "The force is strong with this one."

Still *Star Wars* has most certainly come to Singapore and will soon take up residence in an office complex that provides a highlights reel of classic science fiction and dystopian cinema. Fusionopolis is part *Blade Runner*, part *Minority Report*, part *Conquest of the Planet of the Apes* (the area is a dead ringer for Century City in Los Angeles) and even part *Robocop*.

Opened in October 2008, Fusionopolis is a member of the "opolis" groovy gang that marks its territory around the mushrooming research and development business park of one-north. Developed by JTC Corporation, the once quiet colonial corner of Buona Vista is now a magnet for the finest foreign and local brains to nurture those developing across the road at the National University of Singapore. The focus of Fusionopolis is on IT, media, physical sciences and engineering so the attraction to a company like Lucasfilm Animation Singapore, whose 400 employees have outgrown their rented Changi home, is obvious.

A public and private partnership, Fusionopolis already plays host to the Agency for Science, Technology and Research (A*STAR) and SPRING and, apart from Lucasfilm, will be joined by dry and wet laboratories to test new technologies.

It's all very groundbreaking and commendable, but do all the names have to be so geeky? From the Lucasfilm site, I peered up at Fusionopolis's current focal point, a pair of towers joined by what can only be described as a giant silver gym ball (all that was missing was a giant *tai tai* wobbling around on top under the instruction of a personal trainer). The buildings are named Symbiosis and Connexis respectively and the etymology of both words is fascinating, deriving from the Ancient Greek for "too much time in labs and textbooks".

I wandered into the lobby that connected the two towers and onto a Kubrickian movie set. Ironically, Lucas complained that sci-fi movies usually depicted a clean, sanitised and largely deserted universe and *Star Wars* was a dirty, cluttered congested reaction to that utopia. Fusionopolis was a pre-*Star Wars* creation: glassy, spotless, spacious but vacuous. Apart from the armed and numerous security guards and the lovely girls at the information counter, there was no one around. The emptiness recalled childhood evenings watching *Buck Rogers in the 25th Century*, a post-modern metropolis that had forgotten to include people. Fusionopolis was quite similar. All that was missing was that metal robot that waddled behind Buck and said, "Biddi-biddi-biddi."

To its credit, the complex was trying to foster a work-live-learn, all-under-one-roof environment. I noticed a couple of preschools and crèche-type facilities catering presumably to parents working upstairs in the same building. That was if anyone actually worked in either of the towers. I saw not a soul. With Lee Kuan Yew's long-held belief in the irrefutable inequality of genetics, I imagined

Fusionopolis's workforce being engineered in incubators on the higher levels, fed mathematical formulae through drips and forced to listen to English in one ear and Mandarin in the other whilst having subliminal images of science experiments flashed at their eyeballs. For some, that's a dystopian nightmare. For others, that's the average Singaporean tuition centre.

I hurried quickly along Portsdown Road and then Biopolis Road before a deceptive drizzle turned into yet another flash flood. The geek's hand was present on the side of every building in Biopolis. I passed Centros, Chromos, Genome and various other monikers that must have been put forward by biomedical scientists who spend more time with Bunsen burners than human beings. Of course, my cheap potshots stem from my innate envy of those in the life-saving business. A couple of smaller blocks, Neuros and Immunos, were homes to neuroscience and immunology research. I also passed a humbling sculpture. Called *SARS Inhibited*, the outdoor artwork celebrated the incalculable achievements of the Biopolis scientific community in tackling the SARS virus in 2003. The sculpture is based on the sub-molecular data of SARS, allowing visitors to literally walk through the virus. This is what these guys really do when they're not coming up with silly names for their buildings. Had I keeled over beside the sculpture, there would have been no shortage of scientists with the basic knowledge required to keep me alive. No one ever says, "There's been a terrible accident. Quick, send for the novelist."

There are seven buildings within the biomedical complex, but I only poked my head in the Matrix because that was the only name I recognised. I tried to be cynical and jokey about the names on the A*STAR Roll of Honour lists since 2005, which were nearly all Chinese (great for the Chinese, not so good for Singapore's other representatives). I wondered aloud why the seven buildings hadn't been named Sneezy, Dopey, Bashful and the like. But mostly, I was happily out of my intellectual comfort zone.

Singapore is utterly determined to acquire a monopoly on 21st-century research by allocating precious space and private and public funds to corner the market on relevant knowledge. What is so wrong with pulling out all the stops to attract only the world's best? I've lived in towns that cornered the market in chavs and bogans so I know which way I lean. I wandered around Biopolis for an hour and not once did a biomedical researcher block my path and say, "Get out of the way, you fucking homo." This happened to me in Geelong. In fact, this happened to me more than once in Geelong. I was beginning to think it was the clothes I wore. I am not casting aspersions on the Australian chap who revved the engine of his utility vehicle as I crossed the road at the McDonald's drive thru in Geelong. Nor am I questioning his right to pile his dashboard with empty beer cans and call random passers-by "fucking homos". Live and let live, I say. But if I had a choice between my daughter one day bringing home an A*STAR scholar or the tattooed fuckwit in the pick-up truck, I tend to side with Singapore. We only want the best in our house.

So Biopolis, Fusionopolis and Mediapolis (a digital media hub pencilled in for 2015) have established a brains trust to secure Singapore's future as a sexy centre for research and development. Hundreds of millions of dollars have been spent and tenants already include pharmaceutical giants GlaxoSmithKline and Novartis while Procter & Gamble is constructing a $250 million innovation centre. The one-north precinct will continue to evolve, pushing academic and technological boundaries and providing rewarding and, most important of all, relevant jobs for my daughter's generation. But let's put the affix *polis* to bed now. That particular horse has been flogged for long enough. Next time, go with the seven dwarves.

I stood on the kerbside of Buona Vista Road and studied the very deliberate coming together of old and new Singapore. I watched the scientists leave the lab coats by their Petri dishes and scurry across to Rochester Park for lunch. With its modern, functional buildings, Biopolis is a world away from the hidden colonial black-and-white bungalows of Rochester Park and yet they support each other: one is for work, the other for play. At Buona Vista, past and future form a symbiotic relationship (dear me, I needed to get away from one-north).

Rochester Park was built before World War II to house the British military stationed at Pasir Panjang and was handed over to Singapore when the troops withdrew in 1971. Like many of the island's black-and-white bungalows, they were rented out mostly to expatriates with more money than sense for exorbitant sums. At some point, the "gahmen" must have accepted that Helios, Proteos and Centros say many things about a country's progress, except possibly cool, chic and trendy. So the Urban Redevelopment Authority (URA), under strict conservation guidelines, called for food and beverage outlets to take up tenancy. Staff at one-north needed more nocturnal options and cultural and culinary experiences than a food court and Rochester Park was tasked with filling the gaps.

So, who was housed in the first beautifully preserved black-and-white bungalow that I encountered? A bloody Starbucks.

I have no issue with Starbucks. I never go there. Or rather my wife does not permit me to go there. I do not like coffee and she is aware that there is something buried deep within my psyche that always has the potential to explode at a Starbucks counter and shout, "Five dollars for a fucking tea bag and some hot water?"

Fortunately, Rochester Park had not been turned into Any Other Mall in Singapore. I ambled down the leafy, empty street and spotted mostly high-end restaurants, specialising in a mixture of cuisines, from American bar grills to Chinese, Indian and Italian fare. I cannot lie. They were not cheap, but nor were they testicle-shrinkingly expensive either. I noticed a four-course lunch going for $28. That would not be considered unreasonable in Toa Payoh. The only difference was that no Toa Payoh eatery offers a garden. That's the major plus point for Rochester Park's restaurants. They took advantage of the bungalows' gardens and their green canopies to include play areas. Children are not usually interested in the menu, only the entertainment. An obvious point so often overlooked in a cuisine-obsessed country. When families go to dinner, children should be allowed to enjoy themselves too. At Rochester Park, they can.

Such a rare outdoor dining experience for the whole family came at a price at some of the restaurants. I noticed a Chinese place that must have had a discreet sign that read "Valet parking—except for crap cars. You can park at Buona Vista MRT". The restaurant's patrons handed the keys of something shiny and the price of a four-roomed flat over to the valet before heading in for a lunch that wasn't $28. The soothing sound of something brassy being blown in the name of jazz drifted through the trees. Fancy restaurant proprietors tend to make their safe musical choices from the CD section marked "clichéd".

I wandered past an unexpected comedy club. All right, it was a healing cafe but its name made me laugh out loud. Not only was the establishment a healing cafe, it was also ably supported in the healing process by a juice bar that boasted low glycaemic concoctions. I spent much of my adolescence working in my grandfather's East London cafe. My annual earnings were paltry but I would have gladly handed over the lot to witness someone ask my grandad, who survived World War II, if he had ever contemplated adding a juice bar. Or better yet, if his drinks list included anything low glycaemic. He would have replied,

"Low glycaemic? We don't sell anything alcoholic here. We've got Tango or Pepsi. Now pick one or bugger off."

Not everything in new Singapore was wondrous. Some of it was just wanky. But the healing cafe was open to all. Rochester Park's lifestyle and dining outlets might have edged towards exclusive, but they were accessible. At least the black-and-white bungalows were being utilised for something other than a wealthy expat's temporary abode.

The same could almost be said for Dempsey Hill.

As I took the short bus trip from Queensway to Holland Road on the No. 105, I was preparing not to like Dempsey Hill. Apart from its old British army barracks, the site remains a symbolic one to Singaporean men of a certain age. When I mentioned Dempsey Hill to my old mate Dave, who first invited me to Singapore, he shrugged his ignorance. When I referenced the Central Manpower Base of Singapore (CMPB to just about everyone), he perked up. That was the place where boys took the road to manhood on the back of a military truck as they trundled off to their army unit. Where locks were shorn and loved ones left behind, CMPB marked the humble beginnings of national service. Where teenagers bit their bottom lips and parents privately celebrated getting an extra room in the apartment for a couple of years. But that's all gone. The CMPB was relocated to Depot Road in 1989. In new Singapore, middle-aged men can now return to Dempsey Hill and exorcise any lingering army demons with a curry and a crêpe.

National servicemen have been replaced by air-kissing expatriates and *tai tais* poncing about with their pedigreed poodles. At least I initially thought they had. Within months of my leaving in 2006, the Singapore Land Authority (SLA) announced plans to bring the sexy back to Dempsey Road by revitalising some of the former military buildings and turning them into al fresco bars and restaurants. As much as I recognise the architectural elegance of pre-independence buildings, I accept the elitist cliques that they can attract.

I thought my worst fears had been realised when I fought my way through the BMWs and 4×4s and dashed into a butcher's to beat the rain. A bottle of sprite for $3.80 suggested the store's clientele had little time for small change and when a white Porsche later splashed through a puddle to soak my shins, I was ready to leave. How do Porsche owners drive around with straight faces? The Porsche convertible has to be the car equivalent of a big boob job: obvious, expensive, desperate to be seen and admired, but laughed at the moment the owner has left. I couldn't avoid a soaking from the boy racer with small genitalia (I'm assuming this because it makes me feel better, he didn't wave his willy at me through the Porsche window). Decent footpaths are hard to come by around Dempsey Hill. The popular hang-out is well served by buses along Holland Road, but most of its patrons do not use public transport.

I didn't want to like Dempsey's trendy village because the area brought back memories of a lunch meeting I once attended just a little further along the road—paid for by a British organisation just along the road—to pick my brains for an hour. It is impossible to go into too much detail for fear of revealing who was at the lunch. I have no qualms about naming the guy, for reasons that will soon become apparent, but his support team was helpful and considerate. Being the flavour of the month for five minutes thanks to the popularity of my earlier books, I was invited along by British people on high to gauge my opinions on what made Singaporeans tick because the host, despite working and living in the country at a considerable expense to others, did not have the first clue. During the discussion, I said, "Well, when it comes to Singapore's heartlanders, those living in the housing estates, I think that ..."

"Please," he interrupted, gesturing with his hand as if I were a bothersome bluebottle. "I'm really not interested in the chattering classes here."

I excused myself and went to the toilet. I had to. I was hearing the voice in my head scream "I'm from the chattering classes, too, you condescending prick" and had to make sure that it stayed there.

Against all expectations, Dempsey Hill wasn't quite like that. The forest haven still had its share of handcrafted rugs and rare antiques costing more than a taxi driver's annual salary, but some of the menus were reasonable. I noticed a group of younger Singaporeans piling out of a taxi and heading for an Indian set meal. Local families wandered past restaurants, perusing the menus before making a decision. Despite the drizzle, I enjoyed the easy-going ambience. Sticking restaurants, ice-cream parlours and wine cellars on the site of a former army base does work. The breezy summit has retained its old world charm amid the whistling trees, with new Singapore enhancing the area's history rather than demolishing it.

And, most important, Dempsey Hill is still interested in the chattering classes.

Fourteen

CEMETERIES hold little spiritual resonance for me. I am a product of the MTV generation. For a while, I couldn't visit a relative's grave without expecting an emaciated fist to punch through the soil, followed by lots of shoulder popping and someone shouting, "Cos this is 'trilla'." But my cold detachment to cemeteries can be attributed to my macabre mother. When most parents discover that their firstborn son is going to have his first child, they buy a book of baby names so the family can gather and compile a top 10 list. My mother didn't. My mother dragged us around Ramsgate Cemetery.

"Here's a good name," she said one summer's morning, pointing to a crooked, crumbling gravestone. "Johnny Strong. That's a lovely boy's name, little Johnny."

"Mum, he died of syphilis in 1898," I replied, peering through the weeds at the faded inscription. "Do you really want a grandson named after a Kent bloke who died of a sexually transmitted disease in 1898?"

"But you said you wanted names from the interwar generations," she argued. "You said you liked the old-fashioned names."

"Well, let's go to a library and get a book out," I reasoned. "We don't need to pick a name from *Dawn of the Dead*."

"Dawn? I didn't see her. Where's she buried?"

Before I had a chance to explain, she was off again, dragging us past rows of headstones, desperate to pick out a winning name from a list of dead people. But then, my mother loves a good cemetery, always has. She takes great pride in telling people that I was born in the hospital near Highgate Cemetery, famous for its bust of Karl Marx. Mum has never read *Das Kapital*, but knows where its author's body is buried. Wherever she has lived, she has always acquainted herself with the local graveyard, mentally composing fabulous family histories and narratives of its occupants. She loves this relationship. She works out from the grave inscriptions where they went wrong in their lives and they can't argue back.

In old Singapore, my mum's search for cemeteries was already limited. In new Singapore, she might have to rely on a book of baby names.

I took the MRT to Caldecott, a station that did not exist five years earlier and is not in Caldecott, and headed for Bukit Brown Cemetery, which has a nearby station that isn't open yet. The economic numbers do not justify opening the station. Dead people cannot use ez-link cards so visiting relatives must walk from Caldecott or take the bus along Lornie Road. When the dead have been dug up and the area has been redeveloped, then Bukit Brown MRT Station will get the green light. In new Singapore, however, the dead are not willing to go quietly this time. That's why I was eager to visit.

As I left the toots, fumes and traffic of Lornie Road, I turned down Sime Road and then left into Lorong Halwa and savoured the shrilling cicadas, that familiar welcoming call of Singapore's jungle. I spotted some cars parked ahead and a couple of temporary offices and toilets outside the entrance to Bukit Brown Cemetery. Singapore's finest had started early. And then I noticed the handiwork of the Land Transport Authority's contractors—red stencilling. The eye was drawn first to the red stencilling rather than the graves that the red ink was identifying. Stencilled serial numbers have not fared well in modern history. The formal, clinical marking and categorising of human beings and their possessions, dead or alive, through stencilling suggests something sinister—the work of a detached, emotionless, controlling hand. History informs us, our subconscious tells us, that human beings should not be reduced to a stencilled number.

But there they were. On simple whitewashed wooden pegs, numbers had been stencilled in red paint to indicate to the impending, rumbling army of bulldozers which headstones were to be obliterated, almost 4,000 of them (although that figure continues to fluctuate). New Singapore needs a new four-lane dual carriageway to serve a future residential estate expected to be bigger than Serangoon. The development will combine public and private housing spoilt by views of MacRitchie Reservoir and is tentatively pencilled in for 2042 at the earliest (current estimates are between 30 and 40 years) but the Land Transport Authority insists that the dual carriageway is needed by 2016 to relieve rush-hour traffic along Lornie Road.

The road will slice through Bukit Brown Cemetery.

For all its sexy sheen, new Singapore cannot quite shed the image of its uglier big brother.

Despite the island's cashed-up status, Bukit Brown Cemetery is priceless on every level imaginable. Nestled beneath MacRitchie Reservoir, the graveyard is densely vegetated considering it's surrounded by the traffic arteries of Thomson Road, Lornie Road and the PIE. I glimpsed some remarkable birds, mostly black but boasting vivid streaks of either blue, yellow or red. (I admit I'm being shamefully sketchy on the detail but I'd never seen such rare breeds anywhere else on the mainland.) Bukit Brown provides a natural, protective shelter to allow some 85 bird species to thrive in a biologically diverse habitat. Life flourishes after death here.

The elegant hillside graves are the final resting places for up to 100,000 people, making Bukit Brown one of the biggest Chinese cemeteries in the world outside of China (some sources claim it's the biggest). Peering at some of the inscriptions was like reading an MRT map, a street directory and a primary school history book all at the same time. Named after former proprietor George Henry Brown, a ship owner in Singapore in the 1840s, the cemetery includes community leaders, business pioneers and, contrary to some online beliefs, many common folk. Lee Kuan Yew's grandfather Lee Hoon Leong provides an obvious political link but consider these names: Cheang Hong Lim (Hong Lim Park), Chew Boon Lay (Boon Lay MRT), Gan Eng Seng (Gan Eng Seng School), Teh Ho Swee (Bukit Ho Swee), Chew Joo Chiat (Joo Chiat Place), Ong Sam Leong (Sam Leong Road), Ong Boon Tat (Boon Tat Street) and See Ewe Boon (Ewe Boon Road), among many others. In various contexts, we utter these names more often than those of our own relatives. They are all interned at Bukit Brown Cemetery.

Some of these guys were wonderfully eccentric to boot. Go and see the extraordinary edifice that Chew Geok Leong designed for himself—while he was still alive. He supervised preparations for his coffin, his tomb and a pair of Sikh guard statues that were expected to stand guard for all eternity in front of his grave. Unusual, you might say, yet an ostentatious indulgence so common among the insanely wealthy. But dear old Chew decided that his elaborate creations could all be stored in his servants' room. These servants had to sleep with two armed Sikh guard statues at the foot of their beds every night. Chew left behind a decadent legacy, which was great for him and us, but not so great for the servants who woke up in the middle of the night thinking they had snuffed it and gone to heaven.

Enjoying the remoteness of this hilly expanse, I followed a tour mapped out by enthusiastic members of Asia Paranormal Investigators, or API for short. I found myself humming "If there's something strange in your neighbourhood ..." for the rest of the day. But Singapore's ghostbusters are doing sterling work to raise awareness for Bukit Brown's plight. They provide online DIY tours and maps, write blogs calling for the cemetery's conservation and even hang cards and arrows from trees to enable visitors to find the graves of Singapore's colonial luminaries.

As usual, I was lost. Despite the guidance provided thoughtfully by the ghostbusters, I struggled to track down many of the island's pioneers and sought assistance. I stumbled up a well-worn path and came across a couple of young guys examining a headstone. Wearing backpacks, hats and sensible shoes, the Chinese twenty-somethings obviously had plans for a Bukit Brown hike, a bit of an expedition to find the more famous names.

"Excuse me, how are you managing to find all the pioneers in here?" I shouted across several crumbling graves shaded beneath the trees. "Are you following a map?"

"No, we are just following the cards and arrows left around," replied the taller bespectacled one. "Have you seen them?"

"Ah, the ones left by the ghostbusters. Yeah, I've seen them but I can't make sense of them."

"There are a few famous graves up there," he said, pointing towards the hill's grassy summit. "If you head that way, you can't miss them."

"Thanks, guys. So what brings you here?" I asked. "It's an unusual way to spend a Wednesday morning."

"We've been reading the papers, following the news, and wanted to see the place before they started demolishing it."

I pulled a street directory from my rucksack and found the bookmarked page on Bukit Brown Cemetery. I pointed to Lornie Road on the map.

"Can you show me roughly where the proposed road is going to cut through?"

They eyed me suspiciously.

"Why are you so interested in Bukit Brown?" the bespectacled one asked. He did all the talking. "Where are you from?"

"Oh, I live here and I'm writing a book about Singapore."

The bespectacled one stepped towards me. He did not look happy.

"You're from overseas," he said firmly. "Don't you think it's disgraceful that a government can decide to bulldoze a cemetery and tear out our country's history without bothering to consult the people first?"

Well. What could I say to that? I was only trying to find Chew Boon Lay's grave to break the news gently that the East-West MRT line no longer ended at his station.

"You don't think it's any better now?" I ventured cautiously.

"How is it any better? They are still ripping up this place. The government doesn't listen."

"Listen to whom?" I wondered aloud. "Listen to the majority? Where's their Bukit Brown protest? Is it a poor government because it doesn't listen to people like us, or a wily, cynical, but effective, government because it knows roughly what its majority still wants: more money, decent homes, flat screen TVs, lots of Singapore Pools outlets and tuition for their children. I've got friends, Singaporean friends, who honestly couldn't care less about Bukit Brown. They've got bills to pay so why should they care about some dead bodies."

"Don't you think it's terrible?"

"I think it's the same everywhere. I've lived in England and Australia. Some people would care about lost heritage but most would be more interested in who's going to win *The X Factor*. But it's changing in Singapore. You're here and I'm here. All the other volunteers are here documenting the graves. The volume of letters to the papers, the blogs and websites, that is new Singapore. I don't think there would have been so much interest in Bukit Brown 15 years ago. To me, that says new Singapore. You are new Singapore."

And they are, along with the volunteers I met who were painstakingly photographing the graves as they carried out three-dimensional mapping of the affected graves, with plans to record oral histories and compile them for the National Library. They came from universities, institutes, the Singapore Heritage Society and from families who have relatives buried at Bukit Brown. I chatted with a woman as she ate lunch in one of the portable offices. She asked me, pleaded with me, to write a letter to the newspapers, imploring others to back their futile bid to save Bukit Brown Cemetery. They know it is a fight they cannot win. The bulldozers are coming. Golf courses can be spared because their members' wallets shout loudest. No one hears the pleas of the dead. Old or new, some things never change in Singapore.

But in new Singapore, there is a growing resistance to the destruction of the country's physical, historical markers. Public consultation is increasingly expected and demanded (so much so that after I visited, the government agreed to build a bridge over part of the fragile forest to reduce the impact on the flora and fauna). And those volunteers and field workers, numbering close to 300, are determined to record the names, histories and voices of Bukit Brown before they are silenced by the excavator, their beautiful, hand-carved headstones smashed and left in pathetic piles of rubble beside toppled trees and dead shrubbery.

The number crunchers may dismiss such a labour-intensive exercise as naive and tokenistic, but these number crunchers are not as dominant as they once were. New Singaporeans are beginning to look beyond the mere protection of their rice bowl, they are looking … yearning … feeling for something more. Bulldozing parts of Bukit Brown will again offer something less. People need to feel rooted to their country, to maintain an attachment, to want to stay. National Day Parades show off big tanks and fighter jets but new Singaporeans require more than a shiny air force and new MRT lines to feel rooted to their home. They need those historical markers, the physical ties that bind them to their ancestors and their nation's past. Bukit Brown Cemetery gives them that, a fireworks display over Marina Bay doesn't.

As I wandered through the cemetery's rusty iron gates and past those appalling wooden pegs with the red-stencilled numbers again, I found myself marginally more optimistic than when I had arrived. New Singapore revealed itself in the distinct voices of those two Chinese guys. They were the voices of angry young men, amplified by the voices of the angry young women in the portable office. These young Singaporeans can no longer be dismissed as greenie crackpots, heritage zealots or disaffected rabble-rousers. They are dignified, industrious, proactive local heroes. They are my heroes. And they are growing in number. Never mind the practicality of Confucius and utilitarianism of Jeremy Bentham, Singapore's government would do well to heed the warning of David Banner.

Don't make them angry. You wouldn't like them when they're angry. They know they have options. They can leave.

Despite the volunteers' positivity and persistence, I strolled off in search of something more uplifting. I found it at the end of the same road. The meandering Kheam Hock Road (named after Tan Kheam Hock, one of the cemetery's original management committee members) guided me past laughably large private dwellings and led me to Dunearn Road, where I saw a brown sign indicating Jacob Ballas Children's Garden. I had never heard of it. I trekked the pedestrian crossing that covers Dunearn Road, a canal and Bukit Timah Road (Hannibal spent less time crossing the Alps). I passed the sports facilities of the National University of Singapore's Bukit Timah campus and presented myself outside the Jacob Ballas Children's Garden.

At the entrance, a mild-mannered NParks guy stared at me quizzically, like I had a limb missing. I did. I didn't have a child with me. A leaflet pointed out that adults not accompanied by children must join viewing sessions at 9 a.m. or 4 p.m. daily to avoid looking like a pervert. I added the pervert bit, but the leaflet was hardly any less subtle. So I removed my dark glasses, fake moustache and raincoat and vowed to return with a child. (Call me tactless but I grow tired of the intervention of the fun police whenever children are involved. Single men and women are not automatic threats to minors, just as my desire to photograph my daughter taking her first swimming lesson does not make me a paedophile deserving of castration.)

To be precise, two kids—my daughter and I—returned later to see what the Jacob Ballas Children's Garden had to offer. Well, the late Ballas would have been proud. A remarkable man by just about every account, Jacob Ballas was a Jewish-Singaporean who came from a poor background. He went from selling roti, baked by his mother, on street corners to becoming the chairman of the Malaysia and Singapore Stock Exchange. A philanthropist beyond compare, Ballas left behind an estate worth more than $100 million, which was bequeathed to his chosen charities, when he died in 2000. Some of the money was dedicated to all the children of Singapore and was used to create a garden for kids—the first of its kind in Asia—at the northern end of Singapore Botanic Gardens. The Jacob Ballas Children's Garden was opened in 2007.

We loved the place and not only because it was free (although that always helps). The garden fancied itself as an interactive learning and discovery centre for children to appreciate plants, nature and the environment. In other words, a simple introduction to life sciences. There were lots of blocks to build, knobs to squeeze and plenty of water to splash. The multi-storey tree house with its furniture carved from trunks and tunnel slides was far more sophisticated than my allotment camp built in homage to Stig of the Dump. My daughter informed me that she wanted an identical three-storey tree house for Christmas. We live in a two-bedroomed apartment.

We crossed the Indiana Jones-like rope bridge, conducted rudimentary photosynthesis experiments (i.e. we turned some handles), picnicked in the tree house, discovered that fish are deliberately added to rice paddies to control pests and that their crap makes a great fertiliser (I did not know that) and got lost in the maze. My daughter might still be running through the fountains had I not refused to join in the water revelry. A three-year-old splashing in her knickers is still socially acceptable. A 37-year-old gangly man lolloping around in his underwear isn't.

As we shared a bowl of cheesy fries at the kids' cafe outside, where the miniature tables and chairs made me feel like the late Ah Meng at one of her tea parties, I thought about the dichotomy that is Kheam Hock Road. Both ends of the long and winding road represent the frustrating future direction of new Singapore. Just as the charming Jacob Ballas Children's Garden feels so right, the demise of Bukit Brown Cemetery feels so utterly wrong.

Fifteen

I WAS once thrown onto train tracks. Well, when I say thrown, it was more lowered down against my will. Still, the decision to drop me beside a live rail of London Underground's District Line as a train bound for Upminster trundled towards me came as something of a surprise. I had been about to tuck into a well-deserved Curly Wurly, my cheap chocolate treat for getting through another day at a Dagenham comprehensive school unpunished for being the class "boff job".

In my school, a boff job was someone of above average intelligence who refused to follow the herd. (In other words, I didn't play truant, didn't lock the music teacher in the cupboard and didn't hand over my school dinner money to Caroline McHiggins in exchange for what sounded like a "boff job" behind the science bench. I always took a packed lunch.)

The penalty for being a boff job varied from day to day. On the traumatising, infamous, autumnal afternoon in question, this boff job was sentenced by the school bully to face off against a train driver. His name was Pattern. (I'm referring to the big older kid who lowered me onto the train tracks, not the tube driver. I didn't get close enough to read the driver's name tag.)

"Oi, how's it going, Boff Job?" Pattern shouted across the

platform of Becontree Station, swaggering past the graffiti-covered Cadbury's chocolate machine that was smashed for most of my secondary school years.

I feigned deafness and turned away. Pattern was that universally familiar school bully in the upper forms whose stock in trade was skinny first years whose academic potential threatened him because he subconsciously knew that the day would come when that same academic potential would be waiting impatiently in the supermarket queue for Pattern to bag his shopping.

"Oh, hello, Pattern," I mumbled into my Curly Wurly, wondering what form my public humiliation would take that day.

"Give us your Curly Wurly," Pattern barked.

Ah, this was going to be a problem. He could take my freedom but he would never take my Curly Wurly. I had saved my 10p, clung onto it in my pocket all afternoon, in anticipation of a chocolate-coated, swirling caramel feast.

"Er, no, you can't have my Curly Wurly," I muttered, resigning myself to my fate and hoping that Pattern had kept the glue sniffing to a minimum.

He peeled off my school rucksack and dropped it onto the train tracks, a metre below the station platform. In normal circumstances, I might have acknowledged the creativity, the dash of flair even, but there was little time to respond as I found myself swiftly following the schoolbag's trajectory.

"Next time, give me your fucking Curly Wurly," hissed Pattern, glaring down at me from the platform (I never did).

I heard the clicking and clacking of the live rail suddenly spark into life beside my feet. Through the dusky, chilly air, I made out the train's glowing headlights. They were getting brighter. I edged away from the live rail, grabbed my rucksack, threw it over my shoulder, shoved the Curly Wurly between my teeth and clambered up the concrete wall before rolling onto the platform as the train approached. I dusted myself down, got on the nearest carriage and nonchalantly chewed on my chocolate.

No one fucks with my Curly Wurly.

(A couple of weeks later, my older cousin, John Davis, otherwise known locally as The Hardest Kid in Dagenham, provided a postscript. He bumped into Pattern and threw his schoolbag over a fence. And then he threw Pattern over the fence. Do I think my cousin went too far? No, it was only a small fence.)

Twenty-five years later, I found myself recalling my death-defying platform dangle as I stood on train tracks once more. It was strange that an Upminster-bound tube wasn't rumbling towards me. Instead, there was a magnificent steel bridge on my left and a boarded-up brick building on my right. Other than that, I had Singapore's new Railway Corridor all to myself.

On 30 June 2011, the Malaysian railway operator Keretapi Tanah Melayu (KTM) ended operations at Tanjong Pagar, with Woodlands taking over as the terminus for services to and from Singapore. In an elaborate ceremony, Sultan Ibrahim Iskandar of Johor drove the last KTM train out of Tanjong Pagar Railway Station for sentimental reasons. His great grandfather had opened the Causeway in 1923. My grandfather fought in World War II but that doesn't mean I should be let loose with a Sherman tank.

Malaysian trains had trundled out of Tanjong Pagar since 1923, providing commuters with a surprisingly serene, short trip through Singapore's green spine. For that very reason, the narrow strip of land has always been highly prized and highly disputed by the Causeway cousins since independence. The relocation issue was finally settled in 2010. KTM moved out of Tanjong Pagar, parcels of land were bandied about by the two countries like Monopoly board pieces, the tracks were mostly dismantled and returned to Malaysia and Singapore had a rare dilemma and an unusual decision to make. From Keppel Road in the south to the industrial tip of Kranji in the north via some of the island's most expensive real estate in Bukit Timah, there was a lot of land to play with.

The Railway Corridor was born.

From the steel bridge at Bukit Timah southwards, the railway land was opened to the public in late 2011, with the URA launching a competition that called for the best ideas to develop the green link. Residents have a say in where the old track is headed in new Singapore.

Feeling rebellious, I walked over the actual tracks along the steel bridge that crosses Bukit Timah and Dunearn roads. The little stretch of track between the bridge and Bukit Timah Railway Station is almost all that is left in Singapore so I felt duty-bound to step on the old wooden sleepers. A screeching cockatoo soared over the tracks, issuing a reminder of the dense, remote vegetation that comes with the best Bukit Timah real estate that money can buy.

I chatted briefly with a couple of mainland Chinese guys (in new Singapore, it can be difficult to find any Singaporeans) who were photographing the old station. Built in 1915, the small brick building and its quaint waiting room triggered long-forgotten memories of standing outside the waiting room at Dagenham Heathway, a District Line tube station built less than 20 years later with a similar no-frills red brick design. I say outside because the waiting room at Dagenham Heathway Station was usually locked, presumably to avoid vandalism, drunks and people treating the room like a men's urinal. The waiting room was only reopened whenever a fresh coat of paint was applied, presumably for a local councillor to visit to get his picture in the *Dagenham Post*. The waiting room was then swiftly padlocked again, a pointless exercise because it always reeked of stale cider and urine. No such concerns for Bukit Timah Railway Station, which was officially gazetted in April 2011 and will be rightfully conserved.

I stepped off the last of the sleepers to sample a surreal slice of equatorial jungle. I followed a strip of grass laid over the old tracks. It was between 5 and 15 metres wide and bordered on both sides by thick, tall foliage that shielded the millionaires' mansions tucked behind. The walk around Holland Road was so unexpectedly tranquil that the plethora of possibilities for the country's unique green corridor gave way to unhealthy cynicism. Shoeboxes are now sold as suitable homes in Singapore. Having witnessed what Pinnacle@Duxton had achieved on a relatively small parcel of land at Duxton Plain, those anorexic condos currently being passed off as luxurious abodes could fit most snugly along the Railway Corridor.

Such an easy, lazy, myopic vision would literally hack away at Singapore's spine, crippling its physical vitality. As I passed the Greenleaf estate, a solitary expat cyclist—the only person I encountered on the walk—gamely bounced along the boggy terrain, reinforcing the area's potential. The Railway Corridor has the potential to be one of the finest, most accessible walking and cycling trails found in any of the world's leading cities. Even the most laidback of cyclists could manage breakfast in Bukit Merah and a late lunch in Woodlands after a leisurely jaunt through the forest. Build it, and they will come. And they will come, in their tens of thousands. And as I passed the extravagant high-walled houses off Holland Road, where owners have paid fortunes to secure their privacy, I wondered how enamoured they really are by the prospect of a group of pot-bellied cyclists pedalling past and pondering aloud whether or not to eat the half ball being offered on Man U.

The Railway Corridor, however, proved to be so much

more than just a green thoroughfare for trekkers and cyclists. It provided glimpses into different worlds: some gone, like the crumbling Hindu shrines left behind by railway workers, some neglected, some underground but all varied and equally valid. Experiencing Singapore from what was, at times, a subterranean level was most peculiar. Under the vast Commonwealth Avenue flyover, I stepped onto a 1970s New York film set starring Charles Bronson. Graffiti adorned the concrete walls of the flyover, some of which was exceptionally good and deserved a bigger audience than the rare railway walker. The sloped sides of the flyover leant themselves to an instant underground skate park, already being used in an ad-hoc fashion judging by the litter. At the edge of the flyover, three rebellious Caucasian teenagers were taking turns to throw rocks overhead. On closer inspection of their expensive designer labels, they were three wealthy Caucasian teenagers, probably from the bungalows nearby. I have little patience for affluent suburban kids playing out the downtrodden, disaffected "boyz in the hood" routine at the best of times. Watching Western expat teenagers in baggy pants pretending to be Jay Z of Holland V always tempts me to ask, "Sorry to interrupt the gangsta trippin', homies, but does your maid know where you're at?"

They glared at me, perhaps understandably. Vandals do not expect their work to be interrupted beneath Commonwealth Avenue by a lone *ang moh*. They continued to chip away at the ceiling with their rocks, but more tentatively.

"Hello, boys," I said cheerily, stopping to examine their handiwork.

"Hello," one of the rock throwers grunted.

"Are you enjoying yourselves? You seem to be enjoying yourselves. Well, I can see you're busy. I'll leave you to it."

I took out my notepad and made a few scribbles. They

dropped their rocks, picked up their skateboards and left. At the next flyover, I planned to tackle global poverty and famine.

Instead, I was hit with a multiple homicide. After passing my old friends Proteos and Immunos at Biopolis, I stumbled upon a macabre murder scene beneath Portsdown Avenue. There had been carnage at Queensway. The flyover was 30 to 40 metres long and the ground was damp and unstable, with the water often submerging my ankles, but that was the least of my worries. Jackets, shoes, umbrellas, handbags and cases were lying across the muddy pebbles. I ventured closer to examine the belongings, promising myself that if I found so much as a speck of blood, I'd run all the way to the Alexandra police post. Singaporeans were going about their daily lives in their thousands not five metres above my head, but inside the gloomy, filthy flyover, I was very much alone and a trifle concerned.

A male silhouette appeared at the other end of the flyover, ominously framed by the concrete walls. Without thinking, I stepped back from all the personal belongings and scrambled up the sloped, cobbled flyover wall to navigate my way around the soaking, sinking soil and to reassure the silhouette. My haste only heightened his concern. He started running through the caliginous tunnel towards me. I thought he was a murderer. I quickened my uneven pace across the near vertical terrain. Our paths were about to cross.

And then we both pretended that nothing had happened. He surveyed all the bits and bobs and realised nothing was missing, then examined me from head to toe and ascertained that I was not a thief. I spotted the camera he was holding in one hand and the expensive-looking lens in the other and worked out that he was either a professional photographer on a funky urban underground shoot or he was going to batter me to death with his Canon. So we just nodded as we passed each other and continued on our way, like it was the most everyday of occurrences to encounter a stranger beneath a deserted flyover and chase him across its slippery cobbled walls.

As I happily returned to daylight, I smiled at a couple of models standing on the Jalan Hang Jebat side of the flyover touching up their make-up. Tall, slender and blessed with that other-worldly bone structure of David Bowie in *The Man Who Fell to Earth* so popular with modelling agencies, they were dressed as goths, sporting war paint and lashings of lacquer that had been poured onto their heads to make every hair strand stand erect. They were a cross between Lady Gaga and Adam Ant. Where the hell was I?

Eager to leave Zombieland, I picked up the pace, passed the AIA Building and followed the Railway Corridor as it ran parallel with the AYE. The path was a jungle trench. Wading through knee-high *lalang* grass, my ankles rolled in every direction as I struggled to maintain my footing. With the Bukit Merah industrial estate on my left, I had no one but snakes for company. Bodies could be thrown from the AYE and never be found.

By Lower Delta Road, I was seriously struggling. The swampy terrain swallowed my weary feet with every tentative step. I tried to get around one particularly flooded area by crawling up the grassy slope. I slipped, scraped my knees along the cobbles and dropped and soaked my street directory. With dusk closing in, I rolled onto my back to allow the spots in my eyes to clear. Despite being flanked by the bustling AYE traffic and the neighbouring blocks up and away to my left, I was desperately lonely.

The thought occurred to me that I had strayed too far. I was still trudging along the former KTM railway, I knew that, but whether I still had the permission of the Singapore Land Authority was another more serious matter. The colourful, welcoming SLA signs at Bukit Timah reminding visitors that the Green Corridor was "for your recreational use" had stopped abruptly around Holland Road, even though I had kept on searching for them (partly because I was hoping to find one amended to "for your recreational drug use" but I never did).

By the time I had passed beneath the Central Expressway (CTE) near Keppel Road, I was under no illusions. I was still on the right track, as it were, but the public Railway Corridor must have halted some time back. I was aware that my exuberant trekking might have ventured into wayward trespassing but the prospect of retracing my steps back to Bukit Timah, or even Bukit Merah, did not appeal. Indeed, the thought of lying back in an air-conditioned police car and being driven off state land now had a certain allure.

I picked out the cranes and hoists of the port at Keppel Terminal and a sign of new Singapore, the giant billboard advertising Resorts World Sentosa, and knew I was close. The path widened as I passed an old, ghostly station house marked Singapura. Indeed the ghosts of the Malaysian railway surrounded me in the encroaching darkness. Dilapidated shacks, broken shrines and rusty signboards written in Malay were reminders that, ironically, I was returning to old Singapore, which had once housed the magnificent art deco Tanjong Pagar Railway Station. New Singapore was now behind me, facing an undecided future for its green corridor.

I stepped slowly along the railway tracks as I entered the dark, deserted station. Frankly, it was a bewildering experience. With faded posters and signs, paint-chipped benches and litter blowing gently in the dusky breeze on the platforms above me, it were as if I had stepped onto another eerie movie set, the post-apocalyptic *Beneath the Planet of the Apes*. The temptation to fall to my knees, pound the tracks and shout "You maniacs! You blew it up! Ah, damn you! God damn you all to hell!" was overwhelming. But I had a more pressing issue. I was locked in. The station perimeter was surrounded by fences 2 metres high, complete with those small meshed squares that deliberately make footholds and handgrips impossible. As an unsettling murkiness enveloped the station, I was trapped beside its imposing, Gothic, spooky shut-down interior hall. Where were the Asia Paranormal Investigators when I needed them?

I clambered onto the platform and, for the most fleeting of moments, thought I saw an Upminster-bound London tube trundling towards me. Fatigue was failing my mind. Then I thought I picked out a couple of security guards gesticulating wildly and dashing across the bleak, cheerless car park towards me. Hallucinations had taken hold now. Erring on the side of caution, I took off in the opposite direction. Whether they were ghosts or real people, I figured running away was the best option. I was 12 years old and being harassed on a station platform again. All that was missing was a Curly Wurly.

"Hey, you ah! How you get in here, ah?" a voice shouted. "Cannot lah."

They were real people, or Singlish-speaking ghosts. I stopped and trudged towards the car park, wearily anticipating the interrogation. The guard wagged his finger in front of me when I slumped beside his security post at the exit. There is something about people who take pleasure in wagging their fingers in other people's faces, something that makes me want to bite the offending finger off and leave them with a wagging stump.

"How you get in here?" he demanded, rightfully concerned that I had breached his security.

"I walked in," I replied, far too flippantly for his taste.

"Cannot walk in, cannot. There are fences and gates," he pointed out.

"No, I walked in from Bukit Timah. I followed the new Railway

Corridor all the way from Bukit Timah station to this one, and the corridor must have ended at some point and I didn't notice."

"Don't bluff. Bukit Timah so far, lah."

"Why would I possibly make something like that up?"

He conceded that I had a point. He pulled the gate open. I wished him a good night. He did not reply. I did not blame him.

Nevertheless, the Railway Corridor really is something special, an umbilical cord that ties the histories of two neighbouring countries together. Not only must Singapore's green link remain, it should be beautified further with more indigenous vegetation added to keep the landed properties out and maintain a little privacy for all stakeholders. Create not only a lifestyle attraction for walkers, trekkers and cyclists but a legitimate, healthy, practical public transport thoroughfare for Singapore's commuters. In the week that I visited the Railway Corridor, SMRT trains broke down an unprecedented four times. Had a biking path already been laid over the country's spine, Tanjong Pagar office staff could have been home in Woodlands and cycling clips removed before SMRT's packed replacement buses had even shown up.

New Singapore has been gifted an extraordinary trail that must be utilised by all. Build the walking and cycling paths, the skateboard and skating parks and the allotments beside the housing estates of Bukit Merah and Tanglin Halt, maintain the Hindu shrines where possible, preserve Bukit Timah Railway Station and erect information panels and permanent photo experiences to inform future generations of what was handed down to them by old Singapore. The Railway Corridor is filled with the most precious of commodities—land. There is ample space to do all of the above and more. I only ventured along the southern route. From Bukit Timah northwards, there are creative possibilities all the way to the Kranji coastal mudflats. Let the bold development be determined by imagination rather than *kiasuism*.

And most of all, make sure the Railway Corridor is adequately signposted throughout. Those signs make all the difference you know, particularly between trekking and bloody trespassing.

Sixteen

NEW Singaporeans are trying to be more courteous. They really are, particularly when there is the risk of losing face. The MRT, however, has thrown a spanner in the works. I'm referring to that seat in the corner. Reserved for anyone pregnant, with child, with age or with shopping, the seat lurks at the end of each row, seemingly innocent and innocuous, ready to do its good deed for the day for a weary traveller. In reality, it's a veritable minefield of social embarrassments just waiting to blow up in our faces. Life was so much easier in old Singapore. We knew who we were on trains. We were all grumpy bastards. No one gave up their seat for anyone, not even for a one-legged pregnant woman with a dozen shopping bags. Everyone knew where they stood, or sat in this instance, head down in a good book and thinking, Piss off, peg leg, I was here first.

Then new Singapore decided to manipulate the average Asian's obsession with saving face by sticking up highly visible campaign posters above the coveted corner seats. In bright letters accompanied with explanatory diagrams of kind-hearted stick figures offering up their cosy corners for pregnant stick figures, these signs have turned that cosy corner into the electric chair. Few are willing to risk the unexpected shock before a muttering, disapproving audience. On crowded trains, the posters might as well have an arrow pointing at the seat occupier's head and a sign saying "Look at this selfish tosser. He's sitting here, right in front of that perspiring woman, who's either carrying triplets or been impregnated by an elephant, and he's pretending to ignore her by playing Angry Birds. What a wanker."

Not surprisingly, I give my corner seat up to anybody. I practically bundle startled Singaporeans into the vacated seat head first, throwing them around in a way not dissimilar to secret service agents when they are slinging presidents into unmarked cars after assassination attempts.

I prepared to do the same as we rolled along towards Lakeside in the country's southwest. I had the corner seat, but I also had a heavy rucksack, a mitigating factor I thought when I had boarded the near-empty train earlier. The train was now jammed, commuters in the middle of the carriage conjoined by their congealing armpit sweat. A pregnant woman had shuffled her way over to the corner seats, practically straddling herself between the two like an umpire at a tennis court, playing brinkmanship, waiting for either myself or the other corner seat occupier to blink. I got up first and quietly offered her my seat. She turned and peered at me quizzically. She looked confused. I peeked at her belly.

She was not pregnant.

I had offered a young woman my prized corner seat for entirely different reasons. She declined the seat. Being on a packed train, I could not return to the warm corner beckoning my behind. No one around us was conceivably pregnant, over 65 or overburdened with shopping, so the seat remained empty, lonely and adrift, a victim of new Singapore's attempt to create more gracious people in a country preoccupied with face-saving. This is the internal struggle that commuters grapple with daily now. We must give up the seat to the elderly, but how do we define elderly? Is that anyone over 50 or anyone who appears to have only a 50 per cent chance of getting through the MRT trip alive? Is a woman pregnant or, as my mother would say, merely "big-boned"? We cannot ask for a recent BMI reading before vacating our seat.

On reaching Lakeside, I turned from inconsiderate commuter to potential serial killer. I have inherited a rather bombastic street-greeting habit from my mother. When she passes strangers, she invariably offers a breezy "hiya" in a voice that just shies away from sending them into the hedges. She lives on a quiet estate in Kent where such exchanges are commonplace. They are less so in sprawling cities and, if one is being brutally honest, practically negligible in Singapore. Strangers do not generally speak when they pass each other here. Strangers do not generally acknowledge each other unless one of them is on fire. For that reason alone, I greet passing walkers with an enthusiasm that suggests one of us might be tied up and gagged in a car boot before the night is out.

"Hello, how's it going?" I asked warmly as a middle-aged power walker approached along the Jurong Lake Park path.

Well, you would have thought I'd dropped my shorts and cried, "Anyone for noodles?" Her eyes widened, the pace slowed and she stepped awkwardly to her right like a first-time line dancer struggling to keep up with "Cotton Eye Joe".

"Er, hello," she mumbled, still debating whether to pass me or swim around me via Jurong Lake.

"Lovely day for it."

I love saying that. My puerile sensibilities get a perverse kick from its jovial ambiguity. A lovely day for what? A gentle amble around Jurong Lake? A one-way swim in Bedok Reservoir?

"Er, yes, yes," she agreed, her apprehension visibly dissipating. I was not a serial killer. She could see that. There was nowhere to hide a chopper about my person. And she smiled back at me, an invigorating warm smile that added a spring to my step. I reciprocated and we bounced past each other looking like Ronald McDonald.

I had reasons to be in Jurong Lake Park other than disturbing power walkers. Jurong Lake is about to get a makeover to rival Joan Rivers. Her cosmetic surgeon pulled back anything natural, created something artificial and functional in its place and gave the American comedian new material to work with. The government has similar hopes for the Jurong Lake District.

In the next 10 to 15 years, Singapore's neglected west must rival downtown and the only way to achieve that vibrancy, apparently, is waterfront hotels and shopping malls. Obviously there is a shortage of shopping malls in Singapore. As part of the HDB's $1 billion Remaking Our Heartland Programme, Jurong will join Hougang and East Coast in getting sexier. There is already a new shopping mall called JCube (another worthy contender for lame name honours), with a network of park connectors, a healthcare hub comprising a couple of hospitals and the 20-storey Westgate Tower on the way. Jurong will become the largest commercial hub outside the city centre, with shopping malls more than half the size of ION Orchard. This is supposedly a cause for celebration. But the inference is clear. Jurong Lake is a frumpy embarrassment, left on the gym bench on prom night, tapping its feet while more sexed-up neighbours attract handsome, wealthy suitors.

So I expected to find a Plain Jane by the lake. Instead, I discovered a sleepy beauty.

When I left my new power-walking friend, I snapped a photograph of my favourite Singaporean sign to date. It read "Toilet 906 m away". The precise distance threw up two of the more obvious questions. Who measured it? And who cares? Surely, the pedantic accuracy is not going to affect the decision-making process one way or the other. No one is going to stand cross-legged before the sign and say, "Now, if it was 905 metres away, I just might make the toilet in time but 906 metres is beyond my bowels ... Wait, too late, pass me the wet wipes."

I joined a couple of fishermen on the South Promenade and Viewing Deck and shouted my hellos. They replied enthusiastically while I marvelled at the view. With the serene islands of the Chinese and Japanese gardens offering seven-storey pagodas, stone bridges, waterfalls and fountains as a backdrop while the waters lapped the shoreline gently, Jurong Lake provides a thoroughly disarming day out. Not only for fishermen, amblers and picnickers, but also for the hunting herons, the chorusing frogs and a cruising monitor lizard so large that at first glance I honestly mistook the beast for a crocodile. Such fabulous fauna and vistas undoubtedly make the location an attractive proposition for waterfront developments. Whether the current tenants feel quite the same way about sharing their home with drillers and diggers for the next two decades is doubtful. They may just wave a white flag and retreat through the canals to either Selat Jurong or Kranji, which would rather contradict developers' boasts of offering mixed-use properties in a natural setting.

I wandered the length of Jurong Lake Park and back again, passing the adventure playground, the skate park, the Jurong Country Club and the fishing jetties filled with superbly idiosyncratic fishermen. When I offered my customary greeting to one particular fisherman, whose wonky haircut must have been the result of a lost bet, he giggled, mumbled something in Mandarin, took out a plastic toy machine gun from his fishing box and shot me.

Yes, I thought it was peculiar, too.

I raised my hands in mock surrender so he shot me some

more. He even supplied his own machine-gun sound effects. I put my hands down and left the jetty, otherwise I suspect he'd still be standing there shooting me with his toy gun. He smiled at me. I counted six teeth.

I have no idea whether my toothless, gun-toting fisherman will be affected by Jurong Lakeside's radical makeover, but some things will obviously have to go (his toy gun probably being one of them). Space, the reclusive green retreat's finest attribute, will be the first casualty. All Singaporeans in Jurong deserve a bit of legroom, not just those swinging away at the golf course across the lake. Power walkers, kayakers, picnickers, parents playing with their children at the sandpit and fishermen playing with their kids' guns are simply free to be and that's a priceless commodity to have when you're beside the dense housing estates and industrial complexes of Yuan Ching and Corporation roads. Joan Rivers isn't required in Jurong. It's already got Jodie Foster, a quiet, unassuming, natural beauty. And that's sexier than any facelift, no matter how accomplished the men with scalpels. The odd nip and tuck would certainly do Jurong Lake no harm (I'd start with the dilapidated adventure playground) but the waterfront's alluring charms do not need the architectural equivalent of a push-up bra.

I left Jurong Lake Park, studied my street directory, made a startling discovery, jumped on a bus and headed to Tuas. The trip was not planned. I blame my mother-in-law and Sentosa. Whenever my in-laws visited, I always carried out my customary tourist duties, guiding them across Palawan Beach and the suspension bridge to the slither of an unnamed islet that the cartographers of the Sentosa Development Corporation had long ago declared Asia's southernmost point.

My mother-in-law never bought it.

"How can it be the southernmost point of Asia? Those islands are further south," she always said, pointing to Singapore's Southern Islands.

"They are not part of continental Asia, not part of its land mass," I reiterated, on every occasion that we visited. "They are separate islands."

"So is this," she countered. "We had to get across that suspension bridge."

"Yeah, and Sentosa is not part of Singapore," my father-in-law usually chimed in. "So it's an island off an island off an island off Asia. How does that work?"

"Look, do you want to take your photo here or not?"

"Yeah, of course we do. Just make sure you can see the southernmost point bit on the sign."

If my rudimentary map reading was correct, new Singapore might have settled the matter. Land reclamation had overtaken Sentosa. The projected extension of Tuas clearly ventured beneath the islet of Sentosa's Palawan Beach. New Singapore had a new southernmost point of continental Asia and it wasn't far from Lakeside. So I decided, on a whim, to head for Tuas, redraw new Singapore's boundaries and silence my mother-in-law.

Humming The Beatles' "Blue Jay Way" (it's Boon Lay Way's fault), I reached Boon Lay's topsy-turvy public transport hub, where the interchange was air-conditioned but the bus itself wasn't. The bone-shaking time machine, also known as the 182M, was the blue-collar express to Tuas, its exclusively male occupants clearly undeserving of the air-conditioned comfort taken for granted by the white-collar crowd sauntering towards Shenton Way. No such luxury for the poor sods expected to toil in Tuas under the Saturday afternoon sun.

Not that the construction workers concerned themselves with the top deck's temperature. They focused on eating and drinking. Two Chinese guys stretched across the front seat were swigging cans of Coke while an older Chinese uncle, possibly in his early sixties, tucked into *nasi lemak* on the back seat behind me. The boisterous old bruiser of a bus belonged in my Dagenham childhood, taking me home after watching *Jaws 3-D* at the cinema in Romford. All that was missing were empty Stella Artois cans and the odd chorus of "I'm Forever Blowing Bubbles".

The driver bought into my childhood nostalgia, too. He thought he was Stan from the seventies sitcom *On the Buses*, gear-crunching, accelerating and swerving his way along Jalan Ahmad Ibrahim. Thanks to the boneshaker's open windows, my fine Caucasian hair billowed around in the breeze with a gaiety that suggested I had one foot planted in a bowl of water and the other in a plug socket. As we swayed from side to side and the coastal gusts rattled the windows, I struck up a mostly inaudible conversation with Nasi Lemak Uncle about Tuas's land reclamation while continuously holding my dancing hair down lest he confuse me for Doc Brown in *Back to the Future*. He fought a losing battle to keep the rice on his plastic spoon and conducted most of the conversation with a couple of anchovies poking from the corner of his mouth. I never wanted the bus journey to end.

But the loop service reached its southernmost point at Tuas South Avenue 3, where I stepped off, eager to make geopolitical history, both for Singapore and Sentosa. According to my street directory, ongoing land reclamation works being carried out by Penta-Ocean Construction (the Japanese constructor for the MCE gig) would easily make Tuas South the island's southernmost point and I intended to walk on water to get there.

I got nowhere.

Just in case you haven't been to Tuas, the industrial zone does a disservice to dustbowls. Had tumbleweed rolled past me on the pavement, I would not have noticed unless it had bounced up the kerb and smacked me in the face. I was battered about by the searing, sandy, stale air instead. Whatever those trucking guys are paid to transport sand and soil up and down Tuas South Avenue 5 all day, and they rumbled along endlessly before disappearing into a cloud of crap long before they reached the horizon, it is not enough. I squinted and peered down the long, wide white avenue but the sun's reflection, the absence of shade and the omnipresent dust cloud revealed nothing but the fact that the road was beyond me on foot. I continued to trudge along Avenue 5 but I had kilometres ahead of me. Ordinarily, I'd go to just about any length to settle an argument with my mother-in-law but this one was beyond me. I had no distance left to run.

On the roadside, a lone guy sat on a plastic chair under an umbrella, handing out tickets to truck drivers. I hurried over. I wasn't really interested in him, just his umbrella. I joined him beneath the canopy. On hindsight, I probably should have sought his permission first. We were the only two people in a desolate corner of the country and I often forget that I am a tall Caucasian in a predominately Asian country. He did not expect his personal umbrella space to be invaded by Ichabod Crane that afternoon.

"Er, yes, can I help you?" the Indian chap asked cautiously.

"Yes, you see that land reclamation going on down there," I replied, indicating to the distant silhouettes of cranes through the gloomy air. "Can I get to it?"

"Why, lah? There's nothing there. It's just a building site. Trucks, cranes, workers. Cannot go inside."

"No, I guessed that. But I just wanted to say I stood on Singapore's southernmost point. When that work is finished, it will have to be Singapore's most southerly point."

"Yah? So?"

"No, you see, the thing is, my mother-in-law, no, it doesn't matter. I just wanted to go and see it."

"Yah, well, you seen it. It's down there," he said, pointing at the faint crane shapes. "Still cannot go inside. What's the point? You are an *ang moh*. You will be so red."

His logic was incontestable. I thanked him for his time, retraced my steps and got lost. I failed to find a 182M bus stop. I was closer to Malaysia's Johor Bahru than Boon Lay. Alone, tired and hungry, I was disconsolate and disturbed by a couple of stray, salivating dogs on the other side of the road. But then the saint of Singapore's southernmost point appeared. A blue pick-up truck pulled up alongside and the Indian gentleman of a driver, recognising that I had lost my way, offered to drop me at a 182M bus stop. I almost kissed him. But considering my location, circumstances and dishevelled appearance, I settled for a grateful handshake as I clambered aboard.

"I'm a site foreman," he told me, perhaps in an effort to reassure me. He could have told me he was a site fornicator and my opinion of the Good Samaritan would have altered not a jot.

"I'm a writer," I replied.

He wasn't impressed. I noticed some Indian cricket keepsakes on the dashboard.

"Ah, you're a cricket fan," I said.

"Yeah, well, I'm Indian, aren't I?"

"Yeah, well, I'm English so it's football for me," I said as I removed my West Ham baseball cap. "That's my team there, West Ham, do you know them?"

"I don't really follow football but I have heard of West Ham."

And then he laughed. He stopped chuckling long enough to drop me off at the bus stop and we wished each other well. As I joined the waiting industrial workers, I contemplated the profound impact of globalisation upon new Singapore. Most of the men at the bus stop were not Singaporean. They were mostly mainland Chinese, Indian, Bangladeshi and me, of course.

Globalisation's tentacles had reached the farthest flung corner of the growing island. So much so that even a cricket-loving Indian migrant working in Tuas South knew that West Ham were shit.

Seventeen

I HEADED towards the island's northern shoreline to follow in the footsteps of Mas Selamat bin Kastari. For the benefit of overseas readers or any Singaporeans who have been living under a flotation device for the last five years, Mas Selamat is the suspected terrorist formerly known as Singapore's Most Wanted Fugitive. He triggered the biggest—and most unsuccessful—manhunt the country has ever known, generated fear throughout the nation and temporarily exposed the government to international ridicule and domestic vitriol.

Mas Selamat was a 48-year-old man with a limp.

Still, his 2008 escape from the Whitley Road Detention Centre, not far from where I once lived in Toa Payoh, was the most farcical, unintentionally hilarious, getaway since I left home at 13, vowing that my mother would never track me down, only for her to discover me by the back gate two hours later. When Mas Selamat fled on Wednesday 27 February 2008, he left an old, complacent Singapore. When he was recaptured in Johor in April 2009 by Malaysian authorities, he was later returned to a new Singapore. Political apathy was being replaced by jaded cynicism publically and a strident rebellion alliance of sorts in cyberspace. The government could no longer take the ballot box for granted:

votes had to be earned, trust was a serious bone of contention and cabinet hubris needed to be swiftly replaced by a degree of humility. Mistakes had been made and, unlike Mas Selamat, there was nowhere for ministers to hide. By the time the terror suspect was eventually thrown back across the Causeway, the landscape had changed. The man with the limp had unwittingly been one of new Singapore's chief architects. That's a remarkable legacy for a great escape that should have failed at every conceivable level.

Drawing up an outlandish escape route that had more in common with Mr Bean than Steve McQueen, Mas Selamat squeezed through a toilet. Not literally. He wasn't Ewan McGregor in *Trainspotting*. While getting ready for a family visit at the Whitley Road Detention Centre, the Indonesian-born Singaporean asked to be taken to the toilet. Once inside a cubicle, he left a tap running for 11 minutes to fool the guards outside. By the time the guards realised that if Mas Selamat wasted any more water a new agreement with Malaysia might be required, the fugitive had pulled his frame through an unsecured window, lowered and then jumped onto some toilet rolls to break his fall (my mum has always said, "If you've got to go, make sure you've got enough toilet roll before you go."), scaled a fence, hobbled across the PIE and then was spotted in a back road near MacRitchie Reservoir that led to Lorong 1 Toa Payoh. I lived in Lorong 1 Toa Payoh for years. I took that back road to get to MacRitchie many times. In most instances, the road was quiet. Had I met an escaped prisoner with a limp carrying a packet of toilet rolls, I'm sure I might have raised the alarm. Or presumed he was in desperate search for a toilet and guided him towards one with the nearest, easiest access—the one at Whitley Road Detention Centre.

I am not wishing to make light of a serious issue, obviously. Who knows what havoc an unarmed, middle-aged peg leg could wreak upon an unsuspecting community? Still, when Singapore's authorities finally realised something was afoot, the most spectacular MMS alert in multimedia history was sent to every phone in the country. The text read: "Please call 999 immediately if you see Mas Selamat bin Kastari. He is short (1.58 m tall) and limps on his left leg. Thank you." For anyone working in Singapore's security services, in any capacity, that text must have been a real dignity stripper. Had the alert described a muscular, armed brute, a tower of testosterone terror, a suspect in the shape of Schwarzenegger, then there's comfort to be had from being outfoxed by a freakish beast of such superhuman proportions. But the only people usually searching for a man who's "short … and limps on his left leg" are theatrical agents keen to book the back end of a pantomime cow.

I pity any diminutive individual who visited casualty with a leg injury from late February 2008 onwards. He must have been pounced on the moment he limped out of hospital and battered with his crutches. It is no joke. On 7 August 2008, according to reports, a man was spotted "limping like" Mas Selamat and arrested in Tanjung Pandan, Belitung, by Indonesian police. He was not Singapore's most wanted fugitive, he was a book salesman. But his arrest begged the obvious question. How exactly was he "limping like" Mas Selamat? Was he doing an impression?

If so, it was no worse than Mas Selamat's drag act. Reports claimed the escapee was aided by a family member who dressed him in a woman's *tudung*, or headscarf, and disguised him with heavy make-up. So the man suspected of plotting to bomb Changi Airport fled the country as Mrs. Doubtfire. Oh, and he swam across the Johor Straits in a "flotation device". After a nationwide lockdown at all borders and immigration checkpoints, Mrs. Doubtfire evaded the security forces of an entire country by paddling away in a rubber ring.

Naturally, I wanted to visit the northern coastline to examine this interpretation of events. The No. 975 bus dropped me at the rickety fishermen's jetty in Lim Chu Kang, leaving me with a distinctly foul, fishy odour I hadn't wafted since I had to sit next to Ashley Johnston at school. She also had a distinctly foul, fishy odour, so much so that Mr White kept the class behind one day after Ashley had gone home to explain that the poor girl suffered from a rare syndrome that made her vital organs secrete unfortunate smells. We already knew that. It was called BO. But Ashley Johnston and Lim Chu Kang shared a stench so eerily similar, I expected to find her under a straw hat on the edge of the jetty. Instead I encountered a well-weathered angler who had the appearance of man dipped in caramel.

"Er, hello, I'm looking for an old white bungalow called The Pier," I began. "I've heard it's around here."

It's true. I was. It was my secondary reason for being in Lim Chu Kang, which I will get to shortly, but I could hardly say I planned to mess about in the mangroves for a couple of hours by pretending to be an escaped prisoner fashioning a flotation device from the flotsam and jetsam.

"Yah, it's there," he said, pointing across the Johor Straits.

Not 200 metres away, the incongruous, but splendid, colonial retreat jutted out into the sea beyond the mangroves. Its unexpected presence was remarkable. The villa welcomed comparisons to Ian Fleming's Goldeneye home in Jamaica, if Goldeneye had been surrounded by rusty oil drums and stray dogs.

"Can I reach the house through the mangroves?" I asked.

"What for? It's all muddy and smelly, very hard to walk and the house is closed. Can see it from here."

"Yeah, I know, but I wanted to get a closer look. Can I cut through the mangroves?"

He eyed my white trainers and socks and smiled.

"Can, why not? Maybe you can swim back and clean your clothes."

Maybe the old prune could purchase a hat. I thanked the terrifyingly tanned fisherman, jumped off the end of the jetty and made off into Singapore's precious mangroves.

Now, mangroves are tenacious little buggers. Their trees grow where no other tree has been foolish enough to grow before. Their soil (a generous description of the salty, muddy sludge around them) is usually unstable, soft and lacking in decent oxygen. They tolerate tidal salty soakings twice a day. Then there are coastal storms, currents and rivers ferrying in silt during the monsoon season. Most trees would suffocate. Not the mangrove tree. It equips itself with a snorkel and gets on with it. Those snorkels are the roots, tens of thousands of roots, that grow upwards through the swampy ground, allowing the trees to breathe through tiny pores. Those unsightly snorkels are the collective miracle of the mangrove. And I must have tripped over every one of the fuckers.

If I wasn't stumbling, falling and swearing my way through tree roots, my feet were sinking into monstrous mud lobster mounds. The fear of the sludge sucking off one of my trainers only to find a nonplussed mud lobster hanging off a toe didn't leave me. Nor did the smell of Ashley Johnston. She was my constant companion. On the plus side, I was not short of flotation device options. If any critics remain regarding Singapore's anti-litter laws, get a tetanus shot, don a pair of surgical gloves and pick a stream in the Lim Chu Kang swamp. Bottles, buckets, chairs, clothes, slippers, crockery, cutlery, cans, tins, food cartons, oil drums, toilet seats, planks of woods, boat parts and actual boats, tyres and wheels, paint tins, fishing rods, car seats and shopping baskets were only some of the items I recognised washed up, trapped or half buried among the tree roots. If Hannibal turned up with the rest of the A-Team, a spanner and a monkey wrench, he could knock up enough flotation devices to battle the Spanish Armada. The mangroves are actually less polluted now, thanks to the heroic voluntary efforts of coastal clean-up groups. Sadly, there is still much to do. Instead of chasing pretend targets at the nearby Sungei Gedong Camp, national servicemen might spend their time more productively cleaning up their country's coastlines. At least, they'd be more familiar with the terrain when the time came to hunt down a real target.

If Mas Selamat did navigate his way through the island's northern fringes—accounts of his escape vary considerably— then he has the makings of a proficient outward bounds camp instructor. The most accomplished of eco-warriors would struggle with the hazardous tree roots, mudflats, piles of junk and mudskipper mounds under the cloak of nightfall, with or without a limp. I tried to step on the roots, using them collectively as an elevated boardwalk, but their instability had my ankles wobbling like a drunken bride in stilettos. After one particularly awkward sideways tumble, I noticed a plastic board protruding from the sludge. I pulled it from the mudflat, releasing a malodorous blast that melted my eyebrows. Crabs underneath the battered rectangular board scurried off into muddy holes, not amused that I had removed the roof from their latest seafront property. The slimy board, similar to a picnic hamper lid, was as long as my chest and marginally wider. Having gone through a few ad-hoc body-boarding lessons with an Australian mate who, between waves, had pointed out all the recent shark sightings in the area, I figured I had my improvised flotation device. Through the trees, the buildings of Johor Bahru filled the horizon. The distance seemed doable and the Straits were still. I fancied my chances, if only to flee the whiff of Ashley Johnston.

And then, unexpectedly and dramatically, my Mas Selamat expedition ended where his had started—at a toilet. I had the unstoppable urge. If only I had literally followed in the terror suspect's footsteps and set off with a packet of toilet rolls. Fortunately, I found an oval-shaped "toilet" in front of a trunk. Like an intricately woven wicker basket, the dozens of criss-crossing tree roots had created an appropriately-sized box seat about 30 centimetres above the ground. I was back on the Aussie long drop. Surrounded by leaves for the subsequent clean-up operation and a panoramic sea view to boot, the opulence almost matched Mount Faber's Jewel Box. And before anyone tuts disparagingly, my contribution to the mangrove was quickly appreciated by its resident population. I was proud to be one of the few human visitors to leave something behind in Lim Chu Kang that was actually biodegradable. I may not have followed Mas Selamat across the Causeway, but I did improvise in a toilet. Besides, when I ask Singaporeans to sum up the way authorities addressed, publicised and managed Mas Selamat's audacious escape and manhunt, the response is usually the same.

Shit.

At least now I was suitably emptied to venture further into the mangrove to find an old house that hopefully has a role to play in new Singapore.

When considering remote northern coastal locations to hunt down an improvised flotation device, the name Howard Cashin crops up. Born in Haig Road, the late lawyer was one of the colourful Cashins, an Irish family that was one of the oldest to have settled in Singapore. The Cashins went on to own 400 shophouses and several fancy homes in Grange Road, Matilda House in Punggol and the seafront villa hidden here in the Sarimbun mangroves, off Lim Chu Kang. The Cashins' grandfather made much of his money in opium farming and wisely diversified into real estate. Howard Cashin enjoyed life with his family at The Pier, his Sarimbun structure built over the mudflats to take full advantage of the breezy climes of the Johor Straits. In February 1942, the Japanese landings took place there, with the invaders engaging in a sustained battle within the grounds. After World War II, the Cashins repeatedly welcomed the late sultan of Johor, who reportedly liked to pop over for a cup of tea when time and tide were with him. Since Cashin's death in 2009, the property has remained vacant and I was eager to take a gander for a couple of reasons. First, The Pier must be one of the few remaining colonial beachfront properties in Singapore, if not the only one. And second, I admired the online dedication of the island's heritage gatekeepers, those industrious volunteers eager to sustain new Singapore's soul by infusing it with a little of the old.

However, I had to cross a stream to get there. Having snagged every tree root from the Lim Chu Kang fishing jetty, I stood beneath the obscured coastal property, which was mostly shielded by trees and fencing, presumably erected by the SLA, its new landlord. All that stopped me from savouring a rare slice of history was a litter-filled stream. I squelched along its banks, searching for an opening, a natural break, some elevated ground or a muddy path, but there were none. All I discovered was a very large, and very dead, horseshoe crab which I unintentionally flicked into the air, then screamed and performed a spontaneous Native American jig in the mud.

Finally, I found a toppled tree trunk, which erosion had kindly upended and dropped across the stream. I clambered nervously to the top, using the surrounding tree roots as the flimsiest of step ladders, adjusted my rucksack to improve balance, stretched out my arms and thought of *Man on Wire*, the Oscar-winning documentary about that French lunatic's high-wire walk between the Twin Towers of New York's World Trade Center. I was reaching for inspiration, to distract my focus away from my muddy, slimy trainers, the narrowness of the trunk and the very real possibility that one slip would send my testicles through my throat.

Despite a couple of anguished moments when I might have plummeted, ooh, at least 1.5 metres into ankle-deep water, I cleared the trunk, splashed along the riverbank, retrieved my trainer after the mudflats finally pulled it from my sock, chopped my way through some trees, pushed aside *lalang* grass taller than me and reached the fenced perimeter of one of the most stunning properties in Singapore.

And quite possibly the spookiest.

Built behind gardens bigger than my apartment, the house was situated at the end of a long, narrow pier, its tiled floor protected by a red-slate roof. The whitewashed villa stood majestically above the sea, atop girders planted deep into the mudflats. I ventured along the edge of the grounds, fighting constantly with the *lalang* grass, and picked out a balcony through the windows. The late sultan of Johor could have sipped a cup of Lipton's there before an expansive outline of his entire kingdom. No wonder he was always popping over to the Cashins to borrow a cup of sugar. There can be no other property on Singapore's mainland with a superior location, view or environment. I'd like to think that Mas Selamat agreed but there is nothing to corroborate that particular online rumour, sadly. He didn't stop by while he was on the run. Quite clearly, no one has.

The house was empty, run-down and decaying rapidly in the merciless swamp. New Singapore must restore The Pier. Whether the villa is turned into a museum to document the area's farming history and the Japanese landings or becomes an educational extension of Sungei Buloh Wetland Reserve to inform visiting schoolchildren about Lim Chu Kang's ecological value, this fragile link to old Singapore cannot be broken. Like Bukit Brown

Cemetery, The Pier has online support from engaged citizens expecting a more reciprocal relationship with their government. They need to feel anchored to the country and connected to its history. That comes about when the foundations of sites such as The Pier are literally preserved and protected.

And from the oldest to the newest, I dragged myself towards D'Kranji Farm Resort. When I suddenly appeared in Lim Chu Kang Lane 9, from the dead-end side of a one-way street, with my feet and ankles caked in mud and my arms decorated in scratches, an agricultural farmer eyed me and my bulging rucksack suspiciously, probably assuming it was filled with my wife's body parts. But after a two-hour trek that included a quick stand-up wash and a sit-down curry at Bollywood Veggies, the restaurant still boasts the best location in Singapore, I slumped over the reception counter of D'Kranji Farm Resort.

When I last lived in Singapore, this farm resort did not exist. Indeed the mere mention of such a business concept might have generated exaggerated hilarity. More often than not from the very Singaporeans who drag their unwitting children over to a working farm on the outskirts of Perth and pay the landowner for the privilege of cleaning up cowpats. I'm referring of course to the inimitable Australian farm stay, the holidaying rites of passage that many young Singaporeans are compelled to go through when their parents wake up one morning and decide that a 20-minute break from the assessment books spent at the downstairs playground does not constitute a trip to the Great Outdoors. Consequently, an all-inclusive farm stay is booked for the extended family in Western Australia on the strict proviso that Burswood Casino is no more than a taxi ride away.

And then, some bright spark adopted the casino principle of "if they're going to spend it anyway, they might as well spend it here" and established Singapore's first farm stay in 2008. Spread across a distance of six football fields, D'Kranji Farm Resort is Singapore's first $10 million gamble on agri-entertainment. Apart from the ubiquitous karaoke nights, the resort was a risky proposition because it essentially offers nothing other than silence and solitude. With villas backing onto a fruit plantation, the hideaway has more in common with the kampongs of Singapore's regional neighbours. There's really nothing to see here.

The receptionist kindly allowed me to drag my fetid, filthy frame past some of the villas, all of which appeared to have balconies backing onto herb gardens. There was a restaurant using ingredients grown on the premises, with family farm tours offered. The resort, like so many of the Kranji farms reinventing themselves as day-trip destinations, offered a temporary respite from sitting in expressway traffic, standing on buses and suffering the incessant rumbling of encroaching concrete.

The D'Kranji Farm Resort receptionist told me that most visitors are Singaporean. Perhaps it's the inexpensive convenience of a taxi ride to the country and a brief return to a treasured childhood memory. Perhaps Singaporeans want to sample agricultural life without an Aussie farmer complaining that "my sheep are about as useful as tits on a bull". (A Victorian farmer actually said this to me once at a country fair and the imagery just blew my mind.)

Either way, it's sexy. It's about as sexy as Singapore gets and I, for one, cannot get enough of it. I'm talking about Kranji Countryside repositioning itself as a green getaway destination of course, not the tits on a bull.

Eighteen

HOW suspicious do you have to look on the MRT to trigger an alarm? The question piques my curiosity every time I hear the least politically-correct message of this century. As I travelled towards Woodlands, that recorded, slightly monotone but disturbingly erotic, female voice echoed through the carriage. In clipped tones, she said, "If you should see any suspicious-looking person ... kick him in the balls and hit the alarm."

I have no idea what she actually says at the end of the message. I never hear it. I'm too busy scanning the MRT carriage, joining my fellow *kaypoh* commuters in hunting down "any suspicious-looking person". The warning is a hysterical generalisation. If a "suspicious-looking person" is someone perspiring heavily and struggling to sustain a regular breathing pattern, then that's half the carriage. These commuters will have just run up the escalators to leap through the closing doors before they sliced through one of their buttocks. I defy anyone to satisfactorily define "suspicious". Should we wrestle anyone to the ground who has a ticking sound emanating from their person? They might just be hard of hearing and in possession of a very loud watch.

Besides, I have always been a "suspicious-looking person" on trains. From the age of 11, I travelled to and from my grandad's

East London cafe every Saturday morning, knowing that I was going five stops beyond the limit of my school travel pass. From East Ham to Bromley-by-Bow on the District Line, I broke the law every Saturday morning. There was no laxative like it. I would scrutinise every passenger, looking for telltale signs that they might be undercover ticket inspectors. On the rare occasions that a ticket inspector did step into my carriage, I jumped out with all the theatricality of Indiana Jones clearing a canyon.

By the time I reached Bromley-by-Bow station, I was eligible for a "suspicious-looking person" poster campaign. My palms would be clammy and beads of sweat trickled past my ears. Back then, there were no ticket barriers, only a rotund chap squeezed into a glass booth and expected to examine the validity of dozens of train passes flashed at him simultaneously. My travel pass was always a blur. I flashed it with all the speed of David Blaine doing a card trick. But I became a victim of my own agility. I was too fast.

"Oi, hang on, mate," a more alert than usual ticket booth guy once shouted at me as I passed. "I didn't get to see that one properly."

I retreated slowly, a condemned man keeping a date with Albert Pierrepoint. I stared at the tiled floor, checking to see if I had peed on it. I raised my travel pass.

"That's not enough zones, mate," he said. "That only gets you as far as Barking. Where have you come from?"

"Dagenham Heathway," I muttered.

"You've come too far, mate. You need to give me another 30p."

That's the amount I was saving every Saturday, playing the suspicious-looking person routine at 7 a.m. But I was poor. I was cheap. I was desperate. And I could talk. Even at the age of 11, I could concoct quite a cocktail of bullshit when I combined all four.

"Well, I didn't know that. I'm only 11," I cried. "I use this pass to get to school every day. And I'm helping my old grandad in his shop, and I asked the guy at Dagenham Heathway and he said it was OK. He said my train pass was valid. I don't have any money. Look in my wallet. It's empty."

All that was missing was a string quartet.

"Ah, sounds to me like you've been led astray," replied the sympathetic ticket booth guy. "I'll let you off this time. I've a good mind to call that ticket guy. What station was it again?"

"Er, Becontree," I lied, waving my thanks, before sidestepping the drug addicts in the dimly-lit underpass and skipping off to my grandad's cafe, all at the age of 11.

As we chugged along towards Woodlands, I thought about being the most suspicious-looking person on the London Underground tube and smiled. I wiped the sweat from my brow, fiddled with my omnipresent rucksack and studied my fellow travellers carefully. Now I look like the most suspicious-looking person on the MRT.

I had certainly come a long way from those crime-ravaged adolescent years, all the way to Woodlands Waterfront Park. A train and a bendy bus took me to the northern tip of the country, where Sungei Cina meets the sea. Off Admiralty Road West, this *ulu*, or remote, spot used to be known for the old Khalsa Crescent Prison (not one for the postcards), the Senoko Power Station a little further east, a haven for heavy industry and that was about it. But the sea views and adjacent land always hinted at the area's potential. The Woodlands Waterfront Park is a step towards fulfilling it.

In May 2010, the sleepy industrial corner woke from its slumber to find a renovated 400-metre-long jetty (one of the longest in the country), landscaped gardens and a new children's playground built around a two-storey sky walk. A promenade and nature trails were added later, linking the Woodlands Waterfront to the park connectors that stretch 19 kilometres across the northern region. The jetty once served dilapidated warehouses. Now it welcomes nature trekkers, skaters, cyclists, picnickers, sky walk climbers, eco-warriors, fishermen and anyone who wants to peer across the Johor Straits and shout "referee *kayu*" (Singapore returned to the Malaysian Super League the very weekend I visited).

I scurried across the boardwalk in a futile effort to escape the cloudless coastal sunshine, nodded to a father and son fishing tag team and reached the end of the jetty. Positioned to the right of the Causeway, the jetty was built in the 1920s at one of the narrowest points along the Straits. Hotels, building and road signs, cars waiting at traffic lights and people walking along the Johor Bahru coastline were easily visible from the jetty. So close and yet so unnecessarily far, but, hey, that's Singapore and Malaysia.

I wandered around the picturesque promenade but was fighting a losing battle with sunburn so I retreated to a shaded shelter in the spiffy new playground. I admired the children clambering up the rope ladders of the sky walk, hauling themselves onto platforms some 10 metres in the air before dashing along the swaying rope bridges. I got jealous. I looked around. The insufferable heat had kept most sane families away. Just a sprinkling of kids and teenagers were hanging out, on or off the sky walk. I knew what was coming.

Seconds later, I thought I was Jack Sparrow, dragging my 37-year-old gangly frame up a wriggling rope bridge. The sky walk was open to all. At least, I think it was. I had noticed earlier on the Internet that Sembawang GRC MP Hawazi Daipi had been keen on the place when he opened the park. If MPs can climb the sky walk, it must be for grown-ups.

When I reached the top, I admired the sights of Johor Bahru, took some photographs and decided to record proof of my climb for my wife and daughter. I offered my phone to a couple of children at the other end of the rope bridge to take a photo of me but they ran away. In such moments, I curse not carrying my daughter at all times like a get-out-of-jail-free card. Who decided fun was the private property of children? I was indignant. And then I viewed myself through their eyes. I was a lone suspicious-looking person, again, in a kiddies' park handing his camera phone around. I might have run away from me too. I felt like the Gruffalo. Fortunately, some teenage Woodlanders were on hand to take some photos and I wished them well as I returned to the bus stop. I learnt a lesson at the peaceful Woodlands Waterfront that day. If I want to behave like a kid in public places, I need to be accompanied by a real one. Or become an MP.

I flagged the No. 856 bus outside Woodlands Waterfront, hurried along towards Yishun bus interchange a little further east, ducked under the elegant apartment blocks of Yishun Central and picked out the pond. Yet another of the island's water bodies has been revamped as part of the admirable ABC Waters Programme. When Yishun Town sprang up in the 1980s, the pond was created at its centre to collect storm water. Yishun Pond was about as sexy as it sounded. Then in November 2011, the pond was rejuvenated to give residents and patients of the adjacent Khoo Teck Puat Hospital (itself only officially opened in November 2010) something more invigorating. Marshlands, indigenous vegetation and nature trails leading into Yishun Park have all been added around the new centrepiece called The Spiral@Yishun. Apart from another lame marketing effort to get down with the kids by using the funky @ symbol, The Spiral was a welcoming three-storey lookout tower shaped like a butterfly and well worth the visit. I reached the top and savoured the views of the pond and Yishun, an historical, agricultural town I had rarely explored before.

And then, it pissed down.

This was not a refreshing passing shower. This was one of those ceaseless monsoonal thunderstorms that makes you want to cuddle up close with someone under a blanket, watching the hypnotic raindrops dance on the windowpane whilst sharing a marshmallow. I sat beside a damp street directory and endured an army of ants marching beneath my upper thigh and mistaking my groin for a thatched cottage. The rain kept me pinned beneath The Spiral@Yishun's third storey for two hours as water surged into the pond and even cascaded down The Spiral's staircase. Through the sheeting rain, I picked out a siege of herons lurking within the marshland's reeds, desperately seeking shelter. Strangely, I found myself singing Manfred Mann's "Pretty Flamingo" aloud (I had the lookout tower to myself so I wasn't scaring any small children).

Yishun Pond and its resident herons had transported me back to my psychedelic memories of Parsloes Park and its pink flamingos residing on a lake island. I say psychedelic because Parsloes Park was a council-managed park within Dagenham's vast housing estate on the freezing fringes of East London. Miami it was not. But there they were, in the most incongruous of settings, a flamboyance of shivering flamingos, their icepick legs threatening to slip and snap at any moment on the frozen lake as they fixed each other with bemused stares that said "We're supposed to be in the Everglades. What are we doing on a fake East London lake surrounded by Cockneys?"

I never did find out what possessed a park keeper to introduce pink flamingos to my childhood housing estate (or what he was smoking), but I'll always be grateful to him. He gave me pretty flamingos. Yishun Park has given its young ones herons, with a promise to bring hornbills back to the town. There are only 100 hornbills currently living in Singapore, with a small family living in the grounds of the Istana, and the HDB, NParks, Alexandra Health and PUB, the authorities behind Yishun Pond's makeover, have been tasked with encouraging some of these rare birds to return to a more familiar habitat created around the pond. Such exotic fauna and flora should not belong to those only living in landed properties or black-and-white bungalows in Singapore's exclusive districts. Urban youngsters growing up in housing estates deserve wildlife experiences beyond shooing away crows at hawker centres and stepping in pigeon poop. Give the kids in Yishun some hornbills to go with their herons. I had pink flamingos in Parsloes Park and I was blown away, as were the flamingos during the Dagenham winter.

The clouds finally parted long enough for me to continue my water-themed tour of northern Singapore. So I picked up my damp street directory, shook the ants from my undercarriage and set my course for Sengkang.

Returning to Sengkang for the first time since 2006, I had forgotten that the driverless LRT train has a mind of its own. It stops where it wants to stop and goes when it wants to go. The LRT is a petulant little bugger that teases its passengers. The train slows as it rolls into a station, stops at the platform and an announcement says, "This is Kupang station. If this is your stop, pick up your bags and get ready because I'm going to open the doors ... wait for it, wait for it ... No, we're off again, you dopey bastards."

If the MRT is the mother of public transport, then the LRT is the temperamental teenage offspring. I planned to get out at Kupang, the station in Anchorvale Street beside Sengkang Riverside Park. I stood like a pillock in front of the doors as they proceeded not to open. I later discovered that LRT trains skip Kupang due to the lack of development in the area. So I alighted at Thanggam, the next station, and waited for a train to take me back in the opposite direction. I sat beside a mainland Chinese construction worker on an otherwise empty platform. Half an hour later, we were still keeping each other company at an empty station out in the sticks, increasingly concerned by the other guy's motives. Finally, I read a noticeboard explaining that this particular LRT line offered only a one-way service on public holidays. As it was indeed a public holiday, I had no choice but to go full circle as the LRT gave me a tour of Sengkang's half-finished housing estates. With its forward thinking and municipal planning, Singapore is far too clever for its own good. Building stations in anticipation of future developments around the LRT is all well and good, highly commendable even. But when a train stops at a station platform, I expect the bloody doors to open.

More than 45 minutes later, I made for the exit at Farmway Station (I could have walked from Sengkang MRT, my original starting point, in less time) and pursued the shadows along Anchorvale Street. Shade is a rare commodity in Singapore's newest towns. What they lack in mature trees, they more than make up for in bright, glossy reflective concrete pavements. Even the saplings appeared to have sunstroke. When they grow, these trees will provide some welcome respite. Until then, arm yourself with sunscreen in Sengkang.

Outside the Sengkang Sports and Recreation Centre (the place provides a workout just typing its name), I chanced upon the longest queue I had seen for a McDonald's drive-thru outside of Anaheim. No McDonald's will ever out-eat that Californian joint, where non-disabled customers wait in line in motorised wheelchairs holding garden buckets for their free refills. Still, the queue at Sengkang was a fair effort, extending around the sports centre's car park. The Sengkang Riverside Park next door, on the other hand, had no queuing concerns. Disappointingly, I had the place to myself.

Sengkang Riverside Park is a tremendous feat of municipal planning, combining an essential water source with a wildlife habitat. Built beside and across Sungei Punggol, the park includes a constructed wetland of artificial marshes that filter surface run-off and waste water. So visitors get a tranquil park, mangrove birds get a new home and the aquatic, mostly native, plants get to trap and clean most of the crap heading towards the reservoir.

I zigzagged my way across the elevated platform towards the floating wetland, which was opened in November 2010. The man-made island in the middle of the reservoir had a fruity theme, which explained why I was sitting inside a giant plum, or it might have been an enormous Ribena berry. The shelter was complemented by benches shaped as sliced oranges, giving the park a trippy vibe I hadn't felt since the pink flamingos. The wetland was around half the size of a football pitch and wildlife had flocked to the place. Without really trying, I picked out half a dozen herons lurking around the 2-metre-tall reeds, a couple of kingfishers, a bird of prey circling overhead (possibly a Brahminy kite), some turtles and four brutish monitor lizards closing in on the wetland, conjuring memories of Roger Moore in *Live and Let Die*.

I unwrapped my sandwiches and peered through the air holes in the plum/Ribena berry shelter that provided a voyeuristic peep show for the nature enthusiast. A couple of metres away, a monitor lizard cruised towards an oblivious white-breasted waterhen, either looking for a bite or a very confusing mating ritual. I savoured the silence, the solitude, the shade, the scenery and, most of all, my sandwiches. I thought about old Singapore across the reservoir with its cars crawling along the concrete, air conditioners on overload, temperatures and tempers rising, all waiting to get their hands on something warm, limp and greasy from Ronald McDonald. I like this side of Singapore better. If Sengkang Riverside Park, with its emphasis on managing water sources, urban growth and native wildlife in an eye-catching fashion, is the future for this place, then count me in. Take me to the river.

Nineteen

LONG before Al Gore came along, my mother championed the environment. She had energy-saving devices in the house before they became de rigueur. She had her children. My sister and I only had to leave the living room for a sneaky chocolate biscuit in the kitchen and a maternal, protective voice would bellow, "Turn that fucking light off." No one ever said that on *An Inconvenient Truth*. I once left our well-lit bathroom, trousers around ankles, and waddled my way towards the kitchen cupboard to get a fresh toilet roll, only to return to a darkened bathroom, trip over the unsighted mat and tumble towards the bath like a penguin with happy feet. No one was spared by the resident eco-warrior. Rooms often suffered dramatic blackouts with people still in them. The eco-warrior brooked no argument in the matter.

"Who's turned the light out?" my terrified voice often echoed from the bath.

"I did," replied my stern mother. "It's wasting electricity."

"But I'm still in here reading."

"What are you reading?"

"*Adrian Mole.*"

"You've already read that book 10 times. You must think I'm made of money. This house is lit up like a bloody Christmas tree."

"But I can't see in the bath now."

"There's nothing there for you to see, believe me."

There is grainy footage from an old family home video of our family sneaking into her bedroom and switching the lights on as we all cry in unison, "Surprise! Merry Christmas!"

"Turn that fucking light off," she replies.

So my mother would speak very highly of Treelodge@ Punggol, Singapore's first public housing eco-precinct. Opened in December 2010 and home to the one millionth HDB apartment, Treelodge (I'm going with a shorter form to avoid that anal @ again) provides a sneak peek at our children's future homes, an attractive trailer of what is coming soon to a housing estate near you. The seven 16-storey blocks boast groundbreaking innovations for public housing, from centralised recycling rubbish chutes, green roof decks to cool the buildings whose north-south positioning reduces that unremitting sunshine, a jogging path, exercise stations and a children's playground made from recycled materials. My mother's spirit is even present in the guise of solar panels providing the energy to light all common areas. If only the solar panels came with a censor-activated recording that screamed, "Turn that fucking light off." My mother is available for voiceover work.

I climbed the spiral staircase and nosed around the housing estate that new Singapore built. Green overpowers the senses. From the tree-lined walkways and manicured flower beds to the ingenious vertical greenery that covers all seven blocks like an eco-friendly membrane, plants and flowers dominated in every direction. Treelodge provided a fascinating template for the rest of the island's lofty ambitions. It was a housing estate inside a garden, rather than a series of concrete blocks with a patch of grass in front. Residents are provided skinny balconies and planter boxes and encouraged to fill their nooks with something green and living. Such subtle additions beautify the entire complex, adding a Hulk-like skin that does anything but make the visitor angry.

Indeed, there was a discernible kampong feel about the place. I visited on the eve of Chinese New Year and there was a barbecue taking place on the void deck. There was an obvious bond between residents. Punggol is a new town still lacking a major shopping centre and enough schools (both are being built) and is tucked away in the remote rural northeast corner of the country. Punggol people, however, make a very deliberate lifestyle choice. Treelodge residents live there for specific reasons, the right reasons.

Residents like the incomparable Woolee. I stood at the lift lobby reading the posters about the twin chute system when I sensed a middle-aged Chinese man beside me, beaming proudly.

"It's good, right?" he said, nodding towards the information panel about the recycling chute.

"I think it's absolutely fantastic," I replied honestly.

For five years in Australia, I emptied bottles, removed their lids and rinsed them before allocating them to the right dustbin (a green one for garden cuttings, yellow for recyclables and red for regular refuse). Our neighbours were often treated to me shouting, "Our bloody daughter has put her shitty nappy in the recycling bin again." But if I could do that, Singaporeans can easily separate waste from recycling. If ever a country needed to minimise its reliance on landfill, it's the Little Red Dot.

"Come, come, I show you," Woolee cried, suddenly leading me by the arm across the void deck. I had never been invited by a stranger to visit a rubbish chute before. It was a novel experience.

Woolee demonstrated how each chute worked, pointing out which was for waste and which was for recycling. He even went as far as to pull open the chute door and mime throwing in a bag of invisible rubbish. He invited me to take a photo and I gladly accepted his offer.

I took several photographs of a rubbish chute.

"So why are you so interested in Treelodge@Punggol?" he asked, eyeing me curiously.

"Oh, I'm just fascinated by the concept," I replied.

"Really, ah? You want to buy a place here."

"I'm interested sure, but Treelodge only opened in 2010 so I've got to wait five years for the resale flats. Can I ask what sort of price they were?"

"I think one was snapped up recently for $550,000, overlooking the waterway."

"Wow, 550 is not too bad," I replied optimistically. "That's reasonable considering the crazy property prices."

"Hey, they bought it for 550. I buy an apartment at 550, what for I sell it to you for 550? No point, right? I'll sell it for much more than 550."

I was tickled that not everything had changed at Treelodge@ Punggol.

"But do the apartments really save much water?"

"Come, I'll show you."

And with that, Woolee ushered me into the lift and towards his apartment. Being invited into a male stranger's home, moments after meeting him, was not a typical occurrence. I kept my hand in my pocket, my thumb hovering over the call button just in case Woolee opened the door to a bearded chap called Bub and ordered him to bring out the gimp.

Instead, the door opened to reveal a living room full of Chinese people happily preparing for their reunion dinner. Their generous welcome was humbling, particularly after Woolee's unexpected introduction.

"Hello, this is Neil," he said warmly. "I'm going to show him my bathroom."

With unmistakable pride, Woolee guided me through each of

his modern, spacious rooms packed with energy-saving devices. From his daughter's bedroom window, he pointed out the site of the future primary school and the Johor Straits peeking through in the distance. Through another window, he directed me towards the solar panels sitting snugly on the roof, surrounded by greenery. My host ended his tour in the bathroom, where he exhibited the most bizarre toilet outside of Japan. There was a small sink built into the top of a cistern with a single tap on the right. When he flushed the toilet, water also poured through the tap on top and Woolee washed his hands.

"You see, it saves water," he said, clearly as impressed with the green technology as I was. "Before the water flushes through the bowl, some of it comes through this tap. No need to use more water washing hands in the other sink afterwards."

With 712 units in Treelodge, the water savings from this quirky feature alone must be staggering. Take that, Malaysia.

I wished Woolee's family a prosperous Lunar New Year but he insisted on taking me to the next destination, My Waterway@Punggol, which faced Treelodge on the other side of Punggol Drive.

"The waterway is really beautiful," said Woolee. "But you will not see many Singaporeans now. We come out at dusk. Only *ang mohs* like this time of day, right? Don't get burnt."

Considerate to the last, Woolee was a lovely man living in a lovely home and one of the first Singaporeans to truly benefit from the concept of a city in a garden. He has found a green niche to call his own. Treelodge@Punggol was a pilot project, but one that successfully proved that urban growth need not be detrimental to its environment. Every Singaporean deserves a home like Woolee's. I want a home like Woolee's. Aside from its sustainability, that toilet-tap contraption could keep me occupied for hours.

I was rapidly falling for Punggol. Everything was right about My Waterway@Punggol, or the Punggol Waterway (it's neater and I'm not compelled to smash the @ key on the laptop). Calling it the Venice of Punggol is a bit of a stretch, but the scenic reservoir is worth every one of its $225 million. Just think about this for a moment. In the 1990s, the Punggol 21 project was launched to create a self-sustaining waterfront town but the Asian financial crisis checked its momentum. Rather than retreat, the plan was revisited and upgraded to Punggol 21 Plus when the economy recovered. A pipeline was required to connect the Punggol and Serangoon reservoirs. Old Singapore might have knocked up something functional and formulaic, heavy on concrete and low on colour. But the decision was taken for the sleepy village to be turned into a wide-awake water town with Singapore's longest man-made waterway—4.2 kilometres long— as its centrepiece. Three years later, the waterway opened in November 2011. This is no lazy *longkang*. There are five bridges, cycling paths, kayaking outlets, a children's free water splash park, historical trails and a landscaped park running the length of the waterway, which is bordered, of course, by water-purifying plants to filter rainfall before it is discharged into the reservoir.

I was staggered by its foresight and the overriding fact that the waterway was such a damn fine family-friendly park. Plus, the Punggol Waterway was a brilliant bus stop. I crossed Kelong Bridge, its stilt structures a nod to the town's heritage as a fishing village, and sat at a bus stop from old Punggol Road. A new bridge link was built across the waterway to join Punggol Road but the developers retained a portion of the old track within the park complete with bus stop. I love kitschy stuff like that. I sat down and waited for a couple of amblers, a father and son, to approach, whereupon I asked what time the next bus was coming. I said I had been waiting for an hour. I perfected my confused, puzzled stare as they explained matters. I did enjoy myself.

Not far from where I sat, a 7-metre crocodile had been spotted in the Punggol swamp in 1960, according to a *Straits Times* report, three times the length of the estuarine croc I had tracked down in Sungei Buloh Nature Reserve six years ago. The eyewitness's name was not mentioned but he broke the national 100-metre record the same day.

I followed the meandering waterway, nodding to cyclists and sidestepping children on scooters, and realised I was beginning to envy the residents. Some 21,000 public and private homes will rise up along the waterfront and by the time I had reached the children's water play area, I was ready to see show flats. Instead, I jealously watched children running in and out of the fountains and soaking themselves. I was itching to peel off my clammy clothes, run through the cooling fountains and shoot the kids with the water cannons. But my access-all-areas pass, my daughter, wasn't with me and I suspected that I was already on wanted posters around Woodlands Waterfront Park after my sky walk so I trudged on, read the superb heritage murals at Heartwave Wall and then decided to do a little trespassing to reach the island that made Punggol Waterway possible.

Passengers on the No. 84 loop service feel isolated if they are not holding something tall and erect between their legs. The bus to Punggol Point is the fisherman's charter. I was the only one on board without a fishing rod. I was also the only passenger who alighted at the penultimate bus stop. The street directory indicated a Punggol Track 22, but when the dust from the departing bus had settled, I was alone in front of a closed-off muddy path blocked by a barrier. Still, I presumed that was to keep out vehicles so I happily ducked underneath a Keep Out sign and sampled a little of Punggol's rural farming past.

With dusk approaching, the swampy setting proved unsettling. Established trees on both sides of the boggy track afforded the farms on my left some privacy, but they also blocked out the sunlight. Every movement in the long grass had me twitching. Ordinarily, the rare sight of a purple heron rising from a stream beside me and soaring effortlessly for the treetops would have been something to savour. Instead, I found myself producing that sudden yelping noise a small dog makes when you accidentally tread on it.

I hurried ahead and stumbled upon an empty construction site. Large muscular vehicles surrounded me, and the diggers and trucks left tilted atop piles of sand and the area's desolation left me feeling strangely lonely. Finally, I reached a clearing and found what I was looking for—the dam that joined the mainland to Coney Island (or Pulau Serangoon). By damming Sungei Punggol near Marina Country Club and Sungei Serangoon at Coney Island, Singapore created two new reservoirs in July 2011. The island's 16th and 17th reservoirs are linked by the Punggol Waterway that I had just left. These two reservoirs alone will supply 5 per cent of Singapore's water needs. Honestly, if there were another country that took such a profound long-term view of supplementing the supplies in its larder ... well, there isn't, is there?

I planned to break into Coney Island. Fishermen do it all the time. The 45-hectare island is a popular hideaway for intrepid anglers, but one not without risk. In November 2011, lightning struck two fishermen on Coney Island, killing one and severely injuring the other. Clouds loomed overhead, but not enough to pose a threat. Aside from a couple of guys playing with their fishing rods on the Punggol side, I was alone and quickly jogged across the dam. I was greeted by a perimeter fence with barbed wire on top and an SLA warning against trespassing that was too prominent to ignore, even for me. I contemplated a hole in the fence by my feet and had crouched down to gauge its width when a stray dog bolted through and almost sent me into the reservoir. I gave the female stray a wide berth for fear of stumbling upon any pups and losing several toes. A month before I visited, a 20-year-old female jogger was attacked by a pack of nine stray dogs at Punggol Waterway. She barely had time for a tetanus shot before hysterical letter writers and blog posters were demanding death to all dogs. On this tour of Singapore's quirkier corners, I have learnt to walk slowly in the opposite direction. Run away in a frenzied fashion and they will give chase and clamp onto anything dangly. Just leave them be. The dogs were there first.

Having wisely decided not to break in and enter Coney Island and disturb its wolf packs, my day was just about done. I made for the usually dull, dozing Punggol Point. But the old fishing jetty wasn't sleeping, she was alive and kicking. The northeastern point had been sharpened in my absence, the park packed with picnickers, fishing families and cyclists. It was like stumbling upon an old folks' home and finding all the residents twisting their melons to hip hop, swigging cider and groping each other on the sofa.

I had inadvertently discovered the new Punggol Promenade, a 4.9-kilometre-long waterfront trail that started at Sengkang Riverside Park. I had come full circle. Punggol Point Park itself had only opened in November 2011. With a new viewing deck and children's playground, the area was crammed with picnic mats. I peered over the spruced-up jetty and it was almost reassuring to note that the sea remained appallingly polluted, the one constant from my last visit. The sun was setting and the sky glowed in glorious pinks and purples as children ran alongside dogs on the beach while their parents poured out drinks beneath the viewing deck. I was rather thirsty myself and realised I had no change for the vending machine on the promenade.

"Excuse me, do you have change for \$2?" I asked a Malay family stretched out across various blankets in front of the police post. "The vending machine only takes coins."

"Yeah, sure, no problem," said an uncle. "But I don't think the machine is working."

He was right. The machine rejected my coins. Someone touched me on the shoulder. A young policeman had ventured from his post.

"Ah, the machine's not working yet, sir," he said, emphasising the bleeding obvious, no doubt while a dozen illegal immigrants snuck into the country over his shoulder.

"Oh well, looks like I'll be going thirsty until I get back to Punggol," I replied.

I was heading for the bus stop when the police officer called me back.

"The family wants to speak to you," he said, pointing to the picnickers who had changed my \$2 note.

A cross-legged sixty-something Malay auntie waved me over.

"Come here," she said.

She opened a cool box and handed me a can of Coke.

"Take, take," she ordered.

"No, please, there's no need, thanks anyway," I mumbled.

She brushed aside my garbled mutterings with an indifferent wave and returned to serving up food for her family.

"Ah, just take, lah."

"Well, please let me pay you at least."

"It's \$2," shouted the uncle who had just given me change.

Everyone laughed. I giggled and raised the can of Coke, acknowledging my gratitude. The uncle winked back at me.

No drink had ever tasted better.

Twenty

BUYING or hiring bikes has always had its problems. When I was 13, I agreed to buy a Muddyfox mountain bike from an East End drug dealer who occasionally popped into my family's cafe to steal the spoons. When it comes to buying bicycles, drug dealers are seldom considered the go-to people. No one in Singapore ever says, "Oh, you want a new bike for your daughter? No, forget the shops in East Coast Road. I must give you the number of this drug dealer I know."

But I was poor. He was cheap. I needed a bike and agreed to buy his Muddyfox (a trendy brand when I was a teenager), unseen, for £60. He believed that I was good for the money. It's always comforting to have one's honesty validated by a drug dealer. When the cafe had closed one Saturday, I waited expectantly with my uncle for my new purchase to be pedalled along Gillender Street. With the sun reflecting gloriously off Canary Wharf in the background, two silhouettes headed towards us pushing ... something. The drug dealer had brought a friend along, equally scrawny, equally pasty-faced, equally unscrupulous, and the pair of them presented me with my Muddyfox bicycle. Had they handed me an actual muddy fox, I could not have been more underwhelmed. The reason they pushed the bike, rather than pedalled it, was immediately obvious. The bike's rusty frame had long lost the strength to bear the weight of anyone old enough or smart enough to write their own name (which possibly spared the drug dealers). A cheap can of black spray paint had been applied recently, but randomly, covering the chain, the wheels and spokes, in an improvised effort to mask the bike's decrepit state while the tyres clearly belonged to another bike (and probably had done a day earlier).

"There you go, one Muddyfox," said the cheery drug dealer. "That'll be 60 quid then, mate."

I peered across at my uncle uneasily.

"Er, it's not really in the best condition," I mumbled.

"But it's a Muddyfox, mate," he continued, even more upbeat.

"Where exactly? It just looks like a spray-painted old bike."

"Nah, mate. I wouldn't mess you about. That's a Muddyfox frame. That's a 350 quid frame easy."

Eager to own a Muddyfox bike and knowing I lacked the financial means to buy a new one, I accepted and my uncle kindly loaned me the money. (He didn't ask me to pay it back. He knew I'd been lumbered with a heap. Still, I hope he doesn't read this and tap me for £60 now.) I spent weeks and all of my part-time earnings returning the wreck to a roadworthy state. No sooner had I restored the bike, someone climbed over our back fence and nicked it. The Muddyfox was stolen under the cloak of darkness, which made sense. No one would have gone near the bloody thing in daylight.

And I now required pedal power to explore new terrain in Tampines, preferably without the assistance of a drug dealer.

I crossed Tampines Avenue 7 and poked my head in the bicycle hire kiosk in front of Sunplaza Park. A helpful woman pointed me towards some bikes. They were rusty and they were too small. I could hear my uncle's wallet faintly squealing.

"That bike is too small for me, surely," I queried, staring down at the standard-sized bike frame.

"No, no, it's OK, come, see," the woman insisted, calling her repairs guy to adjust the frame to suit my long frame. He raised the seat so high I risked looking like a clown on a unicycle. With an oily spanner in hand, he gestured for me to test the circus vehicle. The seat was indeed just about high enough from the ground, but I was elevated so far above the rest of the bicycle that I expected passers-by to throw me some skittles to start juggling.

"See, it's OK, right? That bike fits," said the proprietor triumphantly. "Actually these bikes can buy, if you want, second-hand, only $60."

I gave the bike a polite examination, picking at the rust on the handlebars with my fingers.

"This bike is not made by Muddyfox, is it?"

"Muddy who?"

"It doesn't matter ... No, I have a bike. I'll just take this one to get around Tampines for now."

With my gangly frame balanced precariously on the ridiculously raised seat, I pedalled slowly through the welcome drizzle of the quiet Sunplaza Park as I made my way towards the Tampines Mountain Biking Trail. To my surprise, I had to sign in with a security guy to use the trail, giving my name, contact details and the time I arrived. A rugged course for the reckless rider surely beckoned at the Tampines Mountain Biking Trail, a mighty mountain for the muscular biker.

It was a hillock.

Or perhaps even a grassy knoll. Either way, it was obviously man-made, manufactured, manicured and micro-managed in that uniquely Singaporean way. There were popular biking courses near my Geelong home within the quite wonderful

You Yangs mountain range, where *Mad Max*, *Ghost Rider* and *The Pacific* were filmed. Course rules and regulations usually consisted of a park ranger pointing to the Flinders Peak summit of the You Yangs and saying, "That's the top. When you get there ... cycle to the bottom again. Is that too complicated for a Pom?"

At the Tampines Hillock Biking Trail, on the other hand, there was a long-winded list of dos, don'ts, definitely-do-nots and expect-to-die-if-you-dos. There were 21 trails, colour coded to indicate their level of difficulty, with marvellous extravagant names like Sideways, Cadaver and Slingshot. It all sounded rather X Games until I glimpsed the highest point of the trail. My daughter has rolled down steeper grassy inclines at public parks.

Still, Tampines offered the island a mountain biking trail more than it did the last time I lived here. The trail has been around for enthusiasts since around 2008, if not earlier, but was extensively improved in early 2010, with a BMX dirt track added next door for the Youth Olympic Games held in August 2010. It was better than nothing. And the track exceeded my cynical expectations. Aware of my rusty circus bike's limitations, I meandered along a green trail for beginners, which was flat and had some traction. It was called the Bunny Loop. Flanked by trees and cooled by the drizzle, I essentially pedalled around the outside perimeter of the entire course, a sensible introduction, but I fancied something tougher and moved inwards and upwards via the blue square trails. These blue bad boys combined steep slopes, narrow tracks and poor traction. They certainly got the blood pumping, not to mention the sphincter.

I took out Deep Purple, The Eel and Sideways before having a crack at the Upper Hamburger. The muddy paths were little wider than my tyres, bordered by jagged rocks that my cheap hired bike was ill-equipped to handle. I left the path on more than one occasion, finding myself in a muddy ditch or long grass.

But I never left the bike. I was proud of maintaining that idiotic tradition. As I struggled to stay with the narrow, sludgy zigzags of the Upper Hamburger trail, I thought of my younger self trying to stay with gravity behind the Dagenham Heathway shopping mall. There was a long, steady descent from the mall beside the public footpath, which offered BMX bandits both a shortcut and an adrenaline rush. It gave me neither. As my friends successfully navigated the slope, my pedals got away from my feet. As I slalomed my way between trees like an Olympic skier, I left the shopping centre, flew through council estate streets for the next five miles, ran over dogs and sent dithering old ladies into their shopping trolleys. But I never left the bike.

I wasn't in a hurry to leave the biking trail. I bounced around, on and off rocks, paths, trenches, ditches and divots for at least an hour. The track was no mountain but it was no molehill either, and Singapore's older towns need such quirky outdoor diversions. Space may not always permit, but Tampines is proving to be something of an environmental pioneer in its ability to incorporate new interactive spaces within its already bustling borders. Sengkang and Punggol have an easier task. They have carte blanche. Entire eco-friendly, sustainable towns can mushroom around new waterways. But Tampines is providing solutions for a more intriguing dilemma for new Singapore—finding ways to sex up an older estate.

The Tampines Mountain Biking Trail provided the workout. Tampines Eco Green provided the warm-down. Just the other side of Tampines Avenue 12, the Eco Green was opened in April 2011 and is another of those enterprising environmental projects often rewarded with a shrug. So rather than explain what it is, I'll point out where it is. To the north of Tampines Eco Green are more than 30 apartment blocks nestled around Paris Ris Drive 1. To the northeast lie at least another 50 blocks while the housing estates around Tampines Avenue 9 dominate to the south. Beyond the biking trail in the west are the heavy industries and retail giants around Tampines Link. At the quiet centre of all that lot is a non-intrusive 36.5-hectare park showcasing the natural habitats of secondary rainforest, freshwater ponds and marshes, which have encouraged more than 70 bird species and other wildlife to the park. Wildlife is protected, nothing is lit after dark, the park furniture is recycled and, best of all, the eco-toilet is a close cousin of the Aussie long drop. All of this is across the road, literally, from tens of thousands of families and apartments.

Existing spaces are being turned green in new Singapore. When I last returned to my childhood town of Dagenham, former green spaces at the end of streets and terraced rows had been turned into one- and two-bedroomed apartments. When I was young, those greens were invaluable. They provided boys with a venue to kiss girls. If a Dagenham guy wants to get it on now, he's got to buy a two-bedroomed apartment first (which is what Singaporean guys have been doing for years). The roles have reversed. The sex-starved have nowhere to go in Dagenham (and yet, strangely, those pregnancy rates refuse to stagnate) while couples now have Tampines Eco Green. Singapore's government will stop at nothing to massage those fertility figures.

But will Singaporeans be trusted to use the place responsibly when they get there? I meandered along the immaculate grassy path, the lawn resplendent in the light rain and stopped by a noticeboard that had 12 do-not signs. Tampines Eco Green is a park. It isn't skydiving over the Grand Canyon. Yet NParks folks are compelled to reinforce 12 do-nots, including the insistence on no bird tapping, with an illustration of a brutish, muscular fist squeezing the life out of a startled sparrow. I was sincerely flattered that NParks assumed I possessed the speed, fitness and dexterity required to catch a kingfisher with my bare hands whilst riding a rusty circus bike with its razor-like seat wedged up my arse, but it was never going to happen.

The issue of trust remains a sticking point in new Singapore. Like the permanently closed Toa Payoh Viewing Tower, public facilities and attractions are built for residents, but they are not always accompanied with a sincere belief that they will be used sensibly. If Australians should be proud of anything, it's their stunning state and national parks. Many happy weekends were spent with our baby daughter strapped to my chest as we hiked, climbed and explored our way across as many of them as possible. A single park ranger often managed territories capable of swallowing Singapore and Johor whole. Some parks had no toilets, not even an Aussie long drop, and one or two had no dustbins. Yet the parks and forests were mostly spotless, with few of those anal do-not signs. They were not required. Common sense sufficed. In Singapore, those signs typify the socio-political chicken and egg conundrum. Are the signs there because Singaporeans need to be spoon-fed? Or are Singaporeans spoon-fed because those signs have always been there? Either way, there remains a distinct lack of public ownership in places like Tampines Eco Green.

At one of the freshwater ponds, I picked out a Brahminy kite on a tree branch. When I visited the Ocean Grove Nature Reserve in Victoria, which shares a similar habitat to Tampines Eco Green, I stumbled upon my first wild echidna. For those of you who have yet to see one of only two egg-laying mammals (monotremes) on the planet, the echidna is possibly the daftest-looking creature in Australia (where there is stiff competition). The echidna belongs in a kindergarten arts and craft session, with its plasticine nose and cute furry ball covered in hand-painted straws. When I spotted the fuzz ball, it did that idiotic freezing thing where it thought, Ssh, if I keep really still, he will not see me looking like a curled-up tribal headdress. I will cease to be visible.

Two distinct groups had made it possible for me to see an echidna up close there and a Brahminy kite here. The Ocean Grove Nature Reserve was the handiwork of independent nature lovers, a group of like-minded residents who came together to provide a green corridor for native wildlife whose native woodland was being bulldozed for housing estates. That was over 40 years ago. Today, the reserve's quaint visitor centre is still manned by volunteers. Tampines Eco Green was conceptualised, devised, landscaped and managed by the government but has yet to fully capture the public imagination.

Perhaps the park needs a McDonald's.

Twenty-one

TIME and low tide wait for no man. I had just over two hours. I had my three-year-old daughter with me. I had no choice. I made a rash and impulsive decision. She was coming with me to Chek Jawa. Chek Jawa is the rocky shore off the southeastern corner of Pulau Ubin, which is off the northeast coast of Singapore. I had just collected her from school near Haig Road, which is off Mountbatten Road in the east, which is not near Chek Jawa. I checked the time. It was already 3.35 p.m. Low tide at Chek Jawa was at 6 p.m., when it would be around 0.5 metres, the ideal height for spotting marine life. I picked up my oblivious little girl and quickened my step towards Mountbatten Road. We needed to be at Changi Point Ferry Terminal further north within 30 minutes to have a realistic shot at catching a bumboat to power father and daughter across Serangoon Harbour, rent a bicycle with a child seat on the back at Pulau Ubin Main Jetty, somehow navigate our way through the unfamiliar jungle terrain and beat the tide off Chek Jawa.

"We're going on a boat adventure," I cried, clutching my daughter to my chest as I trotted along the pavement, frantically flagging approaching taxis and perspiring heavily. "You're going to be Dora and I'm going to be that Boots. Are we ready? Right, *vamanos!*"

"No, Daddy, you know you can't be Boots," she sighed. "You're not a monkey."

She's at that age.

I hailed a taxi, threw in my rucksack, bundled my startled daughter into the back seat and buckled the seatbelt across the both of us.

"Changi Point Ferry Terminal," I mumbled, as we pulled away.

"Ah, Bedok, sure, no problem," replied the chirpy taxi driver.

"No, no, Changi Point Ferry Terminal, beside Changi Village. We want to get a bumboat."

The taxi driver peered at the clock on her dashboard and then up at me in the rear-view mirror.

"You go Pulau Ubin now?" she queried. "It's quite late, no?"

"Daddy, Daddy ..." my little one suddenly interjected.

I raised my forefinger to my lips.

"Not now, just wait, I'm talking to the taxi driver ... Yes, I've got to do some work on the island so I thought I'd take my daughter along. Let her explore the forest."

"Wah, you're a good father, ah," she beamed back at me through the rear-view mirror.

"Daddy, Daddy ..." my daughter continued, tapping me continuously on the forearm.

"Yes, what is it?"

"The taxi driver's not a man, Daddy," she whispered conspiratorially. "The taxi driver is a woman. Is that OK, Daddy?"

"It's fine, just relax. We're on an island adventure."

"You said it was a boat adventure."

"OK, it's a boat adventure first. Then it's an island adventure."

"Daddy, I need to do a wee wee."

We had turned into Tanjong Katong Road. The slip road to the ECP was ahead. My daughter would never hold out along the ECP.

"Sorry, can you pull over, please," I exclaimed. "My daughter needs to pee urgently."

Convinced she was one of the Dukes of Hazzard, the taxi driver screeched across two lanes and slammed on the brakes just metres before Amber Road, allowing me to tumble out of the taxi and position my daughter behind a tree.

Along Changi Coast Road, she had to go again. This never happens on *Dora the Explorer*. We pulled over beside Changi Airport's perimeter fence and she sprinkled the grass in front of a No Trespassing sign at the entrance of a military building. My girl knows how to mark her territory. As we crouched together in front of a military zone, she grinned up at me.

"Daddy, I won't do any more wee wees until we get to the island, OK?"

She lasted as long as Changi Point Ferry Terminal. After a third pee in half an hour and a quick call to book a doctor's appointment for the cascading kid, we waited only five minutes for a bumboat. Thanks to a family of six and the commonsensical approach of the boat's skipper, who was supposed to wait for 12 passengers before departing but had accepted that was unlikely to happen at 4 p.m. and was at least guaranteed a packed charter on his return trip, we were soon bouncing up and down on a blue paint-chipped wooden box seat across Serangoon Harbour.

My daughter's wide-eyed, infectious enthusiasm reminded me what a quaint journey the bumboat provides. Only 10 minutes long, the trip offered fine views of the Changi coastline and passed those gargantuan container vessels. ("It's the Madagascar ship! It's the Madagascar ship! Where's Gloria the Hippo?" my daughter shouted at the confused bumboat driver, whose gap-toothed smile accentuated his sun-ravaged, craggy features.) Most of all, the ride was fun, cheap and real. The bumboat costs $2.50 per person. A two-minute ride on a plastic cartoon character inside a shopping mall, rocking backwards and forwards with all the dramatic dynamism of my nan in an armchair, costs $2. My daughter enjoys those rides, too. But she adored the bumboat.

We arrived at Pulau Ubin Main Jetty and the old spring in the step returned. Returning to the island is always invigorating. Pulau Ubin continues to resist the call of the concrete. Its villagers and its biggest supporters are united in their efforts to keep the kampongs and preserve a fortress of solitude away from the superhuman heroics across the harbour. They can still be cheeky buggers when an *ang moh* enquires about hiring a bike.

"That's six dollars," the young, smiley Chinese guy said.

I giggled. I loved the impudence.

"Come on, ah, you think I got 'tourist' stamped on my forehead, is it?" I replied. "I know I got the backpack, but I'm not a backpacker. I live over there. I want the bike for less than two hours."

"Ok lah, five dollars, because I got to give you the bike with the child seat."

He gave me a photocopied map of the island, without being asked, and pencilled in the route to Chek Jawa. Tarmac roads covered only half the journey. The remote forest in the east had only gravel paths and dirt tracks, some with steep inclines. I admired the sensitive desire to protect the fragile ecosystems and keep human encroachment to a minimum, but I knew the clock was ticking and I wasn't particularly enamoured by the prospect of transporting my little Cleopatra up a rocky, muddy unstable hill.

Still, my blissfully ignorant daughter was eager for the jungle stage of the adventure. (Every adventure must consist of three stages and the jungle was stage two. She constantly chanted, "Boat ... jungle ... Chek Jawa ... boat, jungle, Chek Jawa ..." from the back seat, which will mean nothing to anyone who hasn't seen

Dora the Explorer. Judging by the puzzled looks of villagers, they hadn't seen *Dora the Explorer*.) I pedalled quickly along Jalan Ubin and Jalan Durian (terrific road names), the tyres taking advantage of the tarmac as we pointed out some parakeets in the trees and played animal-spotting games. We even sang songs aloud as we passed locals who waved back. It was glorious.

The hills almost beat me. On two occasions, my skinny calves revolted and I was forced to get off the bike, bend my knees, crouch over the handlebars and push my little girl over the bumpy terrain and deeper into the jungle. I sensed her anxiety. Just an hour earlier, she had left school and skipped out into a familiar world of tarmac, tower blocks and traffic. Like all children, she takes comfort in routine. And now she was being pulled up an uneven slope by her panting father beneath a jungle canopy that was blocking out much of the daylight and making scurrying, scampering, rustling noises in every direction. That made me nervous. She is encouraged to be as independent, resourceful and outdoorsy as possible, particularly in safe, secure and often cosseted Singapore. But as we plunged further into an isolated forest that I had never visited before, let alone with my little one, a thought danced around my dizzying, sweat-drenched head. Had I gone too far with a three-year-old girl?

When a snorting wild boar blocked our path, I suspected that I might have.

The image was dreamy, unreal. It was not possible. I squeezed the brakes slowly and quietly. The hefty creature stood 10 metres away, sniffing the air in our general direction, but otherwise ignoring us. I had seen wild boars before on Pulau Ubin, but never this close and certainly never in the company of my daughter. Paternal instincts kicked in so quickly, they alarmed me. I was terrified. There was precious cargo on board. My straddled legs took a couple of backward waddling steps to ease away from the animal. It glimpsed over at the noise. It was about a metre in length, a greyish brown and obviously well fed. Being late afternoon, it was foraging for food. I had no intention of disturbing its dinner, not with my daughter behind me. Most boars on Ubin are used to human interaction, but if they feel threatened, they can charge. That has never happened on *Dora the Explorer* either.

Eventually, the boar strolled lazily to the other side of the path and continued to scavenge for scraps in the undergrowth. That was my cue. Steering the bike towards the opposite side of the path, I pedalled slowly towards the native mammal. If we kept our heads down and our mouths shut, we would soon be at the Chek Jawa ranger station and laughing about the unexpected twist in the adventure. We approached the wild boar. My daughter passed within a couple of metres of Babe's big brother. Just a few seconds more. We were almost clear.

"Oh, look, Daddy, a warthog, a warthog. See Daddy, a warthog."

My daughter started jabbing a finger excitedly at the animal, which was now peering up at her.

"Look, Daddy, a warthog, a warthog," she shouted. "Pumbaa, Pumbaa, *Lion King*, *Lion King*."

"Ssh, be quiet, mate," I whispered frantically. "You've got to stop talking now."

"It's a warthog, Daddy. Look! A warthog, a warthog," she shouted. "Stop! Have a look! It's a warthog."

"It's not a warthog," I hissed desperately. "It's a wild boar and we don't want to upset it so can you please just be quiet until we get right past it."

"It is a warthog," she cried.

"All right, all right, it's a fucking warthog. Please, stop talking."

There was a brief silence.

"Daddy ... Mummy says you're not to say that word, Daddy. That's a naughty word."

"Sorry, you're right. I shouldn't say that word. I'm really sorry. But let's just keep quiet. I don't want to disturb the wild boar."

"It's a warthog."

"All right, all right, it's a bloody warthog then."

"Daddy ..."

"Yes, I know, I can't say that word either. I'm sorry. Right, we've passed the ... animal ... let's go. Hold on really tight."

As the wild boar moved away from the roadside, adrenalin took hold and I raced towards the Chek Jawa ranger station. The bike stands were a blur. So was the gate that I sped through, along with the sign above the gate that insisted that all vehicles had to be left outside the gate. I hurtled down the path and reached the ranger station.

"Hey, hello, you cannot bring your bike in here," the two park rangers behind the counter chorused in unison.

I unbuckled my daughter and dumped her on a bench with a bottle of Yakult and dropped the map and rucksack beside her. My heart was pounding. She, on the other hand, had never looked happier.

"Do you think that was a mummy or a daddy warthog?" she asked between slurps.

"Er, I'm not really sure. Wild boars are usually boys, but then ..."

"Excuse me, you can't bring your bike in here," the two park rangers chorused again.

I had forgotten about them. I nodded my apologies, opened a bag of crisps, threw them at my delighted daughter who started to devour them gleefully, ordered her to wait on the bench, pedalled furiously back to a bike stand, padlocked the wheel, sprinted back to my little one, slumped beside her on the bench and stole a gulp from her Yakult bottle. I checked the time. It was

4.40 p.m. I had collected her from school only 70 minutes earlier. She finished her drink and I almost lost a finger when I prevented her from shovelling another handful of crisps into her mouth, but we were ready. It was time to see what new Singapore had done with Chek Jawa.

The belated discovery and preservation of Chek Jawa is a familiar, but fabulous, story worth recounting briefly. In some respects, the beginnings of new Singapore were unearthed at the hidden cape of Pulau Ubin, with an active citizenry rousing and organising itself to take ownership of the threatened area and a softer government acceding to conservationists' requests. Ultimately, Chek Jawa is a story of hope, in which environment trumped economy and the simple needs of a natural beauty were placed above the greedy demands of an urban brute. After nature enthusiasts recognised that the unique rugged wetlands had so many largely undisturbed ecosystems in one small area—sandy beach, rocky beach, seagrass lagoon, coral rubble, mangroves and coastal forest—the government agreed to defer land reclamation plans in December 2001. Chek Jawa was spared, in the short term. The 10-year deferment means the bulldozers could now muscle their way through the mangroves at any time, but there are no reports yet of a blueprint to batter the rich biodiversity. Watch this space and pray.

Call me naively optimistic but I believe new Singapore's intervention in 2007 just might have spared Chek Jawa. Nature lovers had been visiting the treasure trove on an ad-hoc basis since 2001, but in July 2007 the country made a firm commitment to the forest's future. The secrets of the six major habitats were made more accessible to the public with little harm done to their residents' homeland. A visitor centre, a viewing jetty, a 21-metre-tall tower above the coastal canopy and, best of all, a 1-kilometre-long boardwalk that includes mangrove and coastal loops allowed visitors to conduct their own DIY wildlife tours without disturbing the inhabitants. The mangroves had their mudskippers, hornbills hovered around the forest, crabs scuttled out of rocky and sandy shore crevices, sea cucumbers and squids hung out at the seagrass lagoon and octopuses could be spotted among the coral rubble, all under the boardwalk, down by the sea. But the tide had to be right. Anything around 0.5 metres was ideal. We were an hour away from that height but the water level was close enough and low enough to see marine life.

Having been cooped up, strapped in and bounced around the child seat above my back tyre, my little tyke savoured her newfound freedom, tearing off down the coastal boardwalk like Bindi Irwin.

"Look, a big black bird," she cried, stopping suddenly to point at the distant seabed exposed by the low tide.

It was a purple heron, next to some egrets, but I was pleased with her eagerness to continue the animal-spotting game after the close encounter with Pumbaa on the path earlier. Further along the boardwalk, we were treated to a fine performance from an orchestra of hundreds of orange-and-white fiddler crabs, each playing its larger claw like a Stradivarius (hence the nickname). People pay a fortune to witness the millions of red crabs on Christmas Island and we had a sandy carpet of fiddlers below us. I'm not pretending the fiddler crabs of Chek Jawa are a natural wonder to rival the annual red crab migration on Christmas Island, but they are well worth the $2.50 bumboat fare.

The same could be said for the mighty mudskippers and monitor lizards sunning themselves in mudflat puddles and on the rocks. Spotting wildlife ensconced cosily in their natural habitat was ridiculously easy. The Mangrove Boardwalk was almost the Night Safari, except it was natural, cheaper and there wasn't a tour party from China shoving cameras against my ear to get a closer shot of something blurred.

I then spotted an awed little girl staring up at the inviting Jejawi Tower. The 21-metre structure obviously provided an incomparable viewing platform, but it was seven storeys up and away from us.

"Let's go to the top, Daddy," she said cheerily, already heading for the first steps.

"I can't, mate. I've still got to cycle back and it's getting late," I replied in vain.

"It's OK, Daddy," cried my fast-disappearing daughter. "I'll climb the stairs myself."

I craned my head back to take in the tower's height. It was far too dangerous for a three-year-old, even one who had turned into Bear Grylls in the previous hour. I sighed, wiped my brow, fished her into my arms and carried her 21 metres to the top. The climb was exhausting, but the view exhilarating. I plopped the little one onto a bench, shared out some crisps, sweeties and blackcurrant juice (unhealthy, I know, but she had been bounced around forest tracks, bypassed wild boars and dragged through mangroves, so she deserved a break). I peered over the platform fence just as a chatter of parakeets soared above the trees beneath me. With dusk sneaking upon us, a red hue hung in the air, the spangles gliding lightly along the sea surface like a concert pianist's fingers. Some yachts dotted the horizon off Changi Sailing Club in the distance while herons and egrets continued to peck at the mudflats in the foreground. From my breezy vantage point, I surveyed Serangoon Harbour, the mangroves under my feet and the forest canopy behind me. I savoured the stillness. The place was just about perfect. Chek Jawa need never change. I smiled at my daughter as she counted out her sweeties into two piles: one for her, one for her Daddy. Soppily, I grabbed her suddenly and kissed her on the cheek. Such moments are so rare.

"Hey, Daddy," she said, smiling back at me, her blue eyes sparkling. "I need to do a wee wee."

But it didn't matter. The ride back to Pulau Ubin Main Jetty was more enjoyable for both of us. Time was on our side. I had made low tide. She had an empty bladder. Plus the return journey was more downhill than up, so I pedalled slowly (ride that brake carefully coming back from Chek Jawa, especially with children on board). We cruised past the splendid Petai Quarry, slowed down in Jalan Sam Heng to gawp at long-tailed macaques, the first wild monkeys my daughter had ever seen, and even picked out two more wild boars through the trees with more confidence.

We returned the bike and I carried my sleepy girl out to the jetty to wait for the bumboat home. The time was 6 p.m. Our adventure had taken just two and a half hours. To keep her awake and stop her from lying beside the dozing feral dogs on the jetty's concrete floor, we summarised our whirlwind trip to Singapore's protected piece of rural paradise.

"So, let's remember what we did," I said enthusiastically. "We took a taxi, then a fast boat and then a bicycle right into the forest, all the way out to sea, and how many animals were there?"

"Three warthogs, two big lizards, lots of mudskippers and orange-and-white crabs, big birds, some butterflies and two monkeys," she said matter-of-factly.

"That's amazing. What was your favourite bit? Was it the big wild boar, I mean warthog, in the road? Was it climbing to the top of the tower? Was it the monkeys? Or was it going really fast on the boat? What did you like best of all?"

She sat up suddenly.

"The sweeties," she said.

Twenty-two

I STOLE a peek at the CCTV camera. I knew they were watching me. They were following my every move. They had to be. I was standing at the entrance to their private, exclusive fortress, taking notes, snapping photographs and eyeing the building. I was most conspicuous. Blue-collar workers passed me in Changi North Crescent, dashing off into the SATS Inflight Catering Centre next door to pack airline meals. Others waited sleepily at the bus stop for the loop service back to Tampines. Meanwhile I continued to examine the deliberately nondescript building, its design, architecture and interiors tailored for new Singapore's specifications. A crane, raised 30 metres in the air, gently eased a crate across the roof. The building's rectangular facade, set back 50 metres from the main road and hidden behind a green fence, was shielded further by eco-friendly brown slats, making the building resemble a huge patio door blind. The drapes kept out the sun. They also kept out prying eyes. Vertical greenery undoubtedly appeased environmental crusaders but they really provided another layer of privacy. There were no discernible windows, not from the street at least. Like detectives behind a one-way mirror in an interrogation room, they see whatever they want. You see only what you're allowed to see.

The sign at the entrance deliberately revealed nothing: The Singapore FreePort. There was a red-and-white, whirly, globe-shaped logo above the name, which again gave little away, quite purposefully. I peered down to the car park up ahead. There were barriers between us, clearly manned by people sitting in front of TV screens, presumably wondering what the note-taking *ang moh* was doing.

I wanted more. I found a number that I had scribbled down in my notepad earlier and thought, Sod it, let's go into the art-collecting business. My nerves jangled as the phone trilled.

"Yes, hello," a polite, well-spoken voice answered.

"Ah, yes, hello, is that The Singapore FreePort?" I stammered.

"Yes, how can I help?"

"Ah, well, the thing is, I was recommended your place by a friend. I have some artworks."

"I see, well maybe you could send us an email at this address, and we can answer your queries."

"Yeah, I could do that ... argh, bloody hell, hang on, argh."

I was covered in red ants, the nippy little bastards. I had leant against a tree, grateful for its shade as I rested one hand on the trunk and held the phone in the other. The biting blighters had marched along my outstretched arm, led their army through my sagging polo shirt sleeve and pitched camp beneath the rainforest under my armpit. One or two had already made it across to my chest, gnawing their way through my nipples when I started a spontaneous jig to shake the buggers off.

"Hello, are you still there?"

I had forgotten about the phone call.

"Yes, I'm still here ... argh ... sorry about that," I said breathlessly through gritted teeth, jumping up and down and slapping my nipples. I looked like a cult. Or something like a cult anyway.

"OK, yes, well, if you'd like to send us an email, then I'm sure we can ..."

"Argh ... Only the thing is ... get off ... I'm an Englishman, you can probably tell from my accent ... shoo, shoo ... and I've actually come down to have a look at the place for myself. Just to see the location ... argh."

"Yes. I can see you."

That stopped me in my tribal ritualistic tracks. He could see me jiggling and flicking away at my body parts in a frenzied state of arousal that might have been giving the wrong impression from 50 metres away.

"You can see me," I muttered rhetorically.

"Yes. You had better come inside."

The barrier magically raised itself. Fort Knox for the fabulously rich had allowed me onto its property. With a dry throat, I nervously set foot on a new Singapore road paved with gold bullion.

If The Singapore FreePort belonged in a movie, *Ocean's Eleven* might have robbed it by now. New Singapore makes no secret of its ambitions to stash the cash of the world's richest, through property and retail investments. Now it wants their knick-knacks, those little keepsakes lying around. You know, Van Goghs, gold bars, things like that. The Singapore FreePort represents the island's plans to carry on where Switzerland has left off. With those pesky European Union regulators insisting on greater banking transparency, Swiss authorities are under pressure to expose tax cheats. No questions asked in Switzerland became some questions asked. As many Europeans faced unprecedented austerity measures, it seemed only fair that the continent's wealthiest pay a little more tax for the Rembrandts, right? No, sod that, they chorused. Isn't there somewhere else to park the paintings, the vintage cars and the cigars, like a

Switzerland of Asia? Somewhere quiet, discreet, peaceful, with a stable government, low taxes and a compliant population that isn't likely to start with all that protesting malarkey and maybe rob our Rembrandts? Changi seemed like the perfect location. It was even beside a golf course. Hence, The Singapore FreePort was born.

In 2010, the largest safety deposit box in the world opened in its own duty-free zone next to Changi Airport. Wealthy art collectors who treasure discretion almost as much as their own anonymity can sell, view or buy pieces with a level of privacy that is breathtaking (and bloody insulting to the average punter who has to travel in and out of the country the conventional way). Interested parties are whisked from the runway in waiting limousines the moment the wheels of their private jets have bitten into the tarmac. Accompanied with a glass of something fizzy and expensive, they are ushered through the CIP (that's "commercially important person", no, I'm not joking) Terminal into The Singapore FreePort to admire their options in private viewing areas, all stored at tax-free rates of course, and can then complete a purchase in a separate meeting room before being driven back to their waiting jets. No questions asked. It's as though they have never been here, just as they desire. I cannot pick up a DVD in Johor Bahru without going through the rigmarole of immigration and customs at Woodlands but an overseas oligarch can pick up a Picasso without setting foot on a travelator and suffering that interminable muzak.

The old oligarch doesn't even have to tell the wives that he's picked up a Picasso. Tenants at The Singapore FreePort register goods with customs by general category only. They just report "a painting". Whether it's the *Mona Lisa* or one of my daughter's finger paintings, the same category applies. The same privacy is guaranteed. Not surprisingly, Goldfinger would need more than

Pussy Galore to get into this place. Swiss engineers and security experts took care of the vaults, which are protected by seven-metric-ton steel doors, and armed guards are provided on request. Getting inside requires scanners, checks and searches of *Mission Impossible* proportions. I had earlier tried to visit with a respected art dealer but the restrictions were too stringent. No expense had been spared to offer the international mega-wealthy peace, protection, privacy and efficiency to store their Jackson Pollock.

Do think about that, Singaporean residents, when you next find yourself queuing at customs to return to your own country.

Still, never mind the Pollocks, I had to convince the management that I was an art dealer. I removed my baseball cap, rather theatrically, and smiled up at the CCTV camera, suggesting, I think, an aura of confidence and innocence. They do this sort of thing in the movies. As I approached slowly along the drive, running over what I might say, I peered across at the FreePort building on my left but there was nothing to see. It was impenetrable, no windows, no gaps, slits or slats to steal a peek. Van Gogh's ear might have been hanging on a wall. No one from the outside world was seeing it.

Two gentlemen in suits appeared. One led his younger colleague, checking his hair and tie as he approached, exuding efficiency. The very attributes that a prospective art expert like me would thoroughly appreciate. I had to get my story straight. I figured on the truth. An undercover investigative journalist once told me that the truth is the safest fallback when you know you're lying.

"Hi there, thanks for meeting me," I said, shaking hands with the two chaps.

"My colleague tells me you might be interested in storing some artworks," said the manager, slipping into charming business mode so quickly and smoothly that I almost missed it. "Do you have paintings?"

"Not really, paintings. No, more classic, rare movie art," I replied truthfully. "I've got some pop culture pieces that need looking after."

I was referring, of course, to my framed Star Wars wallpaper, original and in mint condition, and my limited edition Italian Stallion boxing robe from *Rocky*, complete with matching shorts. My house can go before those two prized possessions.

"Yes, I'm sure we can help with that," the manager said, eyeing me favourably.

I was wearing shorts, but they were complemented by a Batam-bought Ralph Lauren polo shirt. The attire tried to say "just stepped off a yacht" rather than "just stepped in cat shit", which is what my clothing choices usually scream at people. But the white face-Ralph Lauren combination is the right one for new Singapore. The West's wealthiest are most welcome to dump their baubles and bits and bobs here; the seven-metric-ton steel door is always open for the elites of the East, too. (This multicultural country does not discriminate. There are only two classes of people considered in Singapore: those with money and those without.) My wallet had five bucks in it, but my white face and the little horsey man on my left nipple suggested otherwise.

"All you have to do is email me at this address," said the manager, a thoroughly decent Singaporean chap I might add, as I now feel guilty for pulling his leg. "Include all your details, how many pieces, their rough size and so on and we'll work something out."

"So you can't let me inside to have a look around?"

He grinned at me. I had overreached, but our smiles acknowledged that it had been worth a shot.

"No, I don't think so, sir," he added swiftly, already shaking my hand. "I look forward to hearing from you."

I was brushed off and buttered up at the same time. I promised to be in touch, pulled my cap back on tightly—still in character as the shadowy art collector desperate to remain incognito—and returned to the bus stop, once the two men were no longer watching me. I'm sure no one buys a Monet at The Singapore FreePort and then carries the painting under their arm on a bus bound for Tampines.

The bus stop was packed. A shift had ended at the SATS Inflight Catering Centre. I watched as more tired workers trudged towards the bus stop and examined the neighbouring buildings. Both had private road access to Changi Airport at the back of their properties. Vans will use that road to carry airline meals; limousines will carry Van Goghs. The same road, serving two distinct worlds. Separated only by a perimeter fence, they will never meet. That's new Singapore for many of its residents. The two employees at FreePort were warm and courteous. They made me feel important, that I had a chance to belong at some point.

But I was never allowed inside.

So I took the short bus ride along Upper Changi Road East, stumbled along the insufferably long and unshaded Koh Sek Lim Road and kept a date at a new Singapore destination that is open to all.

"Ah, there you are, we were about to call you," replied the sweet guide. "OK, now that we are all here, we can begin the tour. Welcome to NEWater Visitor Centre."

Back in 2003, Uncle Leslie, my indefatigable book distributor, handed me a bottle of water during a Kinokuniya launch and encouraged me to take a swig. The audience laughed. The bottle contained the recently-launched NEWater, or recycled water. I really didn't see what the fuss was about. My instinctive trust told me that the water had already passed every safety test. Common sense made it so, right? Not in Australia, it didn't. In July 2006, with the world watching, residents of the Queensland city of Toowoomba rejected a water recycling scheme in a poll (the city voted 62 per cent against recycling 25 per cent of its water from its own sewage). Fear and yuck factors put paid to the laudable scheme. No one wanted to drink their own pee. And the city's indigenous name of Toowoomba offered too many ways to rhyme with "poo" to make the idea palatable. Still, imagine the billboard slogans at the city's entrance: Welcome to Toowoomba. You're in Shit Creek.

Of course, the short-sighted doom merchants caused carnage, leaving behind a panic-stricken, misinformed city still devastated by drought. Six years on, Toowoomba dams were full and ratepayers were funding an almost A$200 million pipeline to move the liquid gold around. But at some point, it will stop raining again in Australia.

Singapore is not prepared to take such chances. In 1974, the year in which I was born, PUB designed a pilot plant to turn used water into potable water. By the turn of the century, technology had reached the stage to make production costs affordable. Today, there are four NEWater plants, the latest opened in Changi in May 2010.

I was at the Bedok plant to understand how Singapore leads the world in providing 30 per cent of its total demand from recycled water. I had earlier signed up for the tour via the NEWater Visitor Centre website (available to all—school parties, families and casual visitors like myself—free of charge) and joined the group in a plush auditorium for a short film. Yes, it banged the government drum, but the movie made no idle boasts. With no natural aquifers or groundwater, Singapore is labelled a "water-scarce country" by the United Nations. Through its "four national taps"—local catchment, imported water, recycled water (NEWater) and desalinated water—the country makes do.

Putting it into perspective, the lovely tour guide described how Singapore had so little water during the famous drought of 1963 that the government turned the taps off for 12 hours every day. Not a drip came out for half a day. Singaporeans will not go back. Nor will they be bent over a water barrel by the resource-rich Malaysians and handed the Vaseline. I admire that can-do spirit more than I can possibly tell you.

The tour was surprisingly engrossing. I didn't get the science jokes. I was the only non-Indian MBA student in the party so the gags about osmosis sailed over my head. But I got how clean the water is. That point was rammed home repeatedly. There are four processes (ultra infiltration, reverse osmosis, ultra violet disinfection and water conditioning to adjust the pH level) but the water already passes every safety and security test after the first two. In fact, the water is too clean. Everything is scrubbed away, including the minerals, which is why NEWater is mostly used for non-potable applications in heavy industry and in air-conditioning cooling towers in commercial buildings. Think about Singapore. Think about the air conditioning. Think about the water involved. Most of it is recycled. Think about how much natural drinking water is saved.

According to the World Health Organization and UNICEF, some 884 million people—one in eight of the world's population—lack access to safe drinking water. At the same time, water use has increased by more than twice the rate of the world's population growth in the last 100 years. While most countries treat their natural resources like a *tai tai* treats her handbags, Singapore is getting its house in order. I'm not even Singaporean but my pride swelled as I followed the guide around the visitor centre as she explained the cleaning processes. By the time I reached the exit, I struggled to stop myself entertaining the MBA students with a quick burst of "Majulah Singapura".

Feeling euphoric, I nipped across town to Bedok Reservoir Park. I fancied kayaking in a dusky setting and possibly a zip through the aerial course at Forest Adventure, which opened in 2007. With its trapezes, bridges, ladders and enormous zip lines, the offerings at Forest Adventure reminded me of a childhood TV programme called *The Krypton Factor*, which has left me disturbingly obsessed with flying foxes and zip lines ever since (contestants always finished their assault course with one). Both kayaking on and zipping over the reservoir is all part of new Singapore's quest for residents to take public ownership of their water supply. I visited on a Monday. Both were closed on Monday. Do not go on a Monday.

As I wandered around the scenic reservoir, I noticed the deep water warning signs and thought about death. Seven people have been found dead in the reservoir since mid-2011. The reservoir is particularly deep, with a maximum depth of more than 18 metres, and I was struck by how accessible, serene and picturesque the body of water was, giving the area an unfortunate romanticism. There have been understandable calls for fences. But fences alter only the venue, not the state of mind. Economic and educational pressures are inescapable in new Singapore. Students work too hard. Their parents work too hard. With few carrots dangled, the constant stick of cheaper foreign labour looms overhead. Almost everyone I know in Singapore, without exception, works too hard, counterproductively so at times. Still, on a brighter note, the government was quick to allay public concerns in November 2011 that the safety of drinking water had not been compromised after the tragic deaths at the reservoir. We must never lose sight of our priorities.

Like the dusky weather, Bedok Reservoir was leaving me rather gloomy which was hardly the fault of the beautiful, family-friendly park. Thankfully, the Berlin Wall cheered me up. I have been treated to some surprising discoveries in new Singapore but being confronted by the Berlin Wall beside Bedok Reservoir took my breath away. I had not expected to come across a part of the Berlin Wall in one of Singapore's older housing estates. Why would I? But there it was in all its glory. I spotted a smallish black sculpture and read the inscription that explained about the donation in 2010. In my idiotic ignorance, I initially thought that the sculpture was the Berlin Wall and anal administrators had carved it into a daft post-modern shape and spray-painted it black. My poison pen was poised, ready to castigate bureaucratic buffoonery once more when I spotted a sizeable grey block covered with graffiti and encased in a glass exhibit. That was the Berlin Wall.

I peered up at the four blocks of concrete, joined together by an artwork called *Kings of Freedom*. It was painted by German graffiti artist Dennis Kaun and depicted two kings, one with his eyes open to change, the other blindfolded to the wishes of his people. The four blocks once formed part of 45,000 separate blocks joined together between 1975 and 1980. The slabs were 3.6 metres tall, 1.2 metres wide and the artwork terrific. I just stared. I had never seen a piece of the Berlin Wall before. I lived in Europe until I was 21—well, England, but it was almost the same thing—and I needed to come to Bedok to see a piece of the Berlin Wall.

The glass case was a sensible move. Like those heroic German "wall peckers" of 1989, I might have returned later with a penknife. Coming face to face with the Berlin Wall was just like coming foot to turf with the Wembley Stadium pitch when I was 11. On a school trip, we were given a tour of the football venue and we deliberately scuffed our shoes along the touchline, desperate for as much mud to stick to our soles as possible. My piece of Wembley turf stayed with me for about a month until I trod in dog's crap playing football with Duke, our pet Dobermann, in the back garden. The shoes had to be cleaned. I didn't talk to Duke for weeks.

Twenty-three

A PRODUCER for Channel NewsAsia called. She was making a documentary about post-general election Singapore. In a nutshell, they were looking for a new Singapore, or a "new normal" Singapore to borrow the nauseating buzzwords of the day. They sought my views on the general mood towards foreigners and planned to film me at my workplace going about my duties.

"So how do you spend your working day?" the producer asked.

"Most of the time at home banging away on a laptop," I replied, as the producer pictured a pervert.

"And when you're not at the laptop?" she enquired.

"I'm usually out on the road, notepad in hand," I said, far too proudly.

"I see. Is there nothing else that you do?"

The dramatic silence was punctured by a thousand *kiasu* voices in my head, all screaming, "You're a writer, ah? But what do you *really* do?"

I now add that I'm also a part-time property agent. This seems to make them feel better.

But as luck would have it, I had just left the Berlin Wall and was ready to cross the divide. I was off to a political hotbed where residents had made international headlines. For the first time, they had elected an opposition party in a group representation constituency (GRC). New Singapore would not just be casinos and theme parks, the political landscape had also changed.

I was headed for Aljunied.

The documentary crew directed me towards a bench in Hougang Central in front of the Aljunied-Hougang Town Council. On a wall behind, the sign and logo of the town council glowed above my head like a halo. The cameraman noticed an unsightly dustbin propped against the wall over my shoulder. His framing suggested that the dustbin was coming out of my ear so he pushed it out of shot.

"Action!" he called.

"Wait," a voice cried.

A cleaner appeared from nowhere and started sweeping furiously, removing litter that had accumulated behind the dustbin.

"Cannot have that on camera," the cleaner said.

Intrigued, I wandered over to the Chinese uncle and asked why he needed to tidy up.

"Must clean, lah," he said. "Cannot make this place look bad, right?"

My cynicism turned me into Jason Bourne.

"Who sent you?" I asked.

"Wha'?" he replied, confused.

"Who sent you?" I repeated, peeking up at the town council windows.

"No one, lah," he insisted.

I was not satisfied. In Singapore, someone is always sent from somewhere. It's the old queen gag. Why does Queen Elizabeth II think the world smells of fresh paint? Because some lackey is always going crazy with a brush and a tin of whitewash just in front of her. The same applies to Singaporean ministers.

If you fancy a unique trip to a hawker centre toilet when each cubicle does not look like the previous occupant emptied his bowels blindfolded, go during a community event involving a ministerial guest. The transformation is bewildering. Urinals gleam, basins sparkle and the only oblong-like objects left behind in the cubicles are additional loo rolls. At all other times, of course, bribing or maiming is required to procure three sheets of toilet paper.

So I was convinced that the Workers' Party (WP), the opposition now in control of the town council, had sent down the cleaner. The new guys had inherited the old guys' penchant for carefully controlled events topped off with a superficial sheen.

Or what my mother has always called "top show".

"Quick, tidy up the place," she'd shout down the phone at my young self. "We've got family coming around tonight."

"OK, mum," I'd reply, ever the filial son. "But is it a proper tidy-up or a top show tidy-up?"

"Nah, it's all right. It's only the cousins. Top show will do. Just do the usual. Throw all the disposable razors under the bathroom sink and no more craps until after they've gone."

After the Channel NewsAsia crew left, I was still curious. I had to know whether the cleaner was part of a proper tidy-up or a cynical top show tidy-up. I took the stairs to the second floor. The walls had been recently painted. Aha. The town council reception had also been renovated, with new worktops, partitions and that bright fluorescent lighting popular at dentists. The receptionist smiled.

"Hi, this will sound strange, but did you send a cleaner downstairs just now?" I asked.

"I'm sorry?"

Her face answered on her behalf. She was not in on my conspiracy theory.

"I just did this TV interview and a guy cleaned up around us. I wondered if the town council sent him down."

"No, I didn't know you were filming downstairs."

The press relations officer had no idea either. Pride rather than a paymaster had compelled the cleaner to spruce up the home of Singapore's major political opposition. He was proud. Many residents in Aljunied are. They have put their HDB upgrading where their money is. History is theirs, but only for now. It can soon become an historical footnote, an asterisk at the end of a page. Making history of any kind is not without risk. There are always drawbacks.

I stood before one of the drawbacks. It was an empty field beside Hougang Central. At face value, the boggy lawn said nothing. Under the surface, the roots of new Singapore are more fragile. In June 2011, this particular site, along with 25 others used mostly for community activities, was excluded from the Aljunied-Hougang Town Council. The HDB, the landowner, had leased the sites to the People's Association (PA). Before the general election, these sites had been managed by Aljunied Town Council when the town council was controlled by the PAP. Many of the sites are prime locations for grassroots events. In August 2011, the PA told Aljunied-Hougang Town Council Chairman Sylvia Lim that bookings by the Workers' Party, which now controls the town constituency remember, would not be allowed. A gloomy picture had been painted soon after the heady days of change. The news was unfortunate for the residents of Aljunied. Most of all, it was highly ironic.

By any yardstick, a key issue in new Singapore is inclusiveness. Some Singaporeans feel neglected in their own country, overlooked by their own political representatives, brushed aside in the race to bring in more foreign workers and remain economically competitive. These are valid concerns. They are some of the reasons why Aljunied became the first GRC to slip from the government's grasp since the GRC scheme was introduced in 1988. Singaporeans, all Singaporeans, merely asked to be involved again. If Aljunied MPs cannot hold grassroots events for their own residents in their own constituency, how will the locals feel included?

The perceived pettiness was undignified, and perhaps even unnecessary. Apart from the no-longer-open spaces, little else had really changed in Hougang and why should it? VCD shops still promoted three for ten special offers, with those alarming low budget karaoke videos showing singers crooning in front of waterfalls. Lift lobbies displayed the usual warning posters about not feeding birds or cats. There was even a wonderfully terrifying poster for killer litter. In red bold letters, the poster read: DEATH FROM ABOVE, HIGHRISE LITTER CAN KILL. The words were accompanied by a smiling resident dropping a plant pot, a broom, a hammer, a mop and bucket, a sheet and a coat hanger onto an unsuspecting victim below. Litter killers do nothing by half in Aljunied.

I needed to go higher. Hougang Avenue 4 divides the government and the opposition, with the WP's GRC of Aljunied on one side and the PAP's Ang Mo Kio GRC on the other. Depending on one's point of view, each side represents either old or new Singapore. The symbolism was too surreal to miss. I took a side turning beside the Hougang Swimming Complex and stumbled upon an illicit gambling den. Half a dozen aunties sat around a stone table at the void deck playing mahjong. A bubbly uncle patrolled behind them carrying a fistful of dollars. They spoke quickly in dialect, presumably Teochew, but I had no real clue.

"Er, hello, *knee how*," I stammered.

No one was interested in the tall white guy standing beside their table. They were playing mahjong.

"Yah," said Clint Eastwood with his fistful of dollars.

"Is this estate, er, PAP or is it Workers' Party?" I asked, to confused silence. "Is this Lee Hsien Loong or Low Thia Khiang?"

More silence. I took a stab at Mandarin. It might have been less painful had I stabbed myself.

"Er, *wo yao* Low Thia Khiang," I said.

Clint Eastwood smirked. The aunties were horrified. They had misunderstood my intentions. I pointed to the floor and then gestured towards the HDB block above me.

"No, no, no. Er, this Lee Hsien Loong HDB. *Wo yao* Low Thia Khiang HDB."

Losing patience, Clint's hand gestures and smattering of Singlish suggested that he was explaining to me that neither Lee Hsien Loong nor Low Thia Khiang lived in an HDB block here.

I bid them a fond farewell. They didn't care. I loved them for it.

In the end, a laundrette came to my rescue. I crossed Hougang Avenue 4 and enquired about the respective constituencies. The auntie generously gave me her time, directing me to the street and pointing at the junction's traffic lights.

"That one over there PAP, Lee Hsien Loong," she said, pointing towards Clint Eastwood's HDB block.

I hope the prime minister is aware that the auntie mafia is managing an illegal gambling den in his constituency.

"But we are Workers' Party. We are the opposition," she continued.

"Have things changed?" I enquired.

"Change how? Please lah, nothing change," she laughed. "It's no different."

I took a lift to the 10th floor of Block 501 in Hougang Avenue 4 and surveyed the political divide. Of course the woman was right. Discernible differences were negligible. This was not

Potong Pasir, a single member constituency that had once been an opposition stronghold for many years and where I once lived. The checklist that came with voting for the opposition—a lack of upgrading, lifts that did not take aunties to every floor and so forth—was easy to tick off in the late 1990s.

There was only one subtle difference between the two constituencies in Hougang. On the government side of the road, I spotted residents heading into the Hougang Sports and Recreation Centre. Next door was the Hougang Swimming Complex and beside that was Hougang Stadium. That was all on the government side. On the opposition side of the road, there was a grass field.

I sincerely hope elected members get to use that one at least.

In the evening, I loitered around the void deck of Block 173 in Bedok Reservoir Road looking for Low Thia Khiang. I was stalking the guy. The Workers' Party MP, vice-chairman of Aljunied-Hougang Town Council, Teochew titan and long-time symbolic figure for the political opposition was holding a meet-the-people session. Well, he would have been if I had observed the dates properly. He conducted sessions on the second and fourth Wednesday of every month. I had picked the wrong Wednesday. I stopped some teenagers sitting at the void deck playing with their phones.

"Hey, do you know if Low Thia Khiang is holding his meet-the-people session here?" I enquired.

"Don't know," said a teenager, continuing to play Angry Birds.

"Still, it must be cool to live here in Singapore's first ever opposition GRC, right?" I probed, desperate to glean something other than tips on how to catapult a squawking chicken into a load of crates.

He shrugged his shoulders.

"Does it feel any different since the election here?" I tried again, obviously overplaying my hand.

Suspicious, the teenager peered over his phone. He saw the notepad in my pocket.

"Same, same," he replied quickly. "It's all the same, nothing different, nothing different."

I checked over both shoulders to make sure no one from the PAP was taking photographs with a long lens. It might be a new day in Aljunied, but it still feels a lot like old Singapore on the ground.

Unperturbed, I wasn't leaving Aljunied GRC without witnessing a little grassroots action. I cut through Bedok Town Park and spotted a hand-painted dustbin in the darkness. Crude but colourful, the normally dull green plastic had been covered with Singapore's cheesiest landmarks, including the cable car and Merlion. It was street art Singaporean style: neat, nationalistic and controlled. But it was an improvement.

A young Malay couple, holding hands, crossed the footbridge over the PIE and headed my way. They would know.

"Excuse me, this will be a strange question," I began, "but are all the dustbins in the park painted like this one?"

"Yah," said the teenage girl, her toothpaste smile beaming back at me.

"Really? I think it's terrific. Is it an opposition thing? You know, a town council thing, because I've not seen it anywhere else in Singapore?"

"Yah," she repeated, strangely unmoved by my patter about painted dustbins.

"Are all the dustbins in Bedok Park painted like this one?"

"Yah."

"Are you just saying 'yah' to everything I say?"

"Yah."

The couple giggled and went on their way, keen to lose the world's most boring man. I followed the path for a while and the next couple of bins were decorated with hand-painted Merlions, but I stopped when I realised I was staring at dustbins in the dark and scaring joggers. (I later found some painted dustbins in government constituencies, too. The initiative deserves to go national.)

A little later, I reached Bedok North Avenue 1 where people were gathering beneath Block 550. Clearly, the meet-the-people session with Aljunied MP Muhamad Faisal bin Abdul Manap was in full swing. I tried my luck again with a guy walking my way.

"Excuse me, am I in Aljunied GRC?" I asked, feigning my best ignorance. "Is this the opposition's GRC?"

"Yeah, this is it," he replied, smiling.

"Ah, good, I wanted to have a look around. You seem quite happy about it."

He nodded and smirked.

"It was time," he said simply.

"You felt it was time for a change then?" I enquired, rather transparently trying to push buttons.

He put his hand to his mouth

"Yeah, I voted for the opposition," he mumbled.

Bedok North Avenue 1 was nigh on deserted. And still, the opposition voter felt compelled to put his hand over his mouth, presumably for the benefit of the Internal Security Department lip readers sitting at a nearby coffee shop table.

"You voted for the opposition?" I asked.

"Yeah, I did," he clarified.

I had heard him the first time. I just wanted to see if he cupped a hand around his mouth again. He did.

"And nothing's really changed, has it?"

"No, of course not. What did people think was going to happen? It's so funny," the guy said, still smiling. He glimpsed over at the residents waiting in line at the void deck of Block 550.

"Well, that's changed. Look at everyone sitting outside sweating. Under the PAP, they had their meet-the-people sessions in the air con. Now they have to wait outside in the heat."

He was right. I crossed over and watched the elderly fanning themselves as they sat on plastic chairs and watched videos on a cheap TV and DVD player to pass the time waiting to see Aljunied MP Muhamad Faisal bin Abdul Manap. They did not look particularly comfortable. No one complained. When the government ran the Aljunied show, residents used to chat with their local MP at the other end of the void deck inside the Kaki Bukit Park Residents' Committee Centre next door. I wandered over. It was closed. Residents' committees in Singapore were initially set up in 1978 to encourage greater neighbourly interaction and preserve the increasingly elusive kampong spirit. Volunteers mostly help out at the residents' committees to organise programmes, activities and events for those living in the area. One might assume a meet-the-people session with the local MP comes under one of those categories.

Residents' committees fall under the purview of the PA.

Ah.

So residents are being made to sweat, literally, each time they meet their Workers' Party representative. That's not making voters repent. That's like kindergarten kids squabbling over crayons.

Most of all, it's redundant. On foot, I ambled around Hougang, Bedok Reservoir and Bedok North and saw no bolt of lightning. No one was struck down. The cat got the tongue when the eye caught the notepad occasionally. Other than that, life chugged along in Singapore's first opposition GRC as it always has done. With the landmark general election less than a year old, physical differences were impossible to spot. Indeed the housing estates around Bedok Reservoir had obviously been upgraded and their gardens and playgrounds relandscaped, presumably by the previous town council before the election, and yet the voters still got rid of the incumbents.

As I wandered around the elderly and young families waiting in line to chat with their MP, I thought about that voter's comments.

It was time.

New Singapore's changing political landscape is in the mind of a growing number of residents. There is a growing restlessness, an impatience for new policy, a growing coffee shop culture quick to *tekan*, or whack, the government at every opportunity. There is a slow but gradual demand for change from the bottom up. But I wonder what kind of change new Singaporeans really want. What is it time for? Is this about Martin Luther King or Marlon Brando in *The Wild One*? If there is a growing acceptance that Singapore's labour and human rights issues are a cause for embarrassment—and they are—when it comes to the elderly, foreign workers, domestic helpers and homosexuals, then count me in. But if there is a desire to follow Brando and rebel for the sake of rebelling, then I have reservations. What are the protest votes really protesting against? By all means, *tekan* the government for making aunties clean hawker centres into their eighties and for tolerating the rampant property speculation that has made it so difficult for young couples to get onto the first rung of the ladder. I'm not so sure a government deserves to be toppled because of a few MRT breakdowns. If that happened in Australia and the UK, governments would be booted out once a fortnight.

There is always a bigger picture. Mine was painted by a couple of muggings in London, a burglary in Liverpool, a deranged home invader in Manchester, a friend's violent death in an Essex nightclub and a once proud hometown fraying at the seams and edging closer to economic irrelevance. There is much to be gained politically in new Singapore and still plenty to lose. Sure, make the ministers work harder for their inflated salaries. Make them sweat. Demand a level playing field, even for grassroots events in Aljunied. Expect to be included. But kicking out a government because taxi fares go up a few cents is not much different to making residents wilt in the heat to meet their opposition MP.

It's petty.

Twenty-four

I PUMPED the tyres, checked the handlebars, filled the juice bottle, threw the rucksack over my shoulder, checked the route in the street directory again, had a wee, lifted the bike through the apartment, whacked the pedal against the front door, swore for a bit, apologised to my daughter for the swearing, kissed my wife goodbye and promised to come back alive.

There was a tremendous sense of déjà vu.

I pedalled quickly through East Coast Park. If there is a more uplifting Singaporean image on a bright Sunday morning than throngs of picnickers, parents teaching their children to rollerblade, couples holding hands whilst walking their dogs, retirees nodding off into their newspapers and those wheezing families who puff past merrily in those four-seater carriages, then I'm buggered if I know what it is. I'm still not sure about the Billy Whizz solo skaters though. I passed the time picturing myself running the bare-chested, hands-behind-the back brigade off the road. I'm sure others do the same. It is a testament to our remarkable self-restraint that East Coast Park isn't strewn with the bodies of upended solo skaters, their skates sticking above the sand, the wheels still turning.

Following my trusty street directory, I intended to complete the East Coast Park cycling trail past Fort Road, continue through the greenery of Marina East, then pick up the trail again beside the Marina Bay Golf Course, following the reservoir as I made my way through Gardens by the Bay, and finally on to Kallang Riverside Park near the Singapore Indoor Stadium.

A corrugated green fence put paid to that plan. Building work denied entry to the Gardens at Marina East cycling path, which was agonisingly close beyond the fence, so I turned around, changed gears in a huff, shifted my body weight hard onto the right pedal and the chain came off.

This happens to many riders on a weekend jaunt along East Coast Park. But only I get joined at the otherwise deserted end of the cycling path by a bronzed, buffed beefcake strutting along with not a bead of sweat on his hairless chest. As I bent over the bike, perspiration pouring through my head to create a most magnificent Mohican, bare-chested man swung his biceps in my general direction.

"Are you OK down there?" he asked.

I heaved my sopping frame up over the seat and wiped my forehead. I examined my oil-covered hands and realised I'd just splattered an oily black streak across my forehead.

"Yeah, I'm fine, mate, no problem at all," I replied chirpily.

"Are you sure?" he queried, eyebrow cocked quizzically as he examined the chain dangling pathetically beneath the bike.

"Yeah, no trouble. Cheers."

"OK, then. See ya."

In such moments, I thoroughly loathe my Englishness. He was American and willing to help. He appeared physically capable of lifting the mountain bike with a solitary finger and reconnecting the chain with his own teeth whilst discussing the economic turmoil in the eurozone. But I am English and conservative and insecure and stupid and therefore mumbled something about being fine when what I really should have said was, "Do I need help? I'm alone at the end of East Coast Park. There's no one else within a kilometre. My hands and face are covered in grease and my bike chain is sagging like an old man's scrotum. What do you think, Muscles?"

My irritation at my own inertia and general ineptitude spurred me to a little victory. Through gritted teeth and a couple of cut fingertips, I wrenched the chain back on, cut across Fort Road, reached Tanjong Rhu Promenade and spent a further 15 minutes going around in circles. The popular connector of Kallang Riverside Park did not appear to connect to either the river or the park. I could see it in almost every direction but was unable to actually get to it. At the picturesque river-end tip of Tanjong Rhu, I marvelled at the dragon boaters but had no idea how to follow the river to cover the short distance to make the connector.

Another building site, this one colossal, provided a second obstacle. I was screwed by the Singapore Sports Hub. Scheduled to open in 2014, the Sports Hub's original opening date was pencilled in for 2011 but there was not quite the same corporate enthusiasm that was enjoyed by the integrated resorts. (The Sports Hub comes with pitches and tennis courts rather than casinos and blackjack tables, you see.)

When the Sports Hub is complete, I have no doubt that the complex will provide cyclists and joggers with a stunning, comfortable thoroughfare linking the Geylang River at Tanjong Rhu to the Kallang River on the other side of Merdeka Bridge. I was not afforded such luxury and had to negotiate Stadium Boulevard, Mountbatten Road, Nicoll Highway and a muddy slip road to finally join the park connector beneath Kallang MRT.

Like parts of the Railway Corridor beneath the underpasses, Kallang Riverside Park provided a glimpse into the other Singapore—not old, not new, just ignored and neglected. Foreign workers, dozens of them, were milling around the MRT station, holding hands on benches overlooking the river, messing around singing songs and strumming guitars. Some of them were even drinking beer. Letter writers may call this scene outrageous. I call it any public park in Australia where friends gather around a barbeque on lazy Sunday afternoons. Many of those Aussies also work in blue-collar industries, particularly construction. No one there suggests they must avoid public transport during peak hours or live in shitholes on the outskirts of town away from booming property prices. No one there expects them to climb into dank, malodorous rubbish chutes in the midday sun to clean diaper crap off the walls. No one there complains when they meet for a couple of beers after work. No one denies Australian blue-collar workers a day off for fear they may get drunk, get violent, get laid or get pregnant (even though there are examples of all four being achieved by the same couple in the same night).

And yet as I passed my fellow foreign workers hanging out harmlessly by the river, I thought about the recent vitriolic abuse in Singaporean blogs and online postings. Finally, Singapore's government has conceded that a human being is entitled to a weekly day off. Should a maid choose to work on that day off for a few extra bucks, that's her prerogative. But the choice must be hers. I'd like to claim that a heightened sense of morality and social decency were the driving forces behind the eventual change for the greater good, but I suspect economic prudence held sway once more. Working conditions for maids in Singapore had deteriorated to such a shameful extent that the best were wisely flying to more lucrative destinations such as Hong Kong and Taiwan, where they benefit from minimum wage laws and regular days off. I was at least grateful to the employers of the foreign workers around Kallang River. It was Sunday. They had the day off. And they were not robbing or impregnating each other either.

On the other hand, the so-called park connectors were killing me. At Upper Boon Keng Road, I hoisted the mountain bike up a flight of stairs. At Bendemeer Road, I navigated a busy pedestrian crossing. At Serangoon Road, I cursed the ceaseless traffic. In the street directory, the cute pink strips representing the park connector pathways stop and continue either side of Serangoon Road. The cyclist is merely required to stroll nonchalantly across the street, bike at the side, before going on his way. Have the park connector planners ever seen Serangoon Road on Sunday mornings? I turned into Frogger. For anyone below 21, Frogger was a terrific game in the 1980s in which a frog had to cross lanes of traffic and then a river without being hit by motorbikes, cars, lorries, logs and crocodiles in that surreal order. Each time the frog hopped into the first lane, a motorbike would mash him into the pavement. Serangoon Road was no different. With the utmost reluctance, I wheeled the bike over to the nearby overhead pedestrian bridge, refused to look up at the staircase, took a deep breath, lifted the bike against my right shoulder and carried us both to the other side.

By the time I'd reached the PIE at Jalan Toa Payoh, I was ready to quit. As my jaw dropped, my disbelieving eyes examined the monstrous pedestrian crossing that spanned one of the widest stretches of one of the widest roads in Singapore. Three flights of stairs going up, 16 lanes of traffic going across and another three flights of stairs going down again—that's how many obstacles Frogger had to clear whilst lifting a mountain bike with a cumbersome child seat on the back. When I reached the top, I sulkily threw my cap on the ground and sat down. Walkers on the bridge eyed me suspiciously. Sitting cross-legged on the overhead bridge with the cap lying in front of me, I looked like a beggar. By that point, I didn't care. I was shattered. This was not a park connector. A park connector conjures idyllic images of a gentle jaunt along the breezy banks of Singapore's famous waterways. This was an athletic assault course with the odd glimpse of a river. This was not in the brochure.

In February 2012, the government shared plans for a 150-kilometre Round Island Route, which will allow Singaporeans to jog or cycle around the entire country. The route will link up Singapore's cultural, historical and natural attractions via the islandwide park connectors, another attempt to bring sexy to the city. To its immense credit, NParks has already finished 200 kilometres of park connectors and will build a further 100 kilometres in the next five years. All the major parks will be joined by cycling trails along the waterways. In newer estates, such as Punggol, the task is much easier. The connectors can be incorporated into the town's planning from the outset, which is why the new $57 million North Eastern Riverine Loop will be an undoubted success. But carving a path through narrow stretches of land beside older, established estates is no mean feat. Trying to negotiate the connectors, pedestrian crossings and staircases from East Coast Park through to Bishan Park made it clear how difficult this is going to be. East Coast Park was a joy. Tanjong Rhu was delightful, once I knew where I was going. Kallang Park, thanks to the construction of the Sports Hub and blocked road arteries such as Bendemeer, Serangoon and Jalan Toa Payoh, was a nightmare. Slopes and underpasses are required for the parks to truly connect.

With a wider path on the other side of Jalan Toa Payoh, kiddies on bikes, skateboards and scooters returned with their families. I particularly recommend the lengthy CTE underpass just before Braddell Road for anyone tall. There is a clearance height of just 1.8 metres. Crouch and pedal throughout and you'll be fine. Stand tall and pedal and you risk decapitation. The adrenaline rush was better than Universal Studios.

With no further traffic distractions or roads to hurdle, I whizzed along to Bishan Park.

I hadn't visited the place for years. I played football there a couple of times until a kindly Indian chap rested a paternal hand on my shoulder and whispered, "Being an *ang moh*, I think you are struggling with the heat and pace of the game." That was when I decided my days at Bishan Park had come to an end. Originally opened in 1988 to provide the estate with a green lung, Bishan Park was built around a concrete canal and offered enough space for Sunday morning football teams, but it was an otherwise atypical park in the heartlands. In October 2009, the park was closed for a makeover and reopened in March 2012, when I popped in.

I did not recognise the place. Only in Singapore could an unsightly, decaying canal be transformed into a natural river without looking incongruous. The Kallang River snaked its way through the park. Pedalling alongside, wherever I could, I had followed the iconic waterway from Marina Reservoir to where it narrows to a trickle at the very end of Ang Mo Kio Avenue 1. At a cost of $76.7 million, NParks and PUB have turned a concrete drain into a river surrounded by native flora and fauna as well as increased its water level by 40 per cent. On my tour of new Singapore, such achievements have been commonplace.

And Singaporeans are using the outdoor facilities. That was the best part. Teenage anglers waded through the river, holding a net, ankle deep in water. Dog walkers were everywhere. I had never seen so many dog owners in an established housing estate before. Kids flew kites or scooted across the bridges and couples just hung out. I fixated upon one woman who was reading while stretched out on a wooden recliner near the river. She was reading a novel, too, not a "how to be a millionaire in five minutes" or a "rich dad, kill dad" bit of self-help fluff. She was reading for pleasure in a public park beside a river in front of an HDB block without feeling self-conscious. Never mind the rusty playgrounds and stone benches of the heartland parks of yesteryear, this place had more in common with Hyde Park. New Singapore is reaching out for that outdoorsy, greener vibe of East Coast and Pasir Ris and pulling it towards the central, established housing estates of the country. Bishan had never looked more attractive.

Revitalised, I pedalled purposefully towards my own contribution to new Singapore. I returned to my spiritual home. Though I no longer live there, whenever I visit Toa Payoh, I go home. In Toa Payoh Central, I am "John" in the opticians. (They called me by my middle name 15 years ago and I didn't want them to lose face so I've been stuck with "John" ever since. Even when I filmed a segment for a TV documentary there once and the crew called me "Neil", the staff still shouted out "John".) Around the HDB Hub, I am "that *ang moh*" or "*dumpwee*". The residents of Toa Payoh know why. They have given me nothing but warmth and affection.

So I gave them three trees.

In 2007, NParks launched its Plant-A-Tree Programme. I heard about the scheme through my Uncle Leslie who had planted some trees in memory of deceased loved ones. This is a smart move by new Singapore. Green up the place, absorb carbon dioxide emissions, raise environmental awareness and get residents to pay for it. Singapore will no longer allow you to bury your relatives, so buy them a tree instead.

But I had bought three trees for the living. On a previous visit to Singapore, my wife, daughter and I were handed shovels and three saplings, directed towards some pre-dug holes in Toa Payoh Town Park and told to get to work. Watching our daughter fill the hole around her tree using her little plastic shovel remains one of our happiest memories. The trees were deliberately placed beneath the Toa Payoh Viewing Tower, which I once called a bulbous green penis in a previous book. This pleased me tremendously (the location of the trees, not the green penis). And as long as our three trees are in Toa Payoh Town Park, dogs will always be able to cock a leg.

Like a fool, I ignored the increasing rainfall and reminisced beside the trees. I thought about my first night in Toa Payoh and the void deck funeral, and how that story somehow travelled around the world and back. I remembered hanging out with Scott, my old travelling partner, in the town garden, feeding the turtles *ikan bilis*, or dried anchovies, and plotting our career paths. I suddenly felt overwhelmingly grateful to both Toa Payoh and Singapore. These places have given me more than I can say. I felt privileged to be here. I was elated to be back. I had come home.

And then, I fell off my bike.

Twenty-five

THE tour was not supposed to end this way; a ticker tape parade around Marina Bay perhaps, but not like this. My whimsical recollections around the family trees had distracted me from the stubborn storm and the rising water levels along the Toa Payoh Town Park path. When I finally accepted that I still had a convoluted journey of park connectors and pedestrian crossings back to East Coast Park ahead of me, I left the trees and headed for home. I decided to take an abrupt right to avoid a puddle. My temperamental tyre decided to veer left along the greasy surface. My sopping wet brakes screeched in horror, but to no avail, as my back tyre defied its front counterpart by skidding to the right. I was thrown from the bike quite spectacularly. There was that fleeting moment in mid-air when I realised that this was probably not going to end well. Pain was coming. When my left shoulder decided it was a pneumatic drill and tried to spear itself through the pavement, I decided to lie down for a bit. There is street cred to be gained from this sort of thing happening along Nicoll Highway or on the Tampines Mountain Biking Trail, but not in a small public park filled with domestic helpers and aunties.

I felt like a right tit.

I stretched out on the pavement and watched the rain dance hypnotically on my face. I had no intention of getting up, even when I heard concerned voices.

"We saw you fall, it looked so serious," said a seductive female voice. "What can we do to help?"

I peered through the drizzle and made out two Filipino aunties standing over me, cowering beneath umbrellas. Angels. The heavens had opened and sent down two angels.

"I'm so sorry. I can't move my left arm," I replied. "This is so embarrassing. Could you pick up my rucksack, please? It's got my notepad in it and I can't get it wet, so sorry."

"But what about you?" the other woman enquired.

"Oh, don't worry about me. I'm fine, really. It's just my notepad."

"But you're lying in a puddle."

"Ah, that's all right."

Lying in the puddle had distracted me from the searing pain in my shoulder. Had my two angels not persisted in trying to coax me to my feet, I might still be lying there.

"You should really get up," one of the aunties insisted.

She had a point. I was blocking the footpath. I tried to lift my left arm and chuckled incredulously at the insane stabbing sensation in my shoulder.

"So sorry about this, I'm such an idiot, but I can't lift my arm. Maybe I'll just stay here for a bit, if that's OK with you, sorry. You can go, I'll be fine."

I really did say that. Fortunately, my angels had no time for melodramatic martyrdom. Almost telepathically, they both reached out for me.

"Come on, we'll lift you up," they declared, with more confidence than their petite, slender frames warranted.

The angels grabbed my right arm and hoisted me towards them. There was a weight imbalance. They struggled to pass the tipping point. Suddenly, they were falling towards the puddle. How would that look, in a park of canoodling foreign workers, if I buried myself under two Filipino women?

"Let go, let go," I cried.

They released their grip. I slumped back into the puddle and splashed their ankles. They resisted the temptation, I'm sure, to give me a sly kick in the ribs.

"Come on, one more time," they insisted.

We counted to three, rocking backwards and forwards, before a final heave pulled me to my feet. I thanked them profusely. I wanted to hug them but the pair quickly vanished, skipping towards the HDB Hub with nary a backward glance. Good Toa Payoh people had saved me again. I thought about my arm and my inability to raise it above elbow level. I thought about the daunting prospect of getting myself and my bike back to the East Coast. And I thought about taking an axe to those bloody trees.

Two days later, I learnt from a doctor that I had cycled one-handed a further 15 to 20 kilometres from Toa Payoh Town Park to East Coast Park, via the much more agreeable Whampoa Park Connector and then the Kallang Park Connector, with a torn rotator cuff in my left shoulder. I had no idea what a rotator cuff was either, but it sounded macho enough to me. I thought I was well hard. My wife thought I was well stupid.

So my returning tour of a sexier island had begun with an Australian neighbour threatening to smash my face in and ended with my first Singapore sling.

Have you ever tried to pee with an arm sling? I will never again take for granted the responsibility the non-peeing hand performs in pinning down the underpants. Without the hand that plays that holding role, the waistband acts like a guillotine. As I shook myself in front of a urinal, the waistband on my underpants pinged up, cut into my instrument, pushed it northwards and turned me into a sprinkler system. I deliberately soaked myself at the basin to cover the damage from the sprinkler system, opened the door and craned my head to take in the remarkable scale of the Singapore Flyer.

I had always planned to come full circle and finish where I had started at Marina Bay, and what better place to do so than the attraction that continues to bear witness to new Singapore's evolution. Opened in 2008, the Singapore Flyer reaches 42 storeys and is the tallest Ferris wheel in the world. With its air-conditioned capsules, the Flyer is not much different to the London Eye, only 30 metres taller. Singapore has always been borderline obsessed with records: "Let's break the world text messaging record", "Let's make the world's longest table", "Let's hold the most pointless world records because *kiasuism* won't allow our kids to pursue sporting excellence" and so on. The highest wheel title is a dubious achievement. I'm not exactly sure how an extra 30 metres improves the view of Keppel Harbour and the world's busiest container port (there's another one) but I was keen to find out.

First, I took my daughter around the Singapore Food Trail beside the Flyer. Like a retro 1950s diner in New York, the Singapore Food Trail was a "ye olde hawker centre" for tourists. Filled with replica food carts, old F&N metallic posters, black-and-white photos and menus promising original culinary delights from Bugis Street back in the days when transvestites hawked their sex toys to American servicemen (strangely, this side of old Singapore was not replicated), the tourist trap was kitschy, tacky, clichéd and thoroughly over the top. I thought it was marvellous. I shoved my bemused daughter in front of old jukeboxes, Chinese vinyl record covers and food carts for photographs but she was too distracted by the glass Fanta bottles. She walked and burped her way to the Singapore Flyer, swigging from a Fanta bottle like an *ah pek*.

As we had gone on a school holiday, the Flyer queue was longish so we were entertained (if that is the right word, "confused" might be more apt) by the Journey of Dreams attraction. I presumed the multimedia showcase was there to divert those waiting in line. As it came with the price of admission, I had no grounds for complaint. But it also needed to come with a tab of acid. There were lights, psychedelic images, rotating and revolving patterns, vibrantly-coloured circular shapes and confounding cut-outs that were somehow loosely connected to Singapore's dream. I have no idea what Singapore's dream is but it must have something to do with wearing a smiley T-shirt, blowing a whistle, dancing on a podium, waving your hands in the air like you just don't care and shouting "acid". I'd queue to watch that at the National Day Parade.

Finally, I chased my daughter up the slope towards the Flyer and a dramatic flight countdown commenced along the walls, the numbers lighting up as we got closer. She loved that part.

"Quick, Daddy, it's time to fly," she cried. "Five, four, three, two, one ... Blast off!"

And then we hurled ourselves into a capsule that moved at speeds of half a millimetre a minute.

The anticlimax almost overwhelmed my daughter.

"When do we blast off? When do we start moving?" she wondered.

"We're already moving," I replied enthusiastically. "Look, we're going to see all of Singapore from high in the sky."

"Oh! Can I have your pen, Daddy? I want to colour this leaflet."

For first-time visitors to the country, the Singapore Flyer offers an air-conditioned summary of the most obvious landmarks. Merlion Park, the Southern Islands, the Singapore River and

Raffles Place are all easy to spot, a tourism starter pack for the short-term guest. A commentary might have further enhanced the experience. The tourists sharing our capsule would probably have preferred a voice other than my daughter's saying, "Merlion? I've seen it. The Helix Bridge? It's got lots of colours. Marina Barrage? Daddy took me to the water park there. I like the fountains."

She was mentally taking down her own notes on Singapore. I was so proud.

I was also aware that her ticket had cost me almost $20 and she was sitting cross-legged on the capsule floor, hunched over her latest artwork.

"Come and look out of the window," I whispered. "I'll show you the Indonesian islands."

"I can't. I'm colouring the leaflet."

"But I'd like you to see the great views."

"I like colouring this leaflet."

"I know you do but that leaflet didn't cost me $20. It was free."

"Then I can colour it, Daddy."

I pulled her over to the window. We crouched down together and admired the bay. The sun was slowly setting. I pointed out Sisters Islands and explained how they got their name. We watched the hippo and duck boats meander around Marina Reservoir. Joggers ran along the promenade. Kites soared above the curved, grassy roof of Marina Barrage. Human specks peered across at us from the viewing deck atop Marina Bay Sands. In the distance, a Resorts World Sentosa hotel peeked out through the island's surprisingly dense foliage. Over our shoulders, I made out the sky garden connecting the formidable towers of Pinnacle@ Duxton. New Singapore surrounded us at every turn. Memories of my six-month journey enveloped us. Engineers constructing the undersea expressway behind Marina Barrage were a visual reminder that new Singapore's journey had barely begun. It will probably never end. To our right, a lake had been filled and the landscaping transformed since I had previously surveyed Gardens by the Bay from Marina Bay Sands. New Singapore was dating this book before it was even finished.

Is new Singapore a sexier island? Of course it is. But the question is too simplistic. Who is the sexier island for? That is the question that politicians and residents alike will obsess over until the next general election. The high-end boutiques, restaurants and private gaming tables of Resorts World Sentosa and Marina Bay Sands belong in a chapter of *Casino Royale*, but they do not belong to the average Singaporean. They are priced out of their own country's progress. Visit the depressingly deserted Shoppes mall at the Sands on any evening for proof of that. But the high rollers, both local and foreign, have their uses. If an Indonesian *towkay* is willing to drop half a million on a hand of blackjack so my daughter can spend her birthday posing for photographs with Woody Woodpecker at Universal Studios Singapore, then please, Mr Degenerate Gambler, do it more often.

The Singapore FreePort is a ready-made location for a Hollywood heist caper but most locals will never afford the price of admission. Sentosa Cove certainly isn't for the majority of Singaporeans (two weeks before writing this, a seafront property sold for a vulgar $39 million to an Indian national) but Pinnacle@ Duxton and Treelodge@Punggol most certainly are. They represent new Singapore's public housing (and every apartment block should have a recycling chute from now on, guys). So do the Southern Ridges, Bishan Park, the park connectors, Tampines Mountain Biking Trail, the Railway Corridor, Sengkang Riverside Park and the ABC Waters Programme. They are all forward-thinking positive steps for all Singaporean residents. Open up the waterways and the green lungs and let's have some bloody fun.

But Singaporeans still want to belong. Kayaking at Jurong

Lake might encourage residents to take ownership of their water supply but the anger over Bukit Brown Cemetery shows a desire to be included in issues beyond public park management. All the flowing rivers, children's playgrounds, cycling paths and theme parks in the world will not satisfy a disillusioned Singaporean who feels marginalised or taken for granted. A few MRT breakdowns proved that. Singaporeans are rightfully proud of their nation's progress. Throughout a period of global economic uncertainty, no other country has pulled off such a widespread makeover, with so many nips and tucks across the island, in five years. But residents must share in its pleasures and privileges too or Aljunied will almost certainly not be a one-off. Singapore is much sexier now, but she occasionally dresses only to please rich foreigners. She's beautiful, much greener and much more fun than I remember, but still a bit of a Sarong Party Girl.

Still, it's what's under the sarong that counts. And I have no idea where this analogy is going. No country is perfect, and I've lived in a few, but Singapore does a damn decent impression. So allow me to momentarily lift my arm sling, rip my heart from my chest and unashamedly say that I love this country. Australia is known affectionately as the "lucky country", but there is nothing lucky about Singapore, nothing at all. Its success derives wholly from human endeavour, resourcefulness, productivity and knowledge with an overwhelming, almost disturbing, emphasis on education and filial piety. They're not bad values for an impressionable little girl to have, are they?

We just won't focus on the SPG bits.

As the capsule slowly descended, my daughter and I gazed out at the dusky skyline and I noticed that she was playfully tracking the journeys of the duck boats with her forefinger on the window. Our 30-minute flight was ending and I wondered if I might get some preternatural profundity.

"Hey, your Mummy and Daddy are from England but you were born in Australia," I muttered.

"Yes, I know, Daddy," she sighed, staring down at Marina Reservoir.

"But we live in Singapore. If you could live in England, Australia or Singapore, where would you live?"

"Singapore," she answered without hesitation.

I beamed broadly. This was the perfect end to my island journey. My race was run. It was time to pass the baton.

About the Author

Neil Humphreys arrived in Singapore in 1996 with no job, no prospects and no second language and left a decade later as one of the country's bestselling authors. His works on Singapore—*Notes from an Even Smaller Island* (2001), *Scribbles from the Same Island* (2003) and *Final Notes from a Great Island: A Farewell Tour of Singapore* (2006) as well as the omnibus *Complete Notes from Singapore* (2007)—are now considered must-reads by his mother (and much of Singapore). Humphreys then headed for Australia, where he had a daughter and wrote *Be My Baby* (2008), which chronicled his journey to parenthood and was an international bestseller. *Match Fixer*, his first novel, was released in 2010 to critical acclaim, fascinating football fans but infuriating loan sharks and illegal bookies. His second novel, *Premier Leech*, was a dark, satirical take on fame and celebrity in the English Premier League and was chosen as the *FourFourTwo* Football Novel of the Year in 2011. Missing the smaller island and eager for his daughter to learn conversational Mandarin, Humphreys has since returned to Singapore, where he writes for several magazines and newspapers and pops up regularly on football podcasts and TV shows. His daughter already speaks better Mandarin than he does.

Other Books by Neil Humphreys

Notes from an even Smaller Island
Knowing nothing of Singapore, a young Englishman arrives in the land of "air-conned" shopping centres and Lee Kuan Yew. He explores all aspects of Singaporean life, taking in the sights, dissecting the culture and illuminating each place and person with his perceptive and witty observations.

Scribbles from the Same Island
Humphreys is back with yet more observations and ruminations about the oddball aspects of Singapore and its people. *Scribbles* also contains a selection of his work as a humour columnist.

Final Notes from a Great Island
All good things must come to an end, and before Humphreys makes his move Down Under, he revisits all the people and places he loves in his final, comprehensive tour of Singapore.

Complete Notes from Singapore (The Omnibus Edition)
All three of Humphreys' bestselling works, *Notes from an even Smaller Island*, *Scribbles from the Same Island* and *Final Notes from a Great Island*, in one classic, updated book.

Be My Baby: On the Road to Fatherhood

Follow Humphreys on his most terrifying and hilarious journey yet—travelling the unfamiliar road to fatherhood.

Match Fixer

Once a promising graduate of West Ham United Academy and tipped to play for England, Chris Osbourne arrives on the Singapore football scene in a bid to right his faltering football career. But nothing has prepared him for the underground party drugs scene, the bent bookies, dubious teammates and a seductively beautiful journalist who welcome him to life in paradise.

Premier Leech

English Football Clubs are dying but club captain, Scott, couldn't give a toss. As long as he delivers on the pitch, he can do whatever he likes off it. That's the right and privilege of an English Premier League footballer—until he sleeps with his best mate's wife. The tabloids go wild and a team of investigative reporters are hot on the trails of both Scott and his manager, Charlie, who's been lining up a secret takeover with a Saudi businessman more interested in property and blonde hookers than football. In a world where the only currency is fame, how much are they willing to sacrifice to stay in the game?